Vocabulary Richness of Novels and Their Adaptations

MetaLinguistica

Edited by/herausgegeben von András Kertész

Volume/Band 24

PETER LANG

Frankfurt am Main · Berlin · Bern · Bruxelles · New York · Oxford · Wien

Mária Csernoch

Vocabulary Richness of Novels and Their Adaptations

PETER LANG
Internationaler Verlag der Wissenschaften

Bibliographic Information published by the Deutsche Nationalbibliothek
The Deutsche Nationalbibliothek lists this publication in the Deutsche Nationalbibliografie; detailed bibliographic data is available in the internet at http://dnb.d-nb.de.

ISSN 0946-4174
ISBN 978-3-631-61223-1

www.peterlang.de

Table of contents

1. Introduction

1.1. A first-order statistical model

As many things around us in the world, this project should also be viewed in continuity. The original goal was to find a dynamic first-order statistical model which is able to provide a better approximation of texts than those static models which had come to life previously. The model had to be dynamic to be able to create artificial texts which can then be compared to the original, natural language text. Another requirement for the model was to handle languages other than English. First of all, I wanted to analyze Hungarian texts to reveal similarities to and differences from English texts, to see whether a statistical model could be applied to an agglutinating language.

The model, a computer program written in VisualBasic, acquired its name from its main features: **Dy**namic **Mo**del for **C**omputer **A**ided **S**tatistical **A**nalysis of **T**exts (DyMoCASAT).

After finding such a model and creating artificial texts, as many as were needed to rule out the bias of the random selections, the next question was how to take advantage of them.

I wanted to find those sections in the texts which make them unique in terms of their vocabulary. They are called the seasonalities or the vocabulary rich segments of the text. By seasonalities or vocabulary rich segments I understand those sections of the text where the number of newly introduced words is higher than that predicted by the model. These sections of the text make them stand out by being richer in vocabulary than the main body of the text.

This means, in a paradoxical way, the model must not be 'too' good, the artificial texts should not follow the original text too closely because in that case the model would be perfect and the seasonalities which I was interested in would not be recognized. This explains the choice of the first-order statistical model, which only takes the frequency of the words of the original text into account.

As it will be shown here, the difference between the original and the model based artificial texts is able to reveal the seasonalities of the original text. Furthermore, I present evidence that these sections are those which stand out, and do not otherwise fit into the flow of the text.

1.2. Seasonalities of a literary work

After finding such a model, and – based on the model – the text segments corresponding to the seasonalities, the question arose as to what could be the reason for their presence. I found several previously published works which venture to give explanations for this phenomenon, but these opinions are subjective, mainly based on the intuitions of the reader. I was interested in finding more objective explanations – based on quantitative data – for what makes the author of a text increase the number of newly introduced words so intensively that the process makes qualitative changes in the text.

The analysis of newly introduced word types led to the hypothesis that those sections of the texts which are responsible for changes in style, stand for descriptions of characters, places or events, or give lists of names, out-of-context words, etc. in the story, are richer in vocabulary. On the contrary, there is no clear connection between the chapter boundaries – not even at the connecting points of concatenated texts – and the increase in the number of newly introduced words. These segments can appear anywhere in the text, and as the list above shows they carry only marginal information; they are not essential to an understanding of the story. However, these are the segments which make the text unique, which make the text more than a list of facts and events.

To give further proofs of this hypothesis several other analyses on different types of texts – different adaptations of the original texts – were carried out.

As an extension of the above analysis the distribution of hapax legomena was investigated. The question was whether there is any connection between the text segments responsible for the seasonalities of the text and the number of hapax legomena in the same text segments.

1.3. Adaptations

As was mentioned in the previous section, my aim was to explore how the proportion of newly introduced words varies in different adaptations of the same text. The term 'adaptation' is used here to include both intralingual (lemmatization, condensation) and interlingual (foreign language translation) adaptations, whether involving a reduction in text size (condensation) or not (lemmatization, foreign language translation). To carry out the analyses and comparisons of the different adaptations of the same text the very same model had to be used.

Lemmatization

First of all, based on the original, new texts were created where the word types of the texts were substituted by the corresponding lemmas. I believe that the comparison of newly introduced words in the original and the lemmatized texts should bring a long debate to an end. Several linguists had the intuition that to find an explanation for the presence of the seasonalities, analyzing the word types, carrying all their affixes, is not efficient enough. The lemmatization of the texts, however, revealed only minor differences which did not influence the presence of the vocabulary rich text segments. Nevertheless, the minor differences found between the lemmatized and non-lemmatized texts might be a new starting point in the statistical analysis of texts to reveal those tools which the authors use in order to make changes in style, to introduce new characters, places, etc. in their novels; these analyses, however, are beyond the scope of this project.

Foreign language translation

As I mentioned above, the primary aim of this project was to build a first-order statistical model, which is also able to handle languages other than English. In addition to English, Hungarian, German and French were the selected languages.

Unlike other projects in foreign language translation whose main concern is the subtle differences between short segments of the text, this project focuses on global changes in the text. While subtle differences can be revealed by reading and comparing the original and the translated text word by word, sentence by sentence, until the differences and similarities on the discourse level can be lost to the observer in the details. The statistical analysis of a text, on the other hand is, by its nature, not able to reveal these subtle differences, but is able to generate data about global changes in the text. The parameter which can track these global changes in texts is how the number of newly introduced words varies throughout the discourse. In addition, the algorithm introduced here helps us to reveal the localization of the vocabulary rich text segments of the text. With this method we are able to tell how rich the vocabulary of certain segments of a translation is when compared to the original text.

Condensation

Changes on the discourse level are independent of the language. This is equivalent to saying that if there are differences between the distribution of newly introduced words in the original text and its translations they must be due to unfaithful translations – not necessarily incorrect, but different from the original text in vocabulary. To reveal the causes of this discrepancy is beyond this project, since the aim of this project was to pinpoint the similarities and differences on the discourse level.

The next type of adaptation examined was again an intralingual adaptation; the condensed versions of the texts. The condensation process and its results ignited serious debates between its supporters and opponents. Applying the same method to the condensed texts the most important questions were how serious were the changes vocabulary undergoes, what can be gained or lost by the shortening of a text, and whether the condensation constitutes a simple cropping or a more intellectual re-editing. I was also interested to see if this method would enable us to discern the direct source of a second order adaptation, whether a foreign language condensed book is a condensation of a translation or the translation of a condensed text.

In general, my first concern was to find a model which can be used to reveal the seasonalities – the vocabulary rich segments – of a text and compare the results to other previously published, mainly subjective, opinions. After such a model had been built, it was applied to the different adaptations of the very same texts to reveal what changes a text can endure while its seasonalities still remain detectable.

The method applied here highlights several other questions which are far beyond this project. Among them the most demanding, I think, is to account for the loss or the unexpected appearance of seasonalities in the different adaptations of the texts. Once these seasonalities are found and we can focus on these selected text segments, the old or classical method of reading can be applied to reveal the subtle differences.

1.4. Practical usage of the analyses

Beyond the theoretical significance – that we were able to find a method with the help of which we could separate the vocabulary rich segments from the main body of the text –, the practical usage of the method is also remarkable.

In general, the comparison of texts in different languages with this novel method is able to add information to that which is gained by well established methods.

One of the advantages of this statistical analysis is that it operates independently of the fact that translators are free to use words, expressions, structures and the different techniques well known in translation studies. The only expectation here is that in a faithful translation the text segments in the target language should be as rich in vocabulary as they are in the original text. Here the richness in vocabulary does not mean the absolute number of words; it is rather a relative phenomenon, meaning that if the original text was richer in vocabulary compared to the model, the translation should also be richer in those particular text segments to the same degree.

The other remarkable advantage of the method is that both translators and critics are presented with the location and the intensity of the vocabulary rich segments of a text. On the one hand, the method offers a parameter to the translators. Namely, it gives the exact location of the vocabulary rich segments of the original text. Being familiar with the vocabulary rich segments of the original text in advance of the translation process might draw the attention of the translator to these segments. On the other hand, being familiar with the vocabulary rich text segments of both the original and the translated texts means that a new set of parameters is added to the tools of translation criticism. Here we would be able to provide a more objective analysis of the translation(s); we would be able to tell how close a translation is to the original text in vocabulary, or decide which translation is closer to the original text in this respect.

Furthermore, the method has been proved to be satisfactory in deciding from which of the two possible primary translations a secondary translation of the text is derived.

2. Words in a text

2.1. Vocabulary size, vocabulary richness, words, word types, newly introduced word types

Both the vocabulary size and richness of a text are quantitative data which, at first sight, are easy to determine. However, all of us who have ever ventured into this field, have had to realize, sooner or later, that both vocabulary size and richness are highly dependent on the number of words encountered.

In spite of the fact that the concept of 'word' has a major role in countless subfields of linguistics, there is no clear definition of it. A number of linguists have been trying to give a close definition of 'word' but none of them has succeeded fully (for a review see: Singleton; 1999, Schmitt; 2000, Papp; 1974). However, those who gave up the idea of one almighty definition of 'word', and were willing to use several definitions and sub-definitions of it applying to subcategories have had more success. In this short introduction I will discuss briefly those concepts which relate to the statistical analyses of this project.

2.1.1. Character

Before the definition of 'word' is attempted, the definitions of 'character' and 'character set' have to be given. We have to emphasize that the character set used in a computer-aided analysis does not necessarily equal – either in size or the number of elements – the alphabet of the language. To make clear for a program which characters can form a word the characters have to be sorted into two sets:

- valid characters,
- separator characters.

To decide which character goes into which set is highly dependent on the text and on the goals of the project.

2.1.1.1. Valid characters

The set of valid characters are mainly decided based on the alphabet of the language. The one-character letters are kept while the two- or more character letters are counted as two or more individual characters and not added to the character set as separated items. However, other, non-alphabetical items can also be added to the character set. Such characters might be special characters (e.g. apostrophe), numbers, or letters from other alphabets (e.g. á, é, í, ó, ö, ő, ú, ü, ű, ä, ç, ê, è, ë), etc.

2.1.1.2. Separator characters

The primary separator characters are the space character and the punctuation marks. The 'end of text' and 'end of paragraph' characters also serve as separators although they are not necessarily represented by a single character. In special cases numbers, letters from other alphabets and special characters, such as the apostrophe can also serve as separator characters, their inclusion always determined by the topic and goals of the project (see Appendix 6.6.1 for details on how the apostrophe was treated).

2.1.2. Basic terms

The definitions given below are those on which the whole project was based. It was necessary to settle these definitions at the beginning of the project because all methods applied were carried out by computer programs which, by their nature, are very conventional (Snyder; 2008).

- **Token, running word**: a string enclosed between two separator characters.
- **Word type**: a unique item of the tokens. The number of word types provides the size of the vocabulary, while the token per word type quotient is the vocabulary richness of a particular text. The latter is highly dependent on the size of the text.
- **Lemma**: the residue of word types after deaffixation, the root of the word type.
- **Newly introduced word**: a relative phenomenon, which only has meaning at a certain point of a particular text. When the first appearance of the word is detected at a certain point of a text, the word is considered as newly introduced at that point in that text.

2.1.3. Number of words

In spite of the fact that there is no clear understanding of the concept of word, after some simplification of the problem we are able to determine the number of the words in a text. In the following list we give those numbers and their definitions which are necessary to carry out the following statistical analyses of texts.

- **Text size**: the number of tokens in a text (*N*).
- **Vocabulary size**: the number of different word types or lemmas in an *N*-token-long text (*V*(*N*)).
- **Frequency**: the frequency of a word, either word type or lemma, is the number of appearances of that word in the text. If there are *V*(*N*) different words in a text, and each word is marked as w_i, where *i* runs from 1 to *V*(*N*), their frequency is marked as *f*(*i*,*N*) (Figure 1, Appendix 6.1).

$$\sum_{i=1}^{V(N)} f(i,N) = N \qquad \textbf{(1)}$$

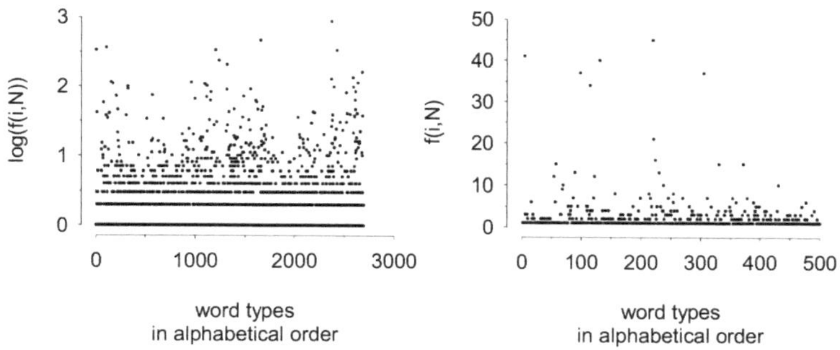

Figure 1. The frequency of word types in the alphabetical order of the word types in Edgar Allan Poe's THE GOLD BUG. There are 13,600 tokens (*N*), 2,694 different word types (*V*(*N*)), and 1,543 hapax legomena (*V*(1,*N*)) in this text. The frequency of word types differs from 881 to 1. The graph on the left shows all the frequencies on a logarithmic scale, while on the right the original values are mapped on a truncated scale.

- **Relative frequency**: the relative frequency of the word w_i is the quotient of the frequency of the word (*f*(*i*,*N*)) and the text size (*N*).

$$frel(i,N) = \frac{f(i,N)}{N} \qquad \textbf{(2)}$$

- **Frequency class**: is a set of words, which have the same frequency in the text. *V*(*m*,*N*) is a frequency class, where *m* is the shared frequency of the words of the set (Appendix 6.1).

The size of $V(m,N)$ is the number of those words which have the same frequency:

$$V(m,N)=\sum_{i=1}^{V(N)} I_{f(i,N)=m}\,, \tag{3}$$

where

$$I_\alpha=\begin{cases}1 & \text{if } \alpha \text{ true}\\ 0 & \text{if } \alpha \text{ false}\end{cases}. \tag{4}$$

$V(1,N)$ frequency class is for the words which occur once in the text (hapax legomena). Typically, 1 is the frequency which is represented by the greatest number of words (Figure 2, Appendix 6.1). $V(2,N)$ is the number of the words which appear twice in the text (dis legomena), $V(3,N)$ is the number of the words which appear three times in the text (tris legomena), and so on. $V(881,N)$ is the number of those words, which appear 881 times in a text. In case of Poe's THE GOLD BUG there is only one such word, the most frequent word of the text, 'the' (Figure 1, Appendix 6.1).

The text size is the sum of products where the size of the frequency class is multiplied by its frequency:

$$N=\sum_m m\cdot V(m,N) \tag{5}$$

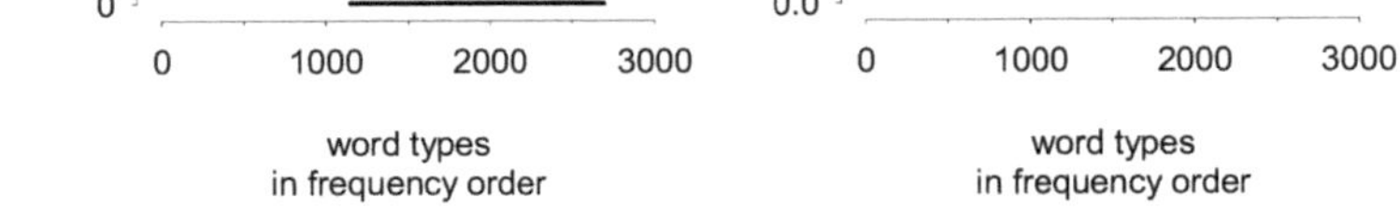

Figure 2. On the left the frequencies of word types in Edgar Allan Poe's THE GOLD BUG are depicted. The frequencies are presented in descending order from $V(881,N) = 1$ to $V(1,N) = 1543$. It is clearly shown that the largest frequency class is the class of hapax legomena ($V(1,N)$), followed by the class of dis legomena ($V(2,N)$), etc. On the right the running integral of the relative frequencies is depicted (*Femp*).

2.1.4. Number and order of words

The analyses detailed in this work are based on literary works and on their adaptations. Four languages – English, French, German, and Hungarian – are involved, among which the first three are known and spoken widely, while the Hungarian language is less frequently used. The other reason why Hungarian was used is that it is an agglutinating language, and as such the texts carry features which might influence the output of the computer aided analyses (Kiefer and É. Kiss; 1994, É. Kiss; 2002).

Before discussing the details of the analyses, I would like to give a short introduction to two special features of the Hungarian language, as compared to the other three well known languages.

Table 1. Changes in the number of word types in the four different languages used in this study. While in English, German and French the affixes do not raise the number of the word types with the appearance of each new lemma, in Hungarian they do, due to the agglutinating character of the language.

Hungarian	English	German	French
a ház 1+1	the house 1+1	das Haus 1+1	la maison 1+1
a ház**ak** 1+2	the house**s** 1+2	**die** Häus**er** 2+2	**les** maison**s** 2+2
a házak**ban** 1+3	**in** the houses 1+1+2	in **den** Häuser**n** 1+3+2	**dans** les maisons 1+2+2
a házak**ból** 1+4	**from** the houses 2+1+2	**aus** den Häusern 2+3+2	des maisons 1+3+2
a háza**ink**ból 1+5	from **our** houses 3+1+2	aus **unseren** Häusern 3+3+2	de **nos** maisons 2+4+2
az ablak 2+6	the window 3+1+3	das Fenster 3+3+3	la fenêtre 2+4+3
az ablak**ok** 2+7	the window**s** 3+1+4	die Fenster 3+3+3	**les** fenêtre**s** 2+4+4
az ablakok**ban** 2+8	**in** the windows 3+1+4	**in den** Fenster**n** 3+3+4	**dans** les fenêtres 2+4+4
az ablakok**ból** 2+9	**from** the windows 3+1+4	**aus** den Fenstern 3+3+4	**des** fenêtres 2+4+4
az ablaka**ink**ból 2+10	from **our** windows 3+1+4	aus **unseren** Fenstern 3+3+4	de **nos** fenêtres 2+4+4

The first consequence of the agglutinating character of the Hungarian language is clearly detectable in Table 1 and Table 4. The number of tokens is the lowest, while the number of word types is the highest in the Hungarian texts.

Another characteristic feature of the Hungarian language is that the order of the words is not strict; words within a sentence can be used in any order. Consequently, by rearranging the words of a sentence we can move the focus to another position, giving new meaning to the sentence. This feature of Hungarian makes the appearance of words more random than in the other languages.

Table 2. Seven Hungarian sentences created from four Hungarian words, and their English, French, and German translations. While in the Hungarian sentences we were able to give different meanings by changing the order of the words, in their translation new vocabulary items had to be used to achieve a similar meaning.

	Tegnap mindenki eljött hozzánk.
English	Yesterday everyone came to our place.
French	Hier tout le monde est venu chez nous.
German	Gestern kamen alle zu uns.
	Tegnap jött el hozzánk mindenki.
English	It was yesterday that everyone came to our place.
French	C'est hier que tout le monde est venu chez nous.
German	Es was gestern, als alle zu uns kamen.
	Tegnap **hozzánk** jött el mindenki.
English	It was our place that everyone came to yesterday.
French	C'est chez nous que tout le monde est venu.
German	Zu uns kamen alle gestern.
	Mindenki eljött hozzánk tegnap.
English	Everyone came to our place yesterday.
French	Tout le monde est venu chez nous.
German	Alle kamen gestern zu uns.
	Hozzánk jött el mindenki tegnap.
English	It was our place that everyone came to yesterday.
French	C'est chez nous que tout le monde est venu.
German	Es war bei uns, wohin gestern alle kamen.
	Eljött hozzánk mindenki tegnap.
English	Everyone did come to our place yesterday.
French	Tout le monde est venu chez nous.
German	Alle waren gestern dabei.
	Eljött hozzánk mindenki tegnap**?**
English	Did everyone come to our place yesterday?
French	Est-ce que tout le monde est venu? / Tout le monde est venu?
German	Kamen alle gestern zu uns?

2.2. Large Numbers of Rare Events

One of the most demanding characteristics of the distribution of word types is the high number of rare words; consequently these distributions belong to the distribution class of large numbers of rare events (LNRE, Khmaladze; 1987). The graphs of the distribution of words are different in shape from the graphs of non-LNRE distributions. In the non-LNRE distributions the graphs reach their maximums at a relatively early stage, while in the LNRE distributions they do not (Figure 2).

The concept of LNRE distributions was developed by Khmaladze (1987). He introduces two formal definitions for the LNRE concept (Baayen; 2001). Let

$$\upsilon(N) = (f(1,N), f(2,N), \ldots, f(S,N)) \quad \textbf{(6)}$$

denote the vector of frequencies of the word types as realized in a sample of N tokens. By increasing N, we obtain a sequence of such vectors,

$$\{\upsilon(N)\},\ N = 1,2,3,\ldots \quad \textbf{(7)}$$

Initially, when N is still small, most word frequencies will be zero, but as we increase the sample size, more and more words will appear with non-zero frequencies. The first formal definition states that

Definition: A sequence $\{\upsilon(N)\}$ is a sequence with large numbers of rare events if

$$\lim_{N\to\infty} \frac{\mathrm{E}[V(1,N)]}{N} > 0, \quad \textbf{(8)}$$

where $V(1,N)$ stands for the number of hapax legomena, while $\mathrm{E}[V(1,N)]$ is the expected number of these words.

According to this definition, we have an LNRE distribution when the growth rate of the vocabulary remains greater than zero even when N is increased indefinitely. It is easy to see that for a fixed finite number of word types S and fixed probabilities of them (π_i, $i = 1, 2, \ldots, S$),

$$\lim_{N\to\infty} f(i,N) = \infty \quad \textbf{(9)}$$

hence

$$\lim_{N \to \infty} \mathrm{E}[V(1, N)] = 0 \quad \textbf{(10)}$$

and

$$\lim_{N \to \infty} \mathrm{E}[V(N)] = S \,. \quad \textbf{(11)}$$

In these circumstances, the vocabulary growth rate will become zero. However, even for distributions with finite *S*, a non-zero growth rate for $N \to \infty$ is not guaranteed, as *N* may grow rapidly with respect to the expected number of hapax legomena. The second definition developed by Khmaladze is more lenient.

Definition: A sequence $\{\upsilon(N)\}$ is a sequence with a large number of rare events if

$$\lim_{N \to \infty} \frac{\mathrm{E}[V(1, N)]}{N} > 0 \quad \textbf{(12)}$$

and

$$\lim_{N \to \infty} \mathrm{E}[V(N)] = \infty \quad \textbf{(13)}$$

This definition explicitly requires *S* to be infinite while requiring that the hapax legomena constitute a non-negligible proportion of the vocabulary.

2.3. Texts in natural languages vs. first-order statistical models

A text written in any natural language is a production of the human mind. As it is, modeling it with a computer program is far too ambitious a goal to set given our present knowledge of human thinking (Russell and Norvig; 1995). At this stage of the development of computer science there is no chance of being able to tackle the whole problem in general. However, by wanting less and finding ways to reduce the problem, breaking it down into simple but still meaningful projects, we might still obtain useful information which can later be pieced together (Prószéky; 1989, Russell and Norvig; 1995, Prószéky and Kis; 1999). One such reduction of the problem is to use first-order statistical models (Herdan; 1964), which, regardless of the syntactic and semantic constrains on word usage, take only the frequency of the words of the original text into account. The parameters which proved to be reproducible with these models are related to vocabulary size (for a review see Oakes; 1998, Baayen; 2001). To follow up the changes in vocabulary size, dynamic models have been proposed (Csernoch; 2006b, 2007b) instead of the former static models (Baayen; 1996a, 1996b, 2001). Based on these dynamic models, artificial texts are created and compared to the original text. Since the model is only an approximation of the original text, there is a discrepancy between the original and the model-based artificial texts. This difference, however, is traceable, and thus we might be able to obtain reliable and important information about changes in the vocabulary of the original text.

To obtain further data on intra- and inter-textual cohesion in the texts, analysis of vocabulary size was not enough. It is the changes in vocabulary that should be focused on. Therefore, analysis of the introduction of new words must be carried out (Csernoch; 2006b, 2007b).

It has been suggested that discourse structure influences word usage when changes occur in the subject matter. Such changes bring about changes in the vocabulary (Baayen; 1996a, 1996b, 2001). Some researchers even suggest that the boundaries of chapters have such a strong influence on the vocabulary that they produce noticeable changes in the number of words (Petőfi; 1990). However, according to Genette's (1995) findings, and using first-order statistical models (Csernoch; 2005, 2006b, 2007a, 2007c, 2007d, 2008a, 2008b), changes in the vocabulary are the results of changes in style, 'longish' descriptions and 'out-of-place' texts within the narrative. A change in topic or the beginning of a new chapter has no direct influence.

2.3.1. The urn model

Several statistical models have come to light over the last couple of decades (Oakes; 1998, Baayen; 2001). Here, I will give the essence of one of them, the urn model, which provides the theoretical background for both Baayen's earlier model and the model used and detailed in this project. These models belong to the category of first-order statistical models, which take only the frequency of the words into account (Beaugrande and Dressler; 2000).

The urn model for word frequency distributions compares the use of words to the sampling of marbles or balls from an urn. Consider an urn containing marbles of various colors. Each color corresponds to a marble type. A particular color may be extremely rare, or it may be represented by a great many individual marbles, the marble tokens. We randomly draw N marbles from the urn, assuming that the outcome of a given trial is completely independent of the outcome of any other trial. (Hajtman; 1971, Meszéna and Ziermann; 1981, Solt; 1971, Baayen; 1996a, 1996b, 2001).

2.3.2. The re-evaluation of the urn model

In Baayen's opinion (1996b, 2001), the urn model is responsible for the overestimation bias, which means that using a model where the polynomial distribution of words is assumed produces a larger size of vocabulary than the observed vocabulary, especially in the first half of the text, (Figure 3 and Figure 4). To reduce the difference between the observed and the predicted vocabulary, instead of assuming the polynomial distribution of the words, their hypergeometrical distribution should be applied (Csernoch; 2005). The difference between the two models seems to be minor, but assuming the hypergeometrical distribution of the words the overestimation is usually not larger than a couple of thousand words at the very beginning of the texts and, more importantly, later on in the text the observed vocabulary fluctuates around the expected vocabulary level (Figure 5).

If we assume that the word types of the texts can be modeled by the different colored balls of an urn, and as many balls of each color are stored as the frequency of the word type (see Equation 1), then for polynomial distributions the balls are randomly selected from the urn and are returned after noting their color (Baayen; 2001, Csernoch; 2006b). The selection of balls is continued until we reach the number of tokens of the original text – model P1. With the assumption of the polynomial distribution of the words, however, there is no clear guarantee that when reaching the desired number of tokens the number of different word types of the observed text equals the number of different word types of the model. Examples of this miscalculation can be clearly seen either in Figure 3 or in Figure 4. (In Figure 3 the examples are taken from Mark Twain's THE ADVENTURES OF HUCKLEBERRY FINN, from now on HUCKLEBERRY FINN (upper panel) and Daniel Defoe's THE ADVENTURES OF ROBINSON CRUSOE, from now on ROBINSON CRUSOE, and in Figure 4 from Mark Twain's THE ADVENTURES OF TOM SAWYER, from now on TOM SAWYER.) In both figures the range of the dashed lines does not reach that of the observed graphs (solid lines) at the end of the domain. The difference between the number of the observed ($V(N)$) and the modeled – i.e. expected – ($EP1V(N)$) word types was the greatest for the number of hapax legomena ($V(1,N)$ vs. $EP1V(1,N)$)).

This drawback of the model can be corrected by a modified version of the model (P2). In order to reduce the difference between the number of the observed and the modeled word types, the number of the word types was artificially increased until the number of the observed word types was reached. However, this had to be carried out in such a way that the relative frequency of the original word types should not be changed. Finally, on the one hand, the number of hapax legomena was increased, with a decrease in the relative frequency of each hapax legomenon; on the other hand, the relative frequency of all hapax legomena was set to constant (in Figure 3 and Figure 4 dotted lines). The method worked but was unique to each text, dependent on the number and the frequency of the word types and of the hapax legomena, which was a great disadvantage of the method, since several trials had to be carried out on each text to reach a relatively good approximation.

The hypergeometrical distribution of the words, on the other hand, can be modeled by an urn where the balls are not returned after their color has been noted – model H. With word types the algorithm is the following. The number and the frequencies of the different word types of the original text are counted and then all the word types found are stored in a one-dimensional array as many times as their frequencies indicate. The size of the array equals the size of the text, i.e. the number of its tokens (Equation 1).

The random selection of a word type beyond inspecting it means erasing it from the array. Using this method the algorithm might slow down towards the end of the process, because as we advance in selecting the words, the places of the erased words are reselected more often than at the beginning. To speed up the algorithm after selecting and deleting the word from the array, the cell was not left in its original location; rather, the array was compressed by moving the elements forward. In the next step a new word was selected from this array, which was one cell shorter.

One of the advantages of model H over P1 and P2 is that the number and frequency of the word types in the model is equal to that of the original text. The other advantage of model H is that while P1 underestimates and P2 overestimates the number of word types throughout the whole text the number of the word types in model H fluctuates around the observed values (compare insets of Figure 4 and Figure 5).

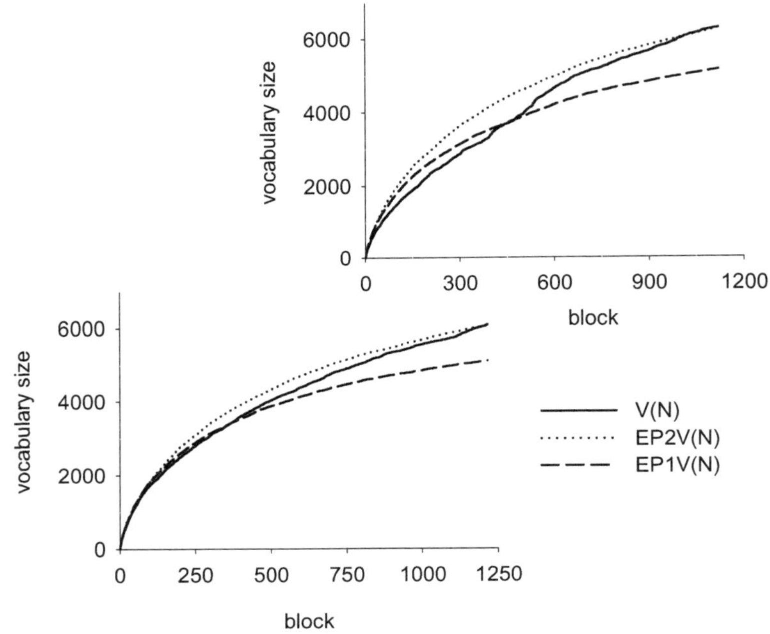

Figure 3. The comparison of the vocabulary size of HUCKLEBERRY FINN (upper panel) and ROBINSON CRUSOE (lower panel). The continuous line is for the measured values, the dashed and the dotted lines are for the values predicted by the models P1 and P2, respectively.

To take advantage of this more precise algorithm, instead of observing the change in the size of the vocabulary, the changes in the number of newly introduced word types was observed.

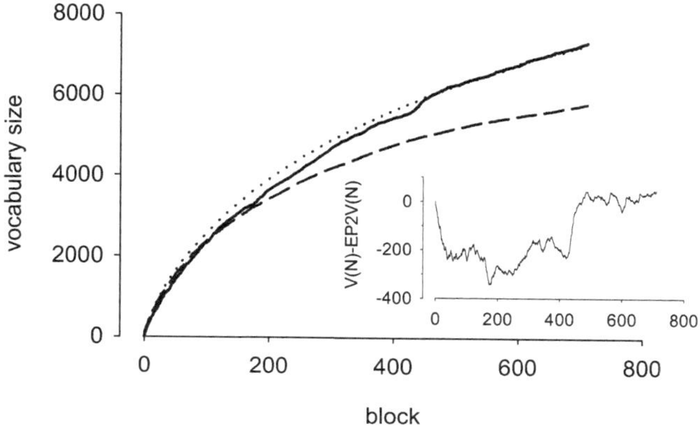

Figure 4. Changes in the size of the vocabulary in TOM SAWYER. The continuous line shows the observed vocabulary of the original text ($V(N)$). The dashed line is achieved by using the original urn mode (P1). It is clear that there is no guarantee that the size of the predicted vocabulary is as large as that of the observed. A modified version of the urn model (P2) is able to generate a vocabulary of satisfactory size. The inset shows the difference between the size of the observed ($V(N)$) and the predicted vocabulary ($EP2V(N)$). Using this model there is a continuous overestimation of the observed vocabulary size.

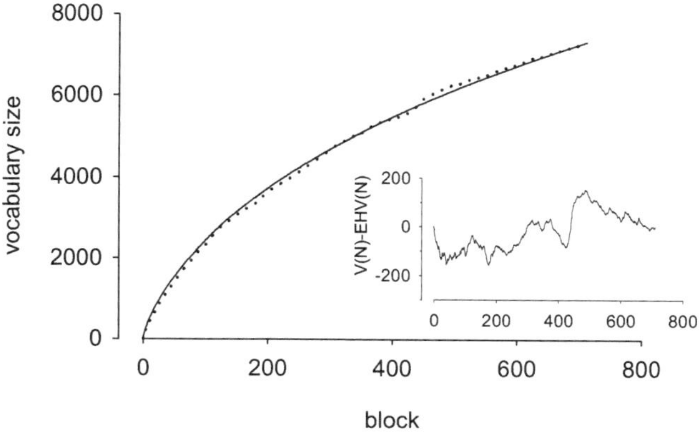

Figure 5. Changes in the size of the vocabulary in TOM SAWYER. The model used here assumes the hypergeometrical distribution of words (H). The continuous line shows the observed vocabulary ($V(N)$), while the dotted line the predicted values ($EHV(N)$). The inset shows the difference between the size of the observed and the predicted vocabulary. Using this model the predicted vocabulary fluctuates around the observed vocabulary.

To be able to observe the changes in the number of newly introduced words (word types and/or lemmas), texts were divided into smaller intervals. Newly introduced words, in this context, are those words which appear for the first time within the particular text in the given text interval (for definition see Chapter 2.1.2). However, to obtain comparable results within a text and between different texts, the method of slicing the texts had to be chosen very carefully.

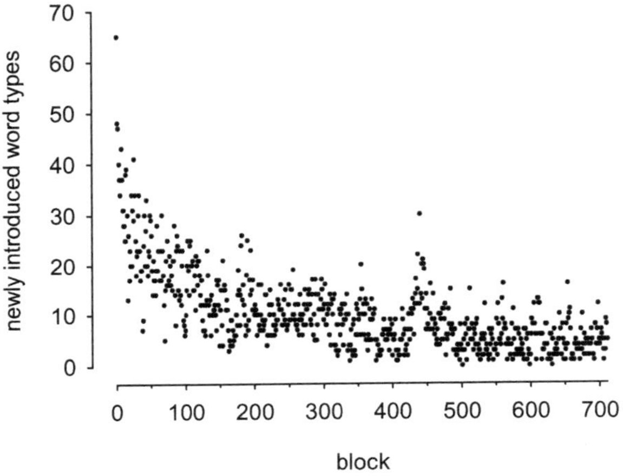

Figure 6. The number of newly introduced word types in TOM SAWYER. The text is divided into one-hundred-token-long text intervals.

Texts divided into equal-number of text intervals – twenty or forty text intervals – (Baayen; 2001), cannot be used here, because for texts with different number of tokens the lengths of these text intervals will be different. Therefore, the number of the newly introduced word types will also be different. Instead, the length of the text intervals should be constant so the number of newly introduced word types becomes comparable throughout a text and also between different texts.

The length of the intervals into which the texts are divided also had to be chosen carefully. First of all, for the length of the intervals a number had to be found which is larger than the average length of the sentences, to rule out the syntactic and semantic constraints of the language. On the other hand, this number cannot be too large because by using intervals of a couple of hundred tokens, the subtle changes in the texts might be overruled and lost for the analysis.

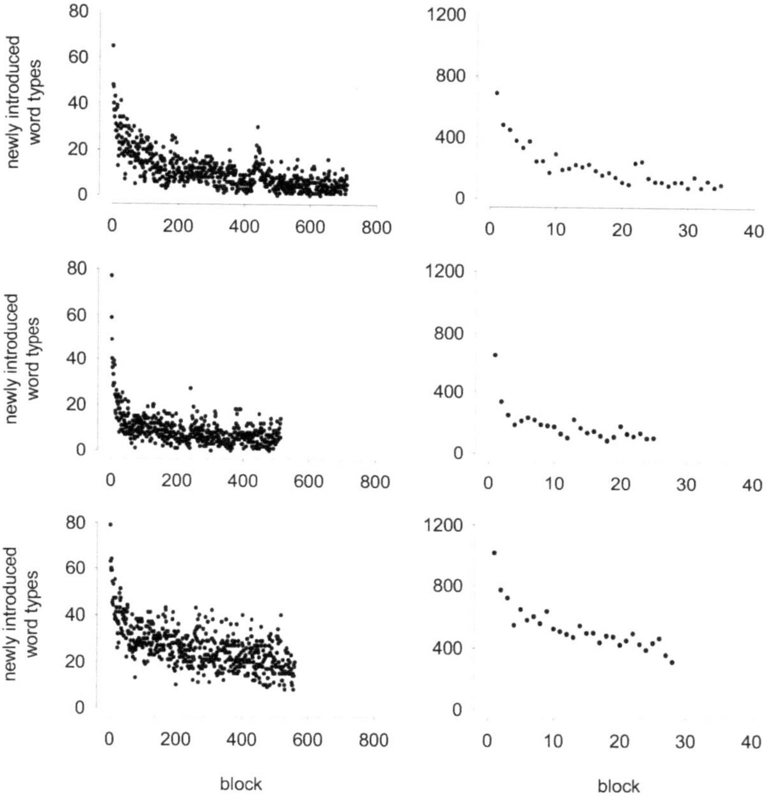

Figure 7. The length of the intervals into which the text is divided has a great influence on the number of newly introduced word types. The graphs on the left use one-hundred-token-long, while the others on the right five-hundred-token-long intervals. The texts are (from top to bottom) TOM SAWYER, Rudyard Kipling's THE JUNGLE BOOK and Kertész Imre's SORSTALANSÁG. By increasing the length of the intervals not only was the noise decreased but the graphs were flattened, with only the primary peaks left detectable; the secondary, but still informative peaks were erased.

2.3.3. Number of the different word types

The other reason why it is not the number of text intervals but rather their length that should be fixed is that by using extensive text intervals, the newly introduced word types might be so small compared to the reused word types that subtle changes might be hidden from the observer. Although Baayen's statement that the 'different word types encountered increases, quickly at first, and ever more slowly' (Baayen; 1996b) might be true generally, it is not always the case

(Figure 6 and Figure 7). The number of newly introduced word types in a text interval is highly dependent on its length (from now on these text intervals will be termed blocks).

At this point, I would like to mention that dividing the text into equal-length text intervals always has to deal with a loss of words at the end of the text. The degree of this loss, again, is the function of the selected length of the text intervals (Figure 8; Equation 14).

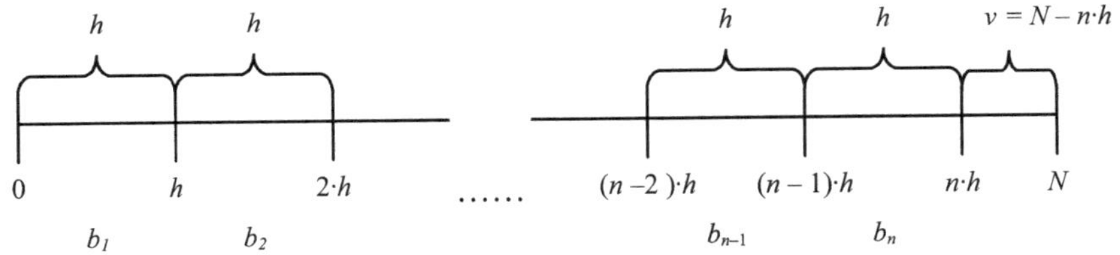

Figure 8. Texts are divided into h-token-long blocks. An N-token-long text contains n blocks, marked as b_i, where $i = 1, \ldots, n$. The loss at the end of the text is less than h token, which is minor in relation to the size of the text.

If we divide an N-token-long text into h-token-long text intervals the text is sliced into b_i blocks, where i runs from 1 to n. The loss is

$$v = N - h \cdot \left[\frac{N}{h} \right] \tag{14}$$

The value v defined above is an equally distributed statistical variable (Hajtman; 1971, Solt; 1971, Meszéna and Ziermann; 1981). According to this, the words left out of the analysis, the expected value of the loss at the end of the texts, is the average of the measured values:

$$\bar{v} = \sum_{i=1}^{r} v_i \tag{15}$$

where r is the number of the texts involved in the analysis.

Considering novels, where N, the number of tokens in a text, is between 40,000 and 400,000 (among the analyzed texts Tolstoy's WAR AND PEACE was the only one that exceeded in the number of tokens the unusually high number of 400,000) the average relative loss (v_r) is

$$\frac{\overline{V}}{400000} < v_r < \frac{\overline{V}}{40000} \quad \textbf{(16)}$$

which is approximately between 10^{-4} and 10^{-3}.

Considering all this, I found that dividing the text into one-hundred-token-long text intervals would provide usable data, and the loss at the end of the text remains infinitesimal compared to the length of the whole text (Equation 14), thus we can generously truncate the text to $h \cdot [N/h]$ token length.

2.3.4. The behavior of the newly introduced word types

The number of newly introduced word types at the very beginning of the text quickly decreases (Figure 6 and Figure 9) but in a totally unpredictable way. There might be text segments where this decrease stops and turns into a sudden increase (Figure 6, Figure 9, and Figure 19). According to Cook (1994), these sudden increases in the discourse might be responsible for making a decision on whether a piece of writing is considered literature or not. He says

> Schemata play a well-documented role in processing text, but certain texts may be complementary and, for an intelligent organism equally important. … discourse may be divided into three major types: 'schema reinforcing', 'schema preserving', and 'schema refreshing'. Discourse of the last type will deviate from schematic expectations. … Discourse which is acclaimed as 'literary' is often this 'schema refreshing' type, and it is this that accounts for the high value placed upon it.

If we accept this classification, we have to deal with texts belonging to the 'schema refreshing' type when we work with novels. Consequently, we cannot expect anything, and there is no way to tell in advance when and for what reason the writer will decide upon a significant change in vocabulary, so it is difficult, though not impossible, to build a model for a literary work.

Assuming the hypergeometrical distribution of words and using the urn model to create artificial text the outcome is also unpredictable, because of the random selection of the words. However, the pattern of newly introduced word types in an artificial text does not vary as much as in a literary work (Figure 9). As a result, the urn model might give us a pattern to which the original text can be compared. We have to keep in mind, however, that applying the urn model only once and comparing its result to the original text might lead to false conclusions. We had to find a method to rule out the unpredictable consequences of random selection. The answer is simple; not only one but several models have to be built on the same assumption and these should be compared to the original text. Using this method we might be able to reveal the 'discrepancies' in the original text.

With this approach, what seemed to be the drawback of the urn model, the difference between the original and the artificial texts, could be turned into a great advantage.

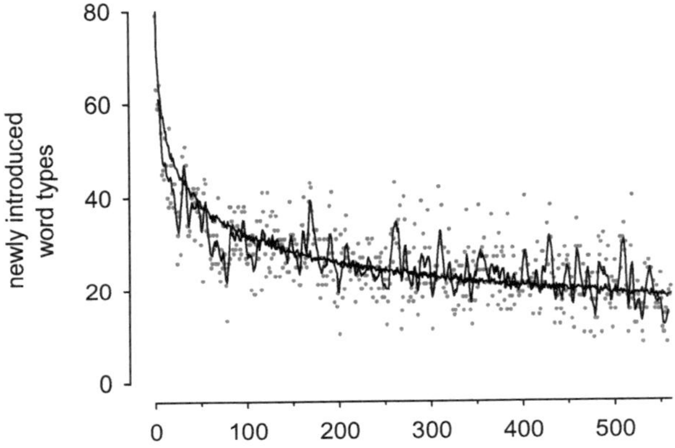

Figure 9. Newly introduced word types in SORSTALANSÁG. The number of newly introduced word types (dots), the smoothed graph of the original text (continuous line with distinct peaks on it), and the newly introduced word types of a model based text (continuous line).

2.4. What is a corpus?

To give a definition of 'corpus', first I decided to look up the definitions in dictionaries and then to see what linguists think about it.

2.4.1. *Definitions of 'corpus'*

Dictionaries of different kinds have the following to say about what a corpus is:

- A complete collection, as of laws or writings of a specified type (James; 1975, in Webster's New World Dictionary).
- A complete and comprehensive collection, as of laws or writings of a specified type (Neufeldt and Guralnik; 1991, in a newer addition of Webster's New World Dictionary).
- Collection, esp. of writings on a specified subject or of material for study (e.g. for linguists, a collection of examples of spoken and written usages (Hornby et al.; 1987).
- A collection of written and spoken language stored on computer and used for language research and writing dictionaries (Macmillan; 2002).
- All the writings or works of a particular kind or on a particular subject; especially: the complete works of an author ([1], Merriam-Webster OnLine).
- A collection or body of knowledge or evidence; especially: a collection of recorded utterances used as a basis for the descriptive analysis of a language ([1], Merriam-Webster OnLine).

The first two definitions are from older Webster's dictionaries and put the emphasis on the completeness of the collection, which is not necessarily accurate. Hornby's dictionary broadens the range to either where the texts can come from or the purposes for which a collection is created. He also mentions that both written and spoken examples might be considered. Macmillan's definition does not say anything about the size; however, it further extends the previous definitions. Here, the mode of storage is mentioned, especially the storing devices of computers as a possible way of making the collection available for further use and for others apart from the creators of the collection.

The last two examples are from the website of Merriam-Webster's electronic dictionary. The first of these definitions does not differ from the old definitions available in printed form. The second definition mentions that not only written corpora can be put together but spoken corpora, too. It also mentions, something which was not present in the older definitions, namely that these collections are mainly for the descriptive analysis of a language.

If we put these definitions together, we can find resemblances to the statements of linguists who have been working with corpora for a very long time.

2.4.2. Corpus and corpora

Sinclair (1995) prefers to define a corpus in a less flexible way in order to make it more useful for the study of language. He defines certain linguistic criteria and characteristics that a corpus is assumed to have: quantity, quality, simplicity, and documentation.

I think that Sinclair was mainly thinking of general corpora (Chapter 2.4.4), a concept which is further strengthened in one of his previous works (Sinclair; 1991). I mostly agree with Kennedy (1998), who gives the following longish description.

> The definition of a corpus as a collection of texts in an electronic database can beg many questions, for there are many different kinds of corpora. Some dictionary definitions suggest that corpora necessarily consist of structured collections of text specifically compiled for linguistics analysis, that they are large or that they attempt to be representative of a language as a whole. This is not necessarily so. Not all corpora which can be used for linguistic research were originally compiled for that purpose. Historically, it is not even the case that corpora are necessarily stored electronically so that they can be machine-readable, although this nowadays is the norm. Electronic corpora can consist of whole texts or collections of whole texts. They can consist of continuous text samples taken from whole texts; they can even be made up of collections of citations. At one extreme, an electronic dictionary may serve as a kind of corpus for certain types of linguistic research while at the other extreme a huge unstructured archive of texts may be used for similar purposes by corpus linguists.

He further gives reasons why corpora are built and accepting that it is not only general corpora which can be compiled makes Kennedy's definition more acceptable.

> Corpora have been compiled for many different purposes, which in turn influence the design, size and nature of the individual corpus....Corpora

which are designed with particular research projects in mind are sometimes called specialized corpora (Kennedy; 1998).

2.4.3. *Corpora vs. text archives*

A distinction is sometimes made between a corpus and a text archive or a text database. Whereas a corpus designed for linguistic analysis is normally a systematic, planned and structured compilation of text, an archive is a text repository, often huge and opportunistically collected, and normally not structured (Kennedy; 1998). The corpus is designed or required for a particular representative function (Leech; 1991).

2.4.4. *Corpora of different kinds*

In the following I first present a list of different kinds of existing corpora of the type that might have served as the sample texts for the first-order statistical model used in this analysis. Following the list of these existing corpora I explain the reason for creating a small corpus of my own.

Corpora can be built for various reasons. The corpus does not have to be complete. In my opinion, to fulfill that criterion is impossible, simply because you can never tell for sure that you would not find further pieces of writing that fit into your collection. To be a linguist and to have well defined aims with your corpus, or have hypotheses to prove it is all very well. However, there is always the possibility that someone else can use an already existing corpus for different goals. And finally, the corpus has to be in machine readable form. Again, in the last couple of decades computers have become so great in number and capacity that machine readability has become a requirement. On the other hand, computer readability is always a difficult question because in many cases we have to face the problem of the incompatibility of computers, storage devices and file formats. Considering all this I made a selection of existing corpora, and give their short description to see what is, in theory, available.

- Diachronic (historical) corpora
  Collections of texts from the same language gathered from different time periods. These periods can be very extensive and this therefore enables us to track changes in language evolution.
- Multilingual corpora
  The term multilingual is used here in a broad sense to include all corpora which are in at least two languages. These corpora can be parallel or

comparable. Corpora of this kind are particularly useful in translation and contrastive studies.

- Do It Yourself (DIY) Corpora

  While there are many ready-made corpora, one may find it necessary to build one's own corpus to address a particular research question.

  - Corpus size

    One must be clear about one's research question (or questions) when planning to build a DIY corpus. This helps to determine what material will need to be collected. Having developed an understanding of the type of data to be collected, and having made sure that no ready-made corpus of such material exists, a source of data needs to be found.

    Assuming that the data can be found then the question of corpus size has to be addressed. There is no easy answer to this question. The size of the corpus needed depends upon the purpose for which it is intended as well as a number of practical considerations.

    The availability of suitable data, especially in machine-readable form, seriously affects corpus size. In building a balanced corpus according to fixed proportions, for example, the lack of data for one text type may accordingly restrict the size of the samples of other text types taken. This is especially the case for parallel corpora, as it is common for the availability of translations to be unbalanced across text types for many languages. While it is often possible to transfer paper-based texts into electronic form using OCR (Optical Character Recognition) software, the process is time-consuming and expensive and is error prone (Chapter 6.6.1). Hence, the availability of machine-readable data is often the main limiting factor in corpus-building (Chapter 6.6.3).

    Another factor that potentially limits the size of a DIY corpus is copyright. Unless the proposed corpus contains entirely out-of-date or copyright-free data, simply gathering available data and using them in a freely available corpus may expose the corpus-builder to legal action (McEnery et al.; 2006).

  - Data capture

    For pragmatic reasons, electronic data are preferred over paper-based materials in building DIY corpora. The world-wide-web (www) is an important source of machine-readable data for many languages.

    The web pages on the Internet normally use Hypertext Mark-up Language (HTML) to enable browsers to display them properly. While the tags (included in angled brackets) are typically hidden when a text is displayed in a browser, they do exist in the source file of a web page. Hence, an important step in building DIY corpora using web pages is tidying up the downloaded data by converting web pages to plain text, or to some desired format (McEnery et al.; 2006).

– Character encoding
  Character encoding is rarely an issue for alphabetical languages (e.g. English) which use ASCII characters. For many other languages which use different writing systems, especially for multilingual corpora which contain a wide range of writing systems, encoding is important if one wants to display the corpus properly or facilitate data interchange (McEnery et al.; 2006).

In view of all this I had no choice but build my own multilingual corpus.

2.4.5. Selected texts

If we accept the definition of corpus given in Chapter 2.4.1 then this chapter could have been entitled 'my corpus', but I felt it somehow too ambitious to do so. It is certain that this collection of texts is a specialized multilingual corpus because the texts I needed were well defined by the goals of my analysis. Thus, I can divide them into three, well distinguishable subcorpora.

Texts collected and analyzed in this project are novels and short stories. What makes this collection special is that not only the original versions of the texts are included but their different kinds of adaptations too (for details see Chapter 4.1.1).

In accordance with translation theories which accept each modified version of a text as an adaptation I decided to examine, in this context, three kinds of adaptations of the original text:

- translation into a foreign language,
- condensation,
- lemmatization.

Both the translation into a foreign language and the condensation are procedures appropriate in particular circumstances aimed at achieving a particular kind of equivalence, and judgments of their success need to be made in terms of the adequacy of the given procedures for achieving those particular ends (Hatim and Mason; 1993). Lemmatization of the texts is a purely theoretical exercise: in this case there is no target group whose needs should be taken into account. Consequently, the three different kinds of adaptations pose different questions.

2.5. Building 'my corpus': sources of texts in electronic form

2.5.1. Texts downloaded from e-libraries

At the very beginning of the project I searched through many multilingual corpora but I was unable to find any which perfectly suited my requirements. After this I searched on-line text archives where fortunately many of the texts were available. I downloaded these texts, then made the necessary editing to fit the texts to my purposes and to the requirements of DyMoCASAT on the input files. The main sources of the texts were the following e-libraries.

- Novels in English are from
  - Project Gutenberg [2],
  - University of Virginia's E-book Library [3].
- Novels in Hungarian are downloaded from
  - Magyar Elektronikus Könyvtár (MEK; Hungarian Electronic Library) [4],
  - Digitális Irodalmi Akadémia (DIA) [5].
- Novels in French are from
  - Ebooks Libres & Gratuits [6]
- Novels in German are from
  - Spiegel Online Projekt Gutenberg-DE [7]

2.5.2. Digitization of texts

Those texts which were not available in digitized form had to be scanned or typed. Both scanning and typing are time-consuming processes. Typing is simple, one has to type fast and well enough to feel fit for such a challenge. Scanning requires other skills and equipment, and in my case this was a more realistic option than typing. Some aspects of digitalization are summarized in Appendix 6.6.

However, in both cases I also needed a printed form of the text. To collect these texts even in printed form was a great challenge. Some of them are from libraries. However, books from libraries are heavily used so the characters in many cases are faded unevenly and the scanner is not able to make corrections to such unevenly dispersed lighter and darker patches.

The other opportunity was the purchasing of new books. Those books which are available through the Internet can be ordered. The serious problem started when the texts were not available through the Internet. In these cases, I had to find other sources to collect the books. Still, I have incomplete analyses due to missing sources.

2.5.3. *Sharing digitized texts*

Because of copyright issues I cannot share these digitized texts with anyone through the Internet. However, there is one text which is out of copyright, ALICE TÜKÖRORSZÁGBAN. While working with the ALICE stories I found both ALICE'S ADVENTURES IN WONDERLAND and THROUGH THE LOOKING-GLASS AND WHAT ALICE FOUND THERE in Project Gutenberg [2], and Petőfi (1990) also gave a detailed analysis of both, but in MEK [4] only ALICE CSODAORSZÁGBAN was available. I found the book, in a relatively good condition, in a library, I scanned it, corrected it, and sent the text to MEK. They made further proofreading and finally put it in their library. Now it is available in MEK for anyone to use [10].

3. Newly introduced words

After digitizing the texts, the same process, using DyMoCASAT (Chapter 1.1), is applied to all of the texts, irrespective of language, length or word level (lemmatized or non-lemmatized). The program to carry out the analysis of newly introduced words was developed by the author. The publicly available programs were not able to produce all the parameters and data which were needed to complete the analyses.

At the beginning of the project a decision had to be made. Two choices presented themselves: to adapt one or some of the already existing programs and accept their deficiencies and make the best use of them, or to write a program which will fit the requirements of the analysis. Finally, the latter opportunity was chosen and the program called DyMoCASAT was created, with all the advantages of a special application designed for a special purpose. Consequently, the program perfectly fits the aims of this project (for details see Chapter 1). The theoretical background to the algorithms and the essence of the program is given in Chapter 3.1 (see also Csernoch; 2004, Csernoch; 2005 and 2007b).

3.1. The essence of DyMoCASAT

3.1.1. Counting and storing words

In this project analyzing the texts means that we have to count the number of words in the text (tokens and word types or lemmas, for word categories see Chapter 2.1.2) and save their location, within the limit of a block (Chapter 2.3.3), for reconstruction (Chapter 3.1.2). To determine the number of words, first the language and the set of valid characters for the language have to be defined.

After the language and the character set are set up, the first step in this process is the analysis of the text. At this stage, the number of the tokens (N) and then the number of different words ($V(N)$) are counted in the text. In the second step the text is divided into equal-length intervals (h is the length of an interval, which is usually one-hundred tokens long), called blocks (Chapter 2.3.3, Figure 8). In these blocks the number of newly introduced words has to be counted and stored (Figure 12 – Figure 16).

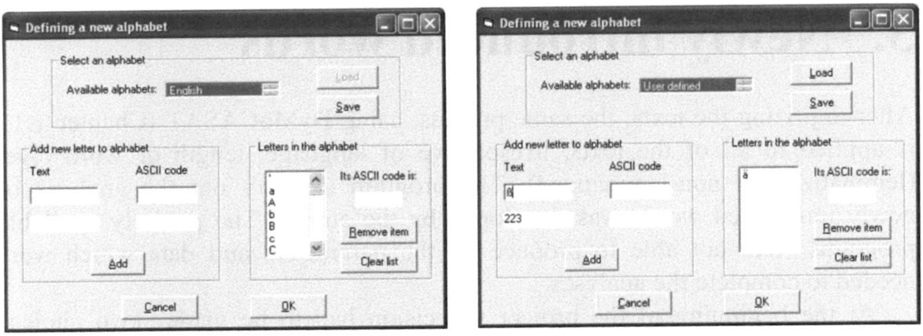

Figure 10. Screenshots from the *Defining a new alphabet* dialog box of DyMoCASAT. This dialog box has two functions. We can upload a chosen character set for further use (left panel). We can remove and add characters to the character set and save it (right panel).

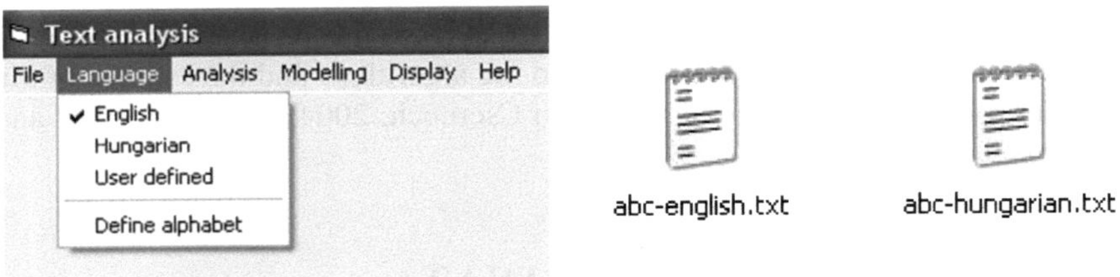

Figure 11. Screenshot from the *Language* menu of DyMoCASAT (left panel) and two sample files of user-defined character sets (right panel). These character sets are simple text files, which contain all the characters which are considered valid characters of the selected language. To be able to use these user defined character sets, first they have to be loaded into the system (*Language* menu, *Define alphabet*, then from the *Defining a new alphabe*t dialog box select the characters set, then choose command *Load,* see Figure 10). After the alphabet is uploaded, it has to be selected as the actual alphabet (*Language* menu, *User defined*).

In each block the different words are identified and the number of times they occur is counted. The amount of data gained from the text with this method required time- and space-consuming data storage. We had to be prepared for further analysis of these data, and had to find a data structure which can be searched with reasonable speed.

The location of each word is stored in a theoretical three-dimensional matrix. The matrix is theoretical, because in practice the data are stored in a number of text files, which is the first dimension of the matrix. The number of files equals the number of the different initial characters found in the text. Each file is identified by these initial characters. The first dimension is the first letter of the word, the second is the position of the word in alphabetical order within that particular character-file, while the third is the number of occurrences of the word in a particular block.

The arrangement of the words starting with letter 'a' in the blocks

	1	2	3	...	n
1	x_{a11}	x_{a12}	x_{a13}		x_{a1n}
2	x_{a21}				
3					
...					
m_a					

The arrangement of the words starting with letter 'b' in the blocks

	1	2	3	...	n
1	x_{b11}	x_{b12}	x_{b13}		x_{b1n}
2	x_{b21}				
3					
...					
m_b					

Figure 12. The arrangement of words starting with the letters 'a' and 'b' in the blocks. The words with different initial characters are saved in separate files. Here, the number of the files is not greater than the number of the valid characters of the character set. Consequently, for each text as many two-dimensional matrixes can be set up as the number of characters in the character set. For each character a maximum number is mapped, which marks the number of words starting with that particular character, where the number of words starting with 'a' (m_a) rarely equals the number of words starting with 'b'(m_b) and the same is true for the other initial characters.

The number of the words starting with letter 'a' in the blocks

	1	2	3	...	n
1	2	1	0	0	1
2	0	0	1	0	0
3	1	0	0	0	2
...					
m_a	0	1	0	0	0

The number of the words starting with letter 'b' in the blocks

	1	2	3	...	n
1	0	0	1	1	0
2	2	1	1	2	2
3	0	0	0	0	1
...					
m_b	0	0	1	0	0

Figure 13. The number of words starting with the letters 'a' and 'b' in the blocks. Not only the place where the words appear, but also their numbers in the blocks are saved.

The appearance of newly introduced words in the blocks starting with letter 'a'

	1	2	3	...	n
1	T				
2			T		
3	T				
...					
m_a		T			

The appearance of newly introduced words in the blocks starting with letter 'b'

	1	2	3	...	n
1			T		
2	T				
3					T
...					
m_b			T		

Figure 14. To decide how many relatively new words appear in the blocks for each word the first occurrence has to be marked.

In Figure 12 – Figure 14, for letters 'a' and 'b', two layers of these matrixes are detailed. The tables show the second and third dimensions of the matrixes.

With this method all the information about the location of the words is stored, so the whole text could be restored within the limit of the length of the blocks, if needed.

While in Figure 12 – Figure 14 the theoretical two-dimensional matrixes of the selected letters are shown, in Figure 15 and Figure 16 their actual representation is presented. The major difference between the measured and the stored data is that in the latter instead of the decimal numeric system a numeric system with radix 26 is used – the number of the letters of the English alphabet. In this numeric system the numbers are substituted with characters. '@', 'A', 'B', etc. standing for zero, 1, 2, etc., respectively (Figure 15 and Figure 16). It was necessary to change to a numeric system with a base greater than ten, because with one-hundred-token-long text intervals there is a good chance that the most frequent words appear more than ten times in a block. With longer blocks this number also increases. The other difference between the theoretical and the stored data, is that in the latter there is no need to store the whole two-dimensional matrix, which would mean $m_a \times n$ cells for letter 'a', and $m_b \times n$ cells for letter 'b', etc. Instead, the last data stored in the real representation is the last non-zero value (Figure 15 and Figure 16).

```
'em
@@@@@@@@@@@@@@@@@@@@@@@@@@@@@@@@@@@@@@@@@@@@@@@@@@@@@@@@@@@@@@@@@@@
@@@@@@@B@@@@@@@@@@@@@@@@@@@@@@@@@@@@@@@@@@@A
'tis
@@@@@@@@@@@@@@@@@@@@@@@@@@@@@@@@@@@@@@@@@@@@@@@@@@@@@@@@@@@@@@@@@@@
@@@@@@@@@@@@@@@@@@@@@@@@@@@@@@@@@@@@@@@@@@@@@@@@@@@@@@@@@@@@@@@@@@@
@@@@@@@@@@@@@@@@@@@@@@@@@@@@@@@@@@@@@@@@@@@@@@@@@@@@C@@@@@@@@@@@@@@
@@@@@@@@@@@@@@@@@@A
```

Figure 15. Two words starting with an apostrophe in ALICE'S ADVENTURES IN WONDERLAND. The first character different from @ indicates the block in which the word appears first and from the value of this character we can calculate the number of occurrences. In this example, *'em* appears twice in the 75th block of the text and once in the 118th block, while *'tis* appears three times at its first occurrence (187th block) and once at its second occurrence (220th block).

```
western
@AA
westward
@@@@@@@@@@@@@@@@@@@@@@@@@@@@@@@@@@@@@@@@@@@@@@@@@@@@@@@@@@@@@@@@@@A
what
B@@@A@@@A@AA@@@@@@BBBBDAB@@DC@BAA@@@@@@A@@AAB@@ABAB@DAA@@@@@@@@@@@@
A@A@@@AA@@@@@@@@@@@@@@A@@@@@@@@@A@@@@@@AA@@@@@@@@A@@@@@@@@A@@@AAA@@
@A
```

Figure 16. A segment of the words starting with letter 'w' from THE GOLD BUG. Here, *western* appears in the 2nd and the 3rd blocks once, *what* appears first in the first block twice, then in the fifth block once, etc.

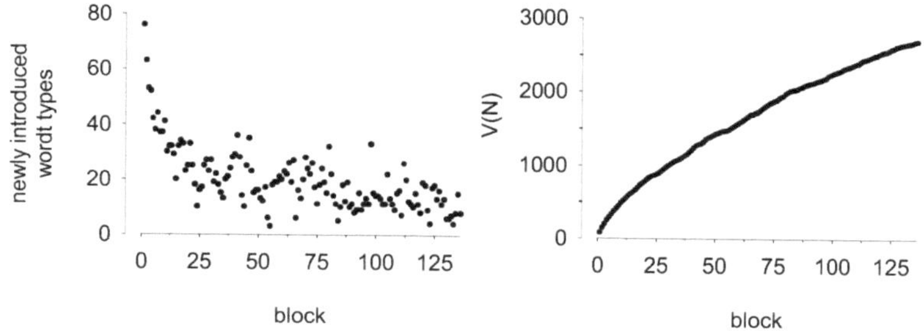

Figure 17. The newly introduced word types (left panel) and the changes in the vocabulary size (right panel) of THE GOLD BUG, using one-hundred-token-long blocks. The sum of the newly introduced word types is the vocabulary size, and by advancing along the blocks at the end we reach the total size of vocabulary.

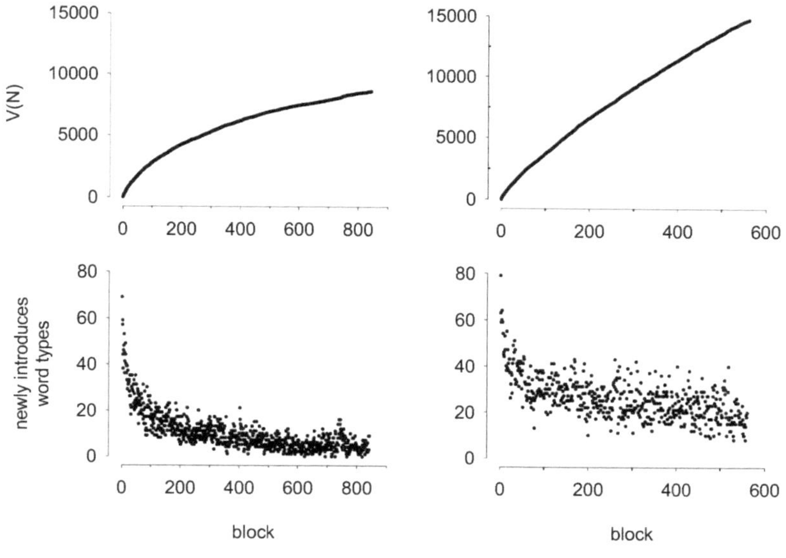

Figure 18. As mentioned and demonstrated with small examples in Chapter 2.1.4 English texts carry the greatest number of tokens, but the smallest number of word types, while in Hungarian it is the other way around, Hungarian texts have the fewest tokens, but the greatest number of word types. In the left panels are the graphs for the vocabulary size (upper panel) and the newly introduced word types (lower panel) of the English THE SCARLET LETTER, while in the right panels are the same graphs for the Hungarian SORSTALANSÁG.

For our analyses, however, not only the location of the words but the location of their first appearance should also be saved. If we compare Figure 13 and Figure 14 the difference between the two matrixes is that Figure 14 stores only the location – the number of the block – of the first appearance of the word. To know how many newly introduced word types appear in a block we have to count the number of first appearances in each block.

In the last step of collecting data a number is assigned to each block – the number of newly introduced words. This is the number of words which are new in the current block compared to previous blocks. Using the variables introduced in Chapter 2.3.3, i marks the number of the blocks, where i runs from 1 to n (i =1, …, n). The value of $f(i)$ marks the number of newly introduced words to each block (Figure 6 is the first of this type in this work). Henceforth $f(i)$ stands for function of newly introduced words.

In general, the number of newly introduced word types follows a monotonic decay (Figure 19). However, we can find sections where this monotonic decay is reversed and a sudden increase then a sudden drop can be detected in the number of newly introduced words. We are interested in finding the location of these sections and finding reasons for their presence (Figure 20, left panels).

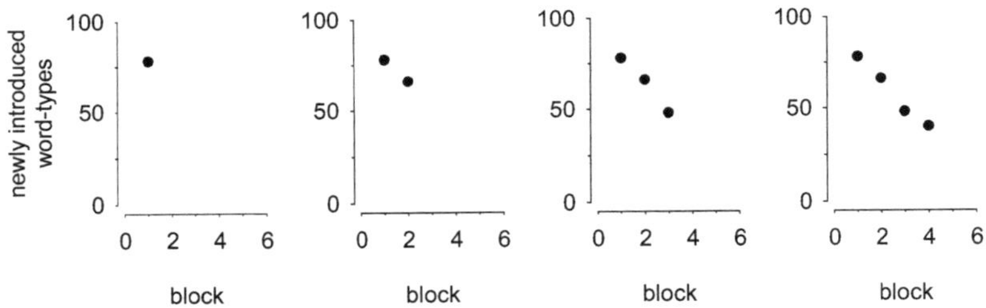

Figure 19. The number of newly introduced word types in the first four blocks of the condensed version of THE DA VINCI CODE. As the graphs show, in general, newly introduced word types follow a descending tendency.

To rule out accidental increases in the function of newly introduced word types ($f(i)$, Figure 21 left, upper panel) a smoothing process was applied. The result is the function $fp(i)$ (i =1, …, n), which follows the same pattern as $f(i)$, but the short, accidental peaks are eliminated (Figure 21 left column, middle panel, for the details of smoothing see Chapter 3.2).

Since the discrete values of function $f(i)$ are replaced by function $fp(i)$, the graph shows more clearly the tendency the newly introduced words follow.

3.1.2. Creating artificial texts

After analyzing the text using DyMoCASAT a first-order statistical model was built, based on the assumption that words appearing in a text are hypergeometrically distributed (Csernoch; 2006a, 2006b). To build this model, a random selection of words was made whose outcome was an artificial text (see right panel of Figure 20). This artificial text contains as many word types (and lemmas) as the original text, with exactly the same frequencies.

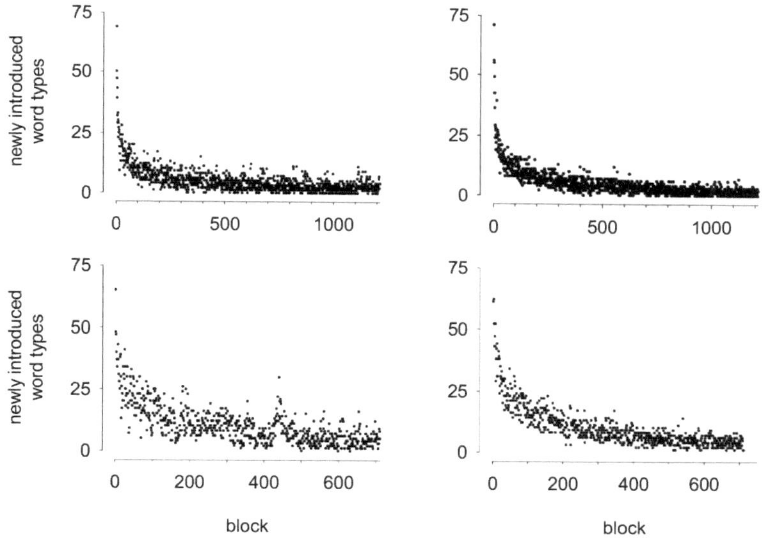

Figure 20. The number of the newly introduced word types of ROBINSON CRUSOE (upper left panel) and TOM SAWYER (lower left panel). The number of newly introduced word types of the model-based artificial texts of the two novels (right panels). These artificial texts are created with a random selection of words, based on the assumption that the words are hypergeometrically distributed. Consequently, these artificial texts have the same number of word types with the same frequencies as the original texts.

The artificial text was analyzed using the same method applied to the original text. In the last step of collecting data the number of newly introduced words of the artificial text was counted in each block. Random selection, however, by its very nature might cause unpredictable changes in the number of newly introduced words (Figure 20). To rule this possibility out, a hundred artificial texts were created and averaged ($F(i)$; Figure 21 left, lower panel).

3.1.3. *Determining the significant changes in newly introduced words*

The next step in the process was to determine the differences between the number of newly introduced word types of the original and the artificial texts. The difference is calculated as the difference in the values of the graph of the smoothed and of the artificial text ($fp(i)$ and $F(i)$, respectively; Figure 21 right, upper panel).

The sudden increases in the number of vocabulary items are represented by protuberances on the difference graph. This protuberance graph is unique to each text, like a fingerprint. If we learnt how to read them we would be able to distinguish the texts by looking at their graphs (similarly to identifying a sound file by its wave graph) and able to follow the general changes in vocabulary by visualization. To select those protuberances which represent significant changes in the vocabulary of the text we have to set the significance level. The mean (M) and the standard deviation (SD) of the differences of $fp(i) - F(i)$ were calculated and mapped on the same coordinate system for better visualization (Figure 21 right middle panel).

The values considered distinguishable are those which exceed the $M + 2SD$ value (Figure 21 right lower panel). We are interested in these significant protuberances. We wanted to find them, and we succeeded, as detailed in this chapter; in the next chapter we will give details of their behavior and try to find explanations for their presence (for details see Chapter 4, Csernoch; 2005a, 2007b).

The result of the analysis is always a graph (Figure 21 right upper panel – Figure 21 right lower panel). The flow of this graph is unpredictable, since there is no clear evidence as to what it is that makes a writer increase the number of newly introduced words, and at what point in the story. The corresponding graphs for such pieces of literature usually provide significant protuberances in the graphs. These protuberances have at least two distinguishable parameters, length and intensity. The length of a protuberance is the number of tokens or blocks ($token = 100 \cdot block$) where the protuberance is above the significance level (Table 14); henceforth these set of blocks are called text segments. To refer to a particular text segment the number of the starting and the ending block is given. Beyond these numbers, to be able to distinguish between the different adaptations of the texts, the source is also marked. Usually, the abbreviation for the source refers to the language of the text – H for Hungarian, E for English, F for French and G for German –, to make more precise distinctions, if necessary, other marks are used, e.g. the name of the author, translator, editor. Finally, intensity is defined as the height of the protuberance, which is the local maximum of function $fp(i) - F(i)$, indicating the degree to which the peak of the protuberance is above the mean of the function.

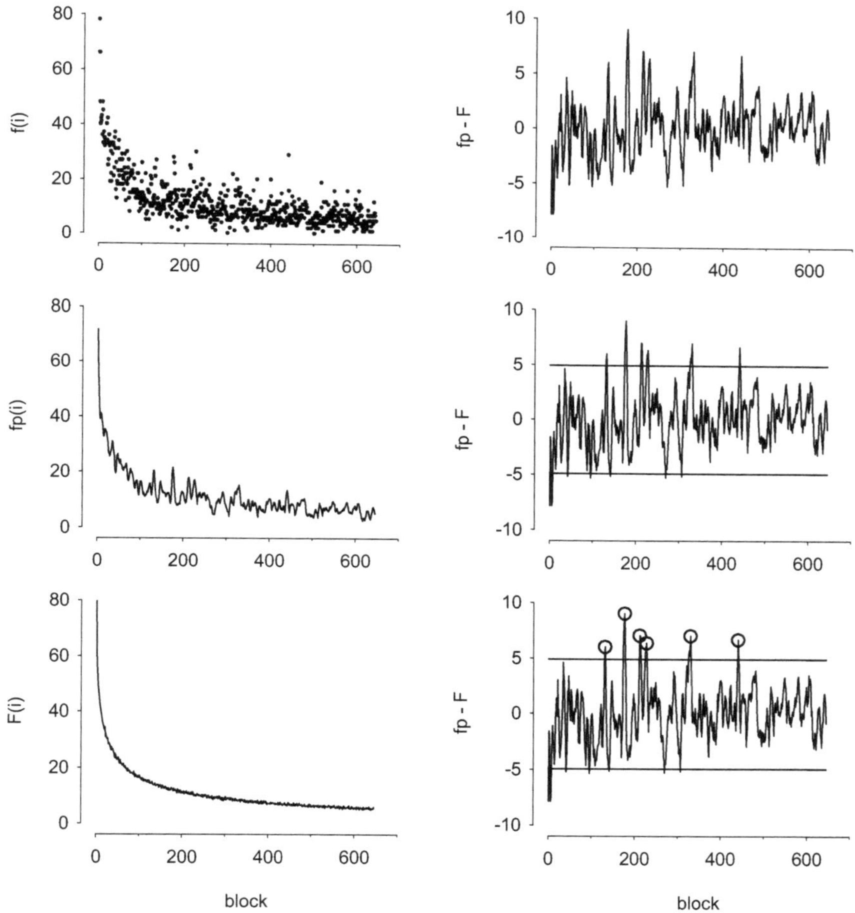

Figure 21. The major steps in the process of analyzing the newly introduced words with DyMoCASAT (condensed English version of THE DA VINCI CODE). First, the newly introduced words were counted in each block (left upper panel, $f(i)$), then this function was smoothed (left middle panel, $fp(i)$). In the third step 100 artificial texts were created and the number of newly introduced words was averaged for each corresponding block (left lower panel, $F(i)$). The difference between the averaged artificial and the smoothed function was calculated (right upper panel). The level of significance was determined as M ± 2SD (right middle panel). Those protuberances were considered significant which exceed the significance level (right lower panel).

3.2. Smoothing the graph of newly introduced words

The results of the smoothing process with different parameters are demonstrated in Figure 22. The raw, non-smoothed graph returns all of the peaks, where an increase in the number of newly introduced word types is present. Even the short, uncharacteristic protuberances appear on the graph (Figure 22 upper panel). To reduce the noise of the graphs a smoothing process was applied. The method of least squares and polynomial smoothing was used because the process leaves the relative position of the peaks untouched. I would like to emphasize that this smoothing process works well with discrete and equally distributed domains, which is exactly the case in this analysis (Worthing and Geffner; 1959, Guest; 1961). The effect of the different number of base-points of the smoothing is demonstrated in the lower panels of Figure 22.

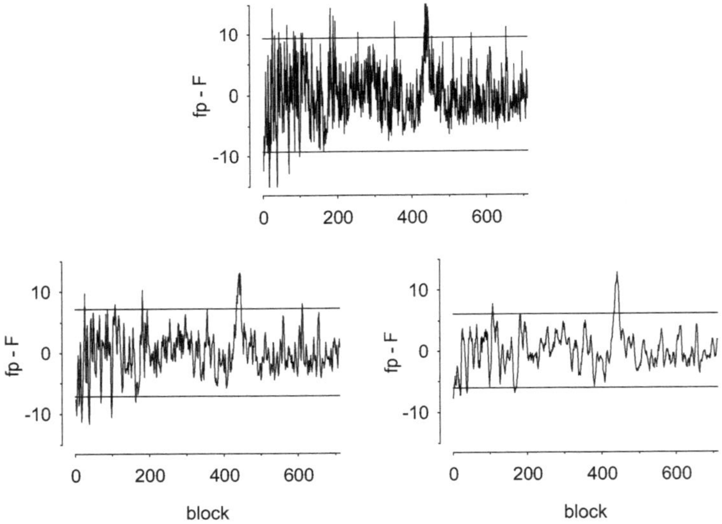

Figure 22. The differences between the observed and the predicted number of newly introduced word types. In the upper panel the raw data of the observed number of word types are used in the difference. Below, in the left panel a 7-point smoothing process was applied to the raw data. In the right panel a 14-point smoothing was applied.

3.3. Word types vs. lemmas

To generate lemmatized texts some of the English and Hungarian texts were tagged and lemmatized with an automatic Part of Speech tagger and lemmatizer program (for details see Appendices 6.2 – 6.4, Csernoch; 2010). Both the selected English and Hungarian texts were fully tagged. To the original word types the programs added the lemmas, and all the possible affixes attachable to the lemma were marked. Finally, the programs selected the one affix which was most likely to be correct in the context.

```
leaveVV theAT hotelNN aAT fortunateJJ coincidenceNN langdonNN beVB feelVV
anythingRR butRR fortunateJJ andCC coincidenceNN beVB aAT conceptNN hePP
doVD notXX entirelyRR trustVV asCSA someonePN whoPNQ haveVH spendVV
hisAPPGE lifeNN exploreVV theAT hiddenJJ interconnectivityNN ofIO
disparateJJ emblemNN andCC ideologyNN langdonNP viewVV theAT worldNN asII
aAT webNN ofIO profoundlyRR intertwinedJJ historyNN andCC eventNN theAT
connectionNN mayVM beVB invisibleJJ hePP oftenRR preachVV toII hisAPPGE
symbologyNN classNN atII harvardNP butCCB theyPP beVB alwaysRR thereRL
buryVV justRR beneathII theAT surfaceNN iPP assumeVV langdonNP sayVV
thatCST theAT americanJJ universityNN ofIO parisNP tellVV youPP whereCS
iPP beVB stayVV theAT driverNN shakeVV hisAPPGE headNN interpolVV
interpolVV langdonNP thinkVV
```

Figure 23. The 37th one-hundred-token-long text interval of the lemmatized English THE DA VINCI CODE. The original word types are replaced by the corresponding lemma and the POS tag of the lemma.

```
EiffeltoronyN feléNU azPro kérdezV hogyCon meghágPre eClit márAdv Langdon
csakAdv bámulV nemAdv nemAdv mászikV mégAdv fölPre aDet toronyN
FranciaországN szimbólumN azPro hiszV tökéletesA Langdon szórakozottanAdv
bólintV aDet szimbólumkutatóN gyakranAdv állapítV megPre hogyCon egyNum
olyanPro országN amelyPro aDet macho tempóN szerelmesA természetN ésCon
azDet olyanPro apróA termetN miattNU kisebbségiA érzésN küzdőMIF vezetőN
híresA mintCon napóleonN vagyCon kisA pipiN keresV semAdv találhatV vanV
magaPro illőA nemzetiA jelképN egyNum háromszázNum méterN magasA
phallosznál amikorAdv odaérikPre aDet rue deCon Rivoli kereszteződésN
pirosA váltV aDet lámpaN deCon aDet CitroenN nemAdv lassítV aDet nyomozóN
átsüvítPre aDet kereszteződésN ésCon ráfordulPre aDet faN szegélyezettMIB
rue deCon Castiglione amelyPro
```

Figure 24. The 34th one-hundred-token-long text interval of the lemmatized Hungarian THE DA VINCI CODE. The original word types are replaced by the corresponding lemmas and the POS tags of the lemmas.

For the analysis of newly introduced lemmas, however, not only the lemmas, but the lemmas along with the chosen category of word had to be kept to enable us to distinguish polysemous words. From this point on, the original text is converted into a text where word types are replaced by a string whose first part is the corresponding lemma and the second part is the tag of the lemma (Figure 23 and Figure 24). The analysis and modeling of the lemmatized texts were carried out, and again those text segments were selected where the number of newly introduced words, now lemmas, is higher than predicted.

It should be noted, however, that intentional stylistic changes used by the authors (e.g. to indicate a character's special style of speaking, see Table 3) will be lost with the lemmatization process. This will inevitably lead to a decrease in vocabulary size and usually to a reduction in the number of newly introduced words. As a consequence, vocabulary rich text segments can be lost in lemmatized versions (as will be shown and discussed in Chapter 1.1).

Table 3. Syntactically incorrect expressions from Charles Dickens's DAVID COPPERFIELD and Winston Groom's FORREST GUMP. Through the lemmatization process not only the affixes but words and expressions differing from literary English can also be lost.

Charles Dickens: David Copperfield	Winston Groom: Forrest Gump
anywheres → anywhere	dunno → don't know
Heerd → heard	I says, she say→ I say, she says
fur → for	I be → I was
'twixt, betwixt → between	po ole → poor old
furdest → farthest	srimp bidness → shrimp business

4. Vocabulary rich segments of novels

4.1. Texts and their foreign language translations

4.1.1. List of the analyzed texts

Analysis of the introduction of new words (either word types or lemmas) in the foreign language translations of a text reveals a novel feature of the translated text. Since texts contain several untranslatable elements, and elements which the translator is not willing to reproduce for various reasons, their replacement with other lexical elements is acceptable (Bart and Klaudy; 1985, Simigné; 2006, Rybicki; 2003). From the point of view of translation theory it would be interesting to know how changes in the vocabulary of translations follow the changes of the vocabulary in the original text. With the method described above we can decide whether the translation is as rich in vocabulary as the original text.

To get comparable results texts were chosen, whose foreign language translation(s) was/were also available at least in printed form.

The following texts give the main stream of the analysis:

- a 20th century Hungarian novel (Kertész Imre: SORSTALANSÁG, Kertész; 1975), and its
  - German (ROMAN EINES SCHICKSALLOSEN, Kertész and Viragh; 1996), and
  - English (FATELESS, Kertesz, Wilson and Wilson; 1992) translation,
- a 21st century English novel (Dan Brown: THE DA VINCI CODE, Brown; 2003) and
  - its three full-length translations
    - Hungarian (A DA VINCI-KÓD, Brown and Bori; 2004),
    - German (SAKRILEG, Brown and Poll; 2004), and
    - French (DA VINCI CODE, Brown and Roche; 2004) translation,
  - its two Readers' Digest condensed versions
    - English (Brown; 2004),
    - Hungarian (Brown; 2005),
- a 19th century English novel (Mark Twain: THE ADVENTURES OF TOM SAWYER, Twain; 1876) its

  - Hungarian (TOM SAWYER KALANDJAI, Twain and Koroknay; 1977), and
  - French (LES AVENTURES DE TOM SAWYER, Twain; 2007) translations, and
  - its Readers' Digest condensed versions
    - in English (Twain; 1966),
- another 19th century English novel (Daniel Defoe: THE ADVENTURES OF ROBINSON CRUSOE, Defoe; 1719)
- a collection of English short stories (Rudyard Kipling: THE JUNGLE BOOKS, Kipling; 1961) and its
  - Hungarian translation (A DZSUNGEL KÖNYVE, Kipling, Benedek and Weöres; 1976),
  - three German translations
    - DAS DSCHUNGELBUCH and DAS NEUE DSCHUNGELBUCH edited by Dagobert von Mikusch in 1951 (Kipling and Mikusch; 1951, from now on Mikusch, 1951),
    - DAS DSCHUNGELBUCH and DAS ZWEITE DSCHUNGELBUCH translated by Gisbert Haefs (Kipling and Haefs; 1987, from now on Haefs, 1987),
    - DAS DSCHUNGELBUCH (1987) translated by Wolf Harranth (Kipling and Harranth; 2004, from now on Harranth, 1987) and a
  - French translation (LE LIVRE DE LA JUNGLE, Kipling, Fabulet and d'Humieres ; 1899a and LE SECOND LIVRE DE LA JUNGLE, Kipling, Fabulet and d'Humieres ; 1899b),
- an English novel from the beginning of the 20th century (Baroness Orczy: THE SCARLET PIMPERNEL, Orczy; 1903)
  - its Readers' Digest condensed versions
    - in English (Orczy; 1966),
- two English stories for children (Lewis Carroll: ALICE'S ADVENTURES IN WONDERLAND, Carroll; 1866 and THROUGH THE LOOKING-GLASS AND WHAT ALICE FOUND THERE, Carroll; 1871, from now on ALICE) and their
  - Hungarian translation (ALICE CSODAORSZÁGBAN, Carroll, Kosztolányi and Szobotka; 1974 and ALICE TÜKÖRORSZÁGBAN, Carroll, Révbíró and Tótfalusi; 1980),
  - French translation (ALICE AU PAYS DES MERVEILLES, Carroll ; 2004a and DE L'AUTRE COTE DU MIROIR, Carroll ; 2004b)
- a 19th century Hungarian novel (Gárdonyi Géza: EGRI CSILLAGOK, Gárdonyi; 1899)

Table 4. The number of one-hundred-token-long blocks (*n*), word types (*V*(*N*)) and hapax legomena (*V*(1,*N*)) in SORSTALANSÁG, THE JUNGLE BOOKS, the ALICE stories, THE DA VINCI CODE, and TOM SAWYER and in their foreign language translations.

	n	V(N)	V(1,N)
		Sorstalanság	
Hungarian	561	14740	10253
English	716	6710	3186
German	719	9992	6043
		The Jungle Books (full-length texts)	
English	1171	7452	3124
French	1238	12303	6410
Haefs, 1987	1132	12350	6890
Hungarian	922	20362	13372
		The Jungle Books (adjusted to Mikusch, 1951)	
English	1107	7179	3020
Mikusch, 1951	1079	13570	7683
Haefs, 1987	1070	11811	6590
French	1170	11860	6211
Hungarian	872	19455	12782
		The Jungle Book (adjusted to Harranth, 1987)	
English	453	4306	1911
Harranth, 1987	463	7247	4114
Haefs, 1987	433	6423	3636
Mikusch, 1951	464	7638	4443
		Alice's Adventures in Wonderland and Through the Looking-Glass	
English	562	3879	1515
Hungarian	422	9730	6257
French	608	6248	3120
		The Da Vinci Code	
English	1397	11442	4899
Hungarian	1199	25394	16263
French	1361	14980	7591
German	1452	18539	10581
		The Adventures of Tom Sawyer	
English	711	7331	3556
French	685	9206	5016
Hungarian	581	14038	9280

Texts in different languages, as was expected, contain different numbers of tokens, word types, and hapax legomena (Table 4). This means that they are not comparable based on these absolute numbers. As detailed in Chapter 2.3.2 and 2.3.3, all of the texts are divided into one-hundred-token-long blocks, where the number of the newly introduced word types is comparable.

The Hungarian texts contain the smallest number of tokens but the highest number of word types and hapax legomena. This is the direct consequence of the agglutinating character of the Hungarian language (Chapter 2.1.4). The German texts are about as long as the English texts; however, the German texts contain more word types than the English texts, which is due to the inflective character of the language. Beyond the measured values, the proportion of the hapax legomena, the $V(1,N)/V(N)$ quotient, provides a second proof of the inflective character of the German language. In all of the analyzed German texts the proportion of the hapax legomena is higher than in the English texts. The numbers of tokens in the French texts fluctuate around the English texts, with a higher proportion of hapax legomena.

4.1.2. *Sorstalanság and its translations*

4.1.2.1. *Sorstalanság in Hungarian*

In the original Hungarian SORSTALANSÁG (Kertész; 1975a) six significant protuberances were detected, which refer to vocabulary rich segments of the text. The first five protuberances represent descriptions of places and events, while the last is different in nature from the others since it represents songs, moreover hyphenated songs (Figure 25, H[508–511]). It is remarkable that with the descriptions of new places and events there is also a detectable change in style; however a change in style is the clearest at the sixth protuberance where the style of the song is completely different from the style of the protagonist or the style of the camps. However, regardless of how significant the changes in style are, all the six text segments have only a marginal connection to the story (Csernoch; 2007a).

Figure 25 and Table 5 show the location of the peaks where the significant protuberances appeare. The length of these protuberances (Table 5) is calculated as the distance between the number of the block where the intensity reaches significance level and the number of the block where the intensity drops below significance level (for details see Chapter 3.1.3).

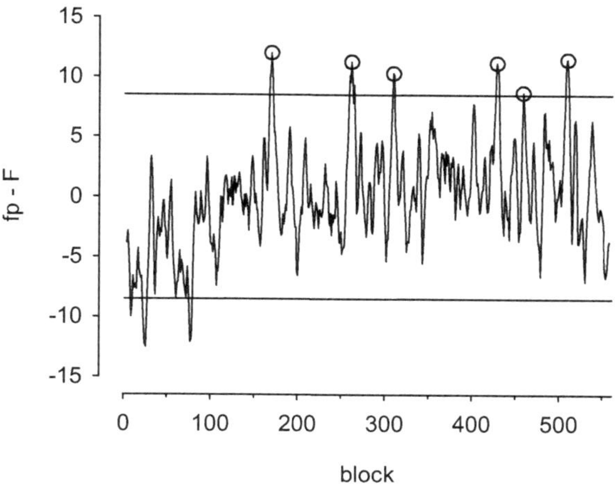

Figure 25. The protuberances of the *fp* - *F* difference graph of the novel SORSTALANSÁG. The circles mark those protuberances whose peaks reach above significance level. Other protuberances are also detectable but their peaks are below the significance level. In this text the number of blocks (*n*) equals 561.

The peaks refer to those events which were distinguished from the other part of the text by the introduction of more word types than expected based on the model. They are the vocabulary rich segments of the text. The arrivals at both concentration camps refer not only to the actual arrivals, but rather to the description of the camps (H[168–171] and H[260–265]). In both cases a detailed description of the surroundings was given. In block H[310–311] a detailed description of the repeated morning activities is given. Here not only the surroundings, but the morning activities are included in the description (H[428–431]). The hospital topic is again a description of the building, the ward, and the patients. 'Pjetyka's cooking' has only a minor role but the words used in this section of the text are so different from the main body of the text that they were able to give a rise in the number of newly introduced word types (H[459]). We do not really expect anything in terms of vocabulary richness at the point of leaving the camp. However, a peak did appear on the graph at this point (H[508–511]). I can suggest at least two reasons for this observation. On leaving the camp the former inhabitants were singing and the word types of the lyrics gave rise to the newly introduced word types. In addition to these relatively new word types, some of the songs were intentionally hyphenated, which further increased the number of newly introduced word types.

Table 5. The text segments of SORSTALANSÁG, which triggered significant protuberances on the graph of the newly introduced word types.

Text segment	Position in text
arriving at Auschwitz	168–171
arriving at Buchenwald	260–265
mornings, factory	310–311
hospital	428–431
Pjetyka's cooking	459
leaving camp	508–511

4.1.2.2. German translation of Sorstalanság, Roman eines Schicksallosen

In the German translation (Kertész; 1975b) six significant protuberances were found (Table 6 and Figure 26). The first of the significant German protuberances – G[209] – appeared earlier than the first Hungarian – H[168–171]. By re-reading the text segments, which generated these two first protuberances it was found that they use similar vocabulary items. It is thus not surprising that there is only a small protuberance – the peak is below significance level – in the German translation – G[222], where the first significant protuberance was found in the Hungarian text.

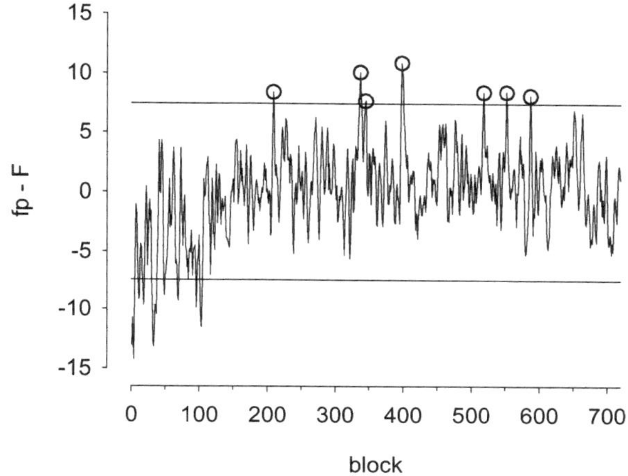

Figure 26. The protuberances of the German translation, ROMAN EINES SCHICKSALLOSEN, of SORSTALANSÁG. In this text the number of blocks (n) equals 719.

Table 6. The significant protuberances of SORSTALANSÁG and its German translation. There are remarkable similarities between the changes in vocabulary in the Hungarian and the German texts.

Text segment	Position in text	
	Hungarian (H)	German (G)
departure of the train		209
arriving at Auschwitz	168–171	222*
arriving at Buchenwald	260–265	336–338
Auschwitz vs. Buchenwald	270	344–345
mornings, factory	310–311	397–400
protagonist's mental state	402*	518
hospital	428–431	552
Pjetyka's cooking	459	587
leaving camp	508–511	651*

* text segments whose protuberances are slightly under significance level

Peaks H[260–265] + H[270] and G[336–338] + G[344–345] are double peaks, found at exactly the same text segments. The only difference between the two double peaks is that in the German text the values between the two peaks drop below significance level, creating two thin protuberances in length, while the two peaks of the Hungarian double peak are closer to each other, generating a wider segment. Peaks H[310–311] and G[397–400] represent the same text segments, the description of morning activities. The fifth significant protuberance of the German translation – G[518] – represents the description of the protagonist's mental state. If we compare the two graphs of Figure 25 and Figure 26, we can see that in the Hungarian text there was also an increase in the size of the vocabulary and the peak almost reached significance level – H[402]. Finally, the last three significant protuberances of the Hungarian text are detectable in the German text also. Two of them are significant (G[552] and G[587]), while the very last one – the hyphenated songs – does not reach significance level in the German text. This can be explained by the fact that in the German digitized text the songs are not hyphenated, so the number of the newly introduced word types generated a movement towards significance level but without the hyphenation did not reach it.

4.1.2.3. The English translation of Sorstalanság, Fateless

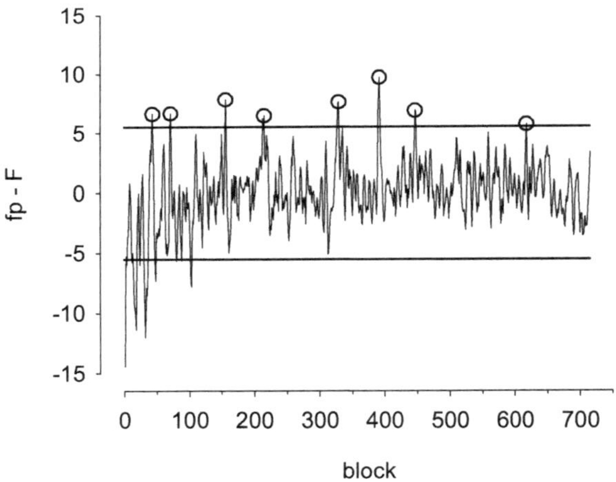

Figure 27. The protuberances of the English translation of SORSTALANSÁG, FATELESS. Compared to the Hungarian and German texts, where the significant protuberances are equally dispersed along the text, in FATELESS towards the end of the story the number of significant protuberances drops markedly. In this text the number of blocks (*n*) is 716.

The English translation (Kertész; 1975c), by counting the tokens, is as long as the German translation, but the number of the word types is about a third and the number of hapax legomena is about half of that in the German translation (Table 4).

Table 7. The peaks of the text segments, which triggered significant protuberances in the graphs of the newly introduced word types of SORSTALANSÁG, in its German, and its English translations.

Text segment	Position in text		
	Hungarian (H)	German (G)	English (E)
Uncle Vili		45*	43
factory in Csepel		73*	71
train's departure		209	156
arriving at Auschwitz	168–171	222*	213–215
arriving at Buchenwald	260–265	336–338	327–329
Auschwitz vs. Buchenwald	270	344–345	344*
mornings, factory	310–311	397–400	390–393
protagonist's physical state			447
protagonist's mental state	402*	518	511*
hospital	428–431	552	
Pjetyka's cooking	459	587	
daily schedule			618
leaving camp	508–511	651*	

* text segments whose protuberances are slightly under significance level

Analyzing the English translation, again, significant protuberances were found at places where 'longish' descriptions were inserted into the text. The major protuberances of the Hungarian and German texts are also present in the English text, but the overlap is not as clear as expected (Table 7, Figure 25, Figure 26, and Figure 27). At the beginning of the English translation two 'new' protuberances appeared – E[43] and E[71] –, which can be found in traces in the German, but not in the Hungarian text. Interestingly, both E[156] and E[213–215] are present, while in the Hungarian and German texts only one of them triggered significant protuberances. The peaks representing the 'arrival at Buchenwald' is clearly there in all three texts – H[260–265], G[336–338], E[327–329]. The double peak of H[260–265] + H[270] is also detectable in the English translation but its second peak does not reach significance level. The description of 'mornings, factory' is again present in all three texts – H[310–311], G[397–400], E[390–393], but E[447] is neither in the Hungarian nor the German text. At the end of the English translation text segments for 'hospital', 'Pjetyka's cooking', and 'leaving camp' do not generate significant protuberances. However, unlike in the Hungarian and German texts, at E[618] a significant protuberance is detected, triggered by vocabulary items describing the 'daily schedule' (Table 7).

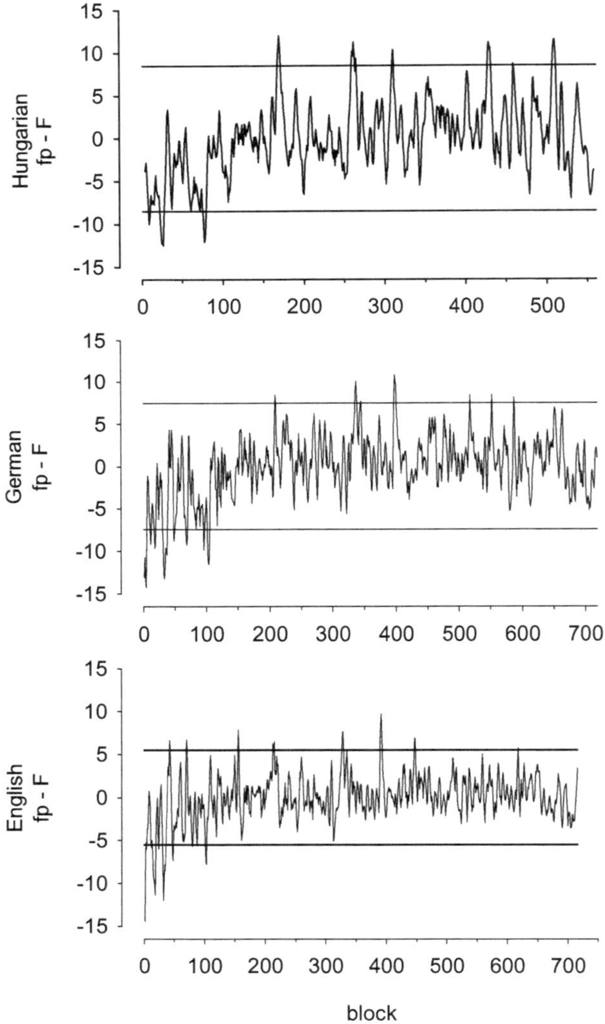

Figure 28. The protuberances of the Hungarian, German and English texts of SORSTALANSÁG. The German translation followed the changes of vocabulary remarkably well, while the English translation seems richer in vocabulary at the beginning of the text and flattened in the second half of the text.

The comparison of the three texts reveals that the German translation follows the original text more closely in the appearance of newly introduced word types than the English text does. Only the major protuberances of the original text are found in the English translation, but new ones, undetectable in the other two texts, are also present. By comparing the graphs of the three texts it is clear that the distribution of the significant protuberances is similar in the Hungarian and German texts, while different from the English text (Figure 25, Figure 26, Figure 27, and Figure 28).

It also became obvious that there is no clear relationship between the launch of new chapters and the rise in the number of newly introduced words, as some had suggested earlier (Petőfi; 1990). These protuberances can occur anywhere in the text, regardless of the chapter-boundaries. This can be demonstrated by the comparison of the chapter-boundaries of the English translation to the other two texts. The English translators (Kertész; 1975c) decided to rearrange the text, by changing the chapter-boundaries from Chapter 6 on, which in our analysis is block E[310], which is not yet halfway through the book. I could not find any acceptable explanation for this change in the structure, but it is clear that the number of newly introduced word types definitely did not increase at these points, so the explanation for the deviances in the vocabulary of the English translation has to be found elsewhere.

4.1.3. The Jungle Books and their translations

4.1.3.1. Texts analyzed in The Jungle Book project

As was listed in Chapter 4.1.1 and Table 4 several different translations of THE JUNGLE BOOK(S) are available. These translations differ in language, but they also differ from each other in several other aspects. Table 8 gives a short summary of the similarities and differences of the texts which are obvious when we take a quick glance at their table of contents.

To my greatest surprise, the different translations of this very popular book were fundamentally different, which for the computer presented insuperable obstacles. To overcome these obstacles the texts had to be normalized. The different translations offered several opportunities for normalization, so several versions of the texts were created to get comparable results (for details see Chapter 4.1.3.1.5).

4.1.3.1.1. The English texts

As stated in the 1981 Signet Classic edition

> …all fifteen stories of The Jungle Books had their original publication in magazines. Macmillan and Company, London and New York, published the first edition of The Jungle Book in 1894; the first edition of The Second Jungle Book followed in 1895 (Kipling; 1981: 334).

In the analysis, this Signet Classic printed edition (Kipling; 1981) and a Project Gutenberg digitized version (Kipling; 2006) were used. The printed version seems to be a good reproduction of the original edition, as stated in its *A Note on the Text*

> This Signet Classic is reprinted from these [Macmillan] first editions. Typographical errors have been corrected, and spelling and punctuation have been brought into conformity with modern English usage (Kipling; 1981: 334).

The digitized version is based on an American edition. Unfortunately, there are differences between the printed English and American versions, so therefore between the analyzed printed and digitized versions. The differences are not vital, but worth mentioning. The title of the seventh story of the first book is different in the two editions.

Appeared in Harper's Weekly on 3rd March 1894, and the Pall Mall Magazine March 1894. Collected in THE JUNGLE BOOK, 1894, with the title Servants of the Queen in the First English Edition and early reprints, but Her Majesty's Servants in the First American Edition. Her Majesty's Servants was used in most – but not all – printings of the Standard Edition (Underwood and Radcliffe; 2008).

The other differences between the printed editions is that some of the names have also been changed, e.g. Mor the Peacock is changed to Mao, the Peacock, Waingunga to Wainganga, etc. However, none of these changes had any influence on the analysis, since the appearance of newly introduced word types was analyzed, therefore it does not matter whether the peacock is called Mor or Mao. Apart from these differences only typographical differences were found, which did not influence our analysis, either.

4.1.3.1.2. The full-length French and German texts

By comparing the tables of contents of the different translations, the French translations (Kipling et al.; 1899a, Kipling et al.; 1899b) and Haefs, 1987 (Kipling and Haefs; 1987) seem to be the closest to the original. These translations follow the original English text both in the number and the order of the stories. As it is, both of them contain the same fifteen stories. LE LIVRE DE LA JUNGLE and DAS DSCHUNGELBUCH have the seven stories from the first book, while LE SECOND LIVRE DE LA JUNGLE and DAS ZWEITE DSCHUNGELBUCH have the eight stories from the second book, and both the French and Haefs, 1987 keep the original order of the stories.

4.1.3.1.3. The German texts cropped to fourteen and six stories

The downloadable German digitized version is based on a 1965 printed edition (Kipling; 1965a, Kipling; 1965b), which is a reprint of Mikusch, 1951 (Kipling and Mikusch; 1951). The third German version in the analysis is Harranth, 1987, published in 2004 (Kipling and Harranth; 2004). In these two German translations the original order of the stories is kept, but one of the stories, *Servants of the Queen*, is missing from both of them. In Harranth, 1987 there is a short explanation for this missing story. This little note at the beginning of the book says that

> Diese Übersetzung beruht auf dem Text der bei Macmillan, London, erschienenen englischen Erstausgabe von 1894 und folgt, anders als die bisher bekannten Bearbeitungen, dem Wortlaut des Originals. Die Aus-

gabe berücksichtigt vornehmlich jugendliche Leserinnen und Leser. Aus diesem Grund wurde darauf verzichtet, das Vorwort und die Erzählung »*Her Majesty's Servants*« zu übernehmen (Kipling and Harranth; 2004: 4).

However, in the afterword the translator says that

> Die hier vorliegende Ausgabe war bei ihrem Erscheinen 1987 nach fast 95 Jahren die erste, die sich bei den Erzählungen und Gedichten streng ans Original hielt, Kiplings Forderung an sich selbst zu achten versuchte kein Wort zu viel und keines zu wenig (Kipling and Harranth; 2004: 218, Appendix 6.5).

These two statements of Harranth are somewhat controversial. It is important to note that originally, THE JUNGLE BOOKS were not meant for children. As Kipling's first authorized biographer, Charles Carrington reported in 1955:

> It would be a shallow criticism of The Jungle Books to call them animal stories for children, though that is the mode in which they first enthrall readers. (Carrington; 1955)

What is certain that *Servants of the Queen* was left out from Harranth, 1987 to create an adaptation fit for young readers. However, as we will see in Chapter 4.1.3.2.6 and Figure 35 the vocabulary has not been at all lightened, on the contrary, in several text segments it is richer than the original text. Just the opposite would be expected from an edition meant for young readers. His original intention, that nothing is left out and nothing is added, is the opposite of what we would expect from a junior edition, not to mention the text segments of the translation which are richer in vocabulary. Other measures, such as the size of the text and the number of different word types, which are the primary data for the analysis, also help to clear up this misunderstanding (Chapter 4.1.3.2.6, Table 10).

The other two controversial statements in this short quotation are that Harranth, 1987 is based on the original Macmillan edition and *Her Majesty's Servants* is left out, which is impossible because this title only appeared in a later American edition. In addition to the missing story of *Servants of the Queen*, as the above quotation suggests, the Harranth, 1987 translation contains only the first book. Altogether, the Mikusch, 1951 translation has fourteen, while the Harranth, 1987 translation has only six stories.

Table 8. The order of the stories in the original English, the French and the German translations (first column), and in the Hungarian translation (second column). The first half of the Hungarian translation contains all of the Mowgli stories, while the second half the other stories. The main references of the Mowgli stories are marked by the arrows, where all but one of the references refer to a story/stories appearing previously to that particular story. In the last Mowgli story – *The Spring Running* – there is a circular reference. Two of the German translations left out *Servants of the Queen*. Besides, the Harranth, 1987 translation contains only the first book.

English, French, German	Hungarian
Book I	
Mowgli's Brothers	Mowgli's Brothers
Kaa's Hunting	Kaa's Hunting
Tiger-Tiger	How Fear Came
The White Seal	Tiger-Tiger
Rikki-Tikki-Tavi	The King's Ankus
Toomai of the Elephants	Letting in the Jungle
Servants of the Queen (∉ M1951*, H1987**)	Red Dog
Book II	The Spring Running
How Fear Came (∉ H1987)	
The Miracle of Purun Bhagat (∉ H1987)	Rikki-Tikki-Tavi
Letting in the Jungle (∉ H1987)	The White Seal
The Undertakers (∉ H1987)	The Miracle of Purun Bhagat
The King's Ankus (∉ H1987)	The Undertakers
Quiquern (∉ H1987)	Quiquern
Red Dog (∉ H1987)	Toomai of the Elephants
The Spring Running (∉ H1987)	Servants of the Queen

* M1951 refers to the Mikusch, 1951 German edition
** H1987 refers to the Harranth, 1987 German translation

4.1.3.1.4. The Hungarian text

The Hungarian translation is in a way special. In the Hungarian translation (Kipling et al.; 1976), based on the 1930 Macmillan edition, all the stories are kept, but originally it was published as a one-volume edition, which is a straightforward consequence of the fact that the order of the stories is changed. The stories in which Mowgli appears are presented first; they are then followed, in the second half of the book, by the other stories. In the stories of Mowgli the original order of the stories is not kept, rather the translator keeps track of the references in the stories to each other. Table 8 compares the original and the Hungarian order of the stories with the main references to the connected stories. The other characteristic unique to the Hungarian text is that the stories and the poems are translated by two writers. Namely, the short stories were translated by Marcell Benedek, while the poems by Sándor Weöres. Although the French translation also has two translators, there is nothing to indicate how they distributed the tasks between themselves. What is known, however, is that they worked together on several other texts.

In the newest Hungarian editions the formerly one-volume book is printed as two separate books. The title of the first one is A DZSUNGEL KÖNYVE (Kipling et al.; 2002, The Jungle Book), while the other book is entitled RIKI-TIKI-TÉVI ÉS MÁS TÖRTÉNETEK. A DZSUNGEL KÖNYVÉNEK MÁSODIK RÉSZE (Kipling et al.; 2007, Rikki-Tikki-Tavi and Other Stories. The Second Part of The Jungle Book). At this point there is a misleading comment on the cover of the book, which says that this second part is based on THE SECOND JUNGLE BOOK. It is clearly not; the statement is incorrect.

4.1.3.1.5. Normalizations

Considering all these differences between the different translations the following four possibilities seemed reasonable for the normalization.

- The comparison of the four full versions – the English, the French, Haefs, 1987, and the Hungarian – in the original order of the stories.
  To get comparable results two German translations – Mikusch, 1951 and Harranth, 1987 – had to be left out and the order of the stories in the Hungarian translation had to be changed back to the original order.
- To include Mikusch, 1951 into the analysis, *Servants of the Queen* is left out of the full length text of English, and the translations of French, Hungarian, and Haefs, 1987.
  Still, the Harranth, 1987 German translation had to be left out, because the second book is not translated in this version.

- In order to include all the six versions into the analysis the texts had to be truncated at the end of the sixth story.
- Changing the order of the stories to match that of the Hungarian.
  Only the English and Hungarian texts were included in this analysis. The question was how changes in the order of the stories influence the distribution of the newly introduced words, especially since the original rather arbitrary order was changed to a more logical order.

4.1.3.2. Results of The Jungle Book project

The analyses were carried out in the order of the normalization listed in the previous chapter (Chapter 4.1.3.1.5). The $fp - F$ graphs were created for those versions where differences were obvious and data provided information. Considering all this, neither the German, nor the French translations were re-ordered to the Hungarian order of the stories.

On the other hand, I found it worthwhile to compare the three German translations, since from such a direct comparison further data and new conclusions could be gained.

4.1.3.2.1. The original English text

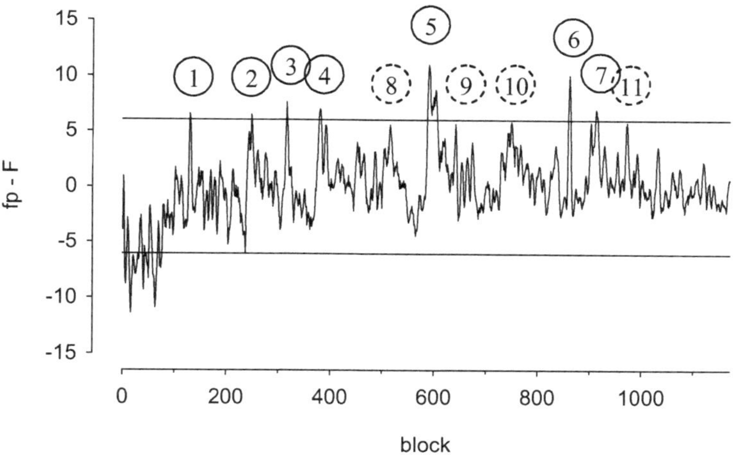

Figure 29. The graph of the changes in the number of the newly introduced word types in the original English text of THE JUNGLE BOOKS. The protuberances reaching over the significance level refer to those text segments which are significantly richer in vocabulary than predicted by a first-order statistical model.

In the original English text seven vocabulary rich text segments were identified (Figure 29, continuous circles), which appear on the graph as protuberances reaching over significance level. Beyond these seven protuberances four more are detectable, which are just below significance level (Figure 29, dashed circles). These protuberances are responsible for text segments which carry more newly introduced vocabulary items than predicted by a first-order statistical model. It was found that all the significant protuberances of THE JUNGLE BOOKS stand for descriptions or lists of names (Table 9). These text segments are richer in vocabulary than the main body of the text.

Table 9. The text segments (third column) which triggered significant (continuous circles) or 'almost' significant (dashed circles) protuberances on the graphs of newly introduced word types. For easier identification, the second column contains the title of the stories in which these text segments appear, followed by the number of the blocks.

	Title of the story	Text segment
1	Kaa's Hunting E[130–131]	King's Palace
2	The White Seal E[249]	Sea Catch, fighting for territories
3	Rikki-Tikki-Tavi E[316–317]	introduction of Rikki-Tikki-Tavi
4	Toomai of the Elephants E[379–382]	introduction of Kala Nag and his mother
8	Servants of the Queen E[516]	Parade-Song of the Camp-Animals
5	The Miracle of Purun Bhagat E[588–607]	Purun Bhagat, Tibet and the pilgrims
9	The Miracle of Purun Bhagat E[642]	A Song of Kabir
10	Undertakers E[750]	village and a list of animals
6	The King's Ankus E[860–864]	treasures
7	Quiquern E[912–916]	North Pole
11	Quiquern E[973]	floe, icebergs

4.1.3.2.2. The French translation

By comparing the significant protuberances of the English and French texts (Figure 29 and Figure 30) it is clear that the major protuberances of the English text are also present in the French translation, but minor differences are also clear.

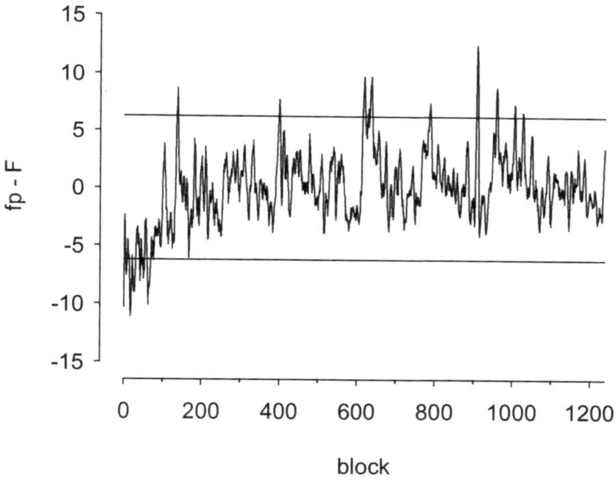

Figure 30. The protuberances of the full-length LE LIVRE DE LA JUNGLE and the LE SECOND LIVRE DE LA JUNGLE, the French translation of THE JUNGLE BOOKS.

The first protuberance, referring to the description of the King's Palace in *Kaa's Hunting*, is present in both texts (E[130–131] and F[136–139]). However, the following two protuberances of the English text (#2 and #3 in Figure 29) are missing from the French translation. These missing protuberances are from the stories of *The White Seal* (E[249]) and *Rikki-Tikki-Tavi* (E[316–317]). In *The White Seal* first the author gives a description of Sea Catch, then Sea Catch himself describes the fight for their territories. In *Rikki-Tikki-Tavi* the story starts with the introduction of Rikki-Tikki-Tavi, the mongoose. Both descriptions are missing from the French translation; they are not even recognizable because the peaks responsible for these text segments do not move up to the significance level. This means that these two stories reuse those vocabulary items which have already been introduced in the previous stories.

The fourth protuberance of the English text from the story of *Toomai of the Elephants* (E[379–382]) is also clearly present in the French translation (second protuberance in the French text, (Figure 30 F[398–401]), which occurs with the introduction of Kala Nag and his mother in the wars they were involved in. One may wonder why this description is clearly present in both of the texts, while the previous two descriptions were lost in the French text. This can be explained by the content of the text segments. In *Toomai of the Elephants* the vocabulary items of war are woven into the description of the animals, while in the other two descriptions it is the animals that are focused on. As such, the vocabulary items used to describe the animals can be replaced by previously introduced items, while this was impossible in case of the war.

The following twin peaks – fifth in the English (E[588–607]), third in the French text (F[616–639]) – are present in both of the texts and are from the story of *The Miracle of Purun Bhagat*. The first of the twin peaks stands for the description of Purun Bhagat, while the second is for the description of Tibet and the pilgrims whom Purun Bhagat met on his way (#8 in Figure 29).

An 'almost' significant peak before these twin peaks (E[516]) is also missing from the French text. It represents the *Parade-Song of the Camp-Animals* following the story of the *Servants of the Queen*. Similar to this 'almost' significant peak there is another one which follows the story of *The Miracle of Purun Bhagat* (E[642], #9) – the connecting poem, *A Song of Kabir* – which is also missing from the French translation.

The fourth peak of the French translation (F[786–789]) is an 'almost' significant peak in the English text (E[750], #10), but it is clearly there. They both stand for the same description of the village and a list of animals introduced in the story of *The Undertakers*.

The next significant protuberance in both texts – (E[860–864] and F[906–911]) – is quite remarkable, since in both languages the length of the protuberance is narrow, but its intensity is extremely strong. This protuberance is from the story of *The King's Ankus*, and the text segment occurs with the descriptions and list of the treasures found under the queen's pavilion.

The following significant protuberances appear in *Quiquern*. In the French text there are four consecutive protuberances, of which three are significant (F[958–962], F[1006–1007], and F[1027–1028])) and the fourth is just below significance level (F[1051]). These should be compared to the protuberances in the English text, where there is only one which is significant and another which is 'almost' significant. The first protuberance of this story in both languages is for the same text segment (E[912–916] and F[958–962]), while the second in the English (E[973]) and the third in the French (F[1027–1028]) are for the same text segment. Interestingly, the second protuberance from this group in the French text (F[1006–1007]) is richer in vocabulary than in the English text, and occurs with the description of the Northern Lights (Aurora Borealis).

4.1.3.2.3. Haefs, 1987 German translation

Haefs, 1987 (Kipling and Haefs; 1987) is the only complete German translation among the three included in the analysis, since it contains all the fifteen stories with the linking poems. In this translation seven significant protuberances were found, which match the number of the protuberances in the English text (Figure 31). The question was whether these protuberances match the text segments of the English text, or not. The simple answer to the question is essentially, yes.

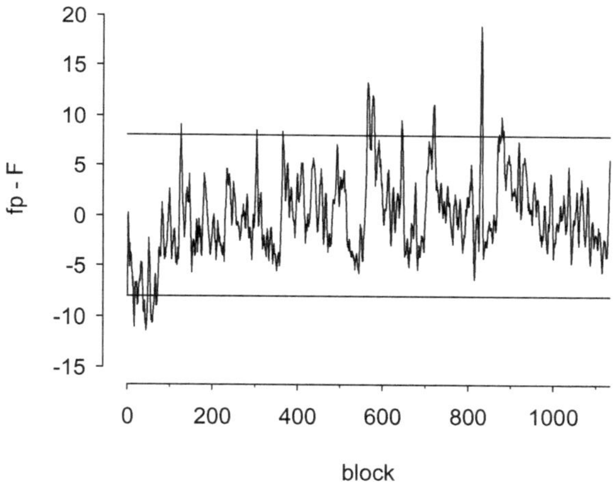

Figure 31. The protuberances in one of the 1987 German translation from Gisbert Haefs, DAS DSCHUNGELBUCH and DAS ZWEITE DSCHUNGELBUCH.

In more detail, the first protuberance of Haefs, 1987 stands for the King's Palace (Haefs[126]). However, the second protuberance of the English text (E[249]) is far below the significance level in Haefs, 1987. The protuberances of the text segments of Rikki-Tikki-Tavi and Kala Nag are also significant in Haefs, 1987 (Haefs[304] and Haefs[365], respectively). These two peaks – similar to the English text – are followed by an 'almost' significant peak of the *Parade-Song of the Camp-Animals* (Haefs[493]). In the second book the twin peaks of Purun Bhagat is again clearly there (E[588–607] and Haefs[563–580]). In Haefs, 1987 the text segment of Purun Bhagat is followed by a peak, which was neither in the English nor in the French text (Haefs[645–646]), and occurs with the poem of the morning song of the wolves in *Letting in the Jungle*. This peak is followed by the introduction of the animals and the village in *Undertakers* (Haefs[717–722]), which was both detectable in the English (E[750]) and significant in the French texts (F[786–789]). The most intensive peak, referring to the list of treasures in *The King's Ankus*, comes next (Haefs[829–833]). Finally, the description of the North Pole triggered a significant peak (E[912–916] and Haefs[878–884]). However, in this version the follow up peak(s) to this first introductory peak are weak (Haefs[933]), except an 'almost' peak, which stands for the description of the Northern Lights (Haefs[919]).

Overall, this translation followed the vocabulary changes of the original text remarkably well.

4.1.3.2.4. The Hungarian translation, with the English order of the stories

As mentioned in Chapter 4.1.3.1.4, the Hungarian translation (Kipling et al.; 1976) follows a logical order of the stories instead of the rather arbitrary order of the English edition. In this chapter the analysis of the re-ordered Hungarian text, following the original order of the stories, is detailed. In Chapter 4.1.3.2.7 the results of the analysis are detailed where the order of the stories follow the order of the Hungarian translation.

The Hungarian translation is the only one which does not have a significant protuberance in *Kaa's Hunting* at the King's Palace (Figure 32 E[130–131]). However, the Hungarian is the only text where around the King's Palace the number of the newly introduced words is kept continuously high. All this is due to the Hungarian Kaa. In the Hungarian version when Kaa speaks the translator tried to mimic the snake's hissing sound, so he replaced three fricatives – [ʃ], [z], and [s] – with a triple-length [s]. While Kaa speaks, the number of newly introduced word types is kept relatively high. Sentence like 'They called me also—yellow fish was it not?' would have been turned into the following snakish sentence by Marcell Benedek. 'They called me also [ôl'sssõ]—yellow fish [fisss] was [wusss] it not?'

To make sure that the missing peak is due to these words with long hissing sounds, the lemmatized version of the Hungarian text was checked. In the lemmatized version the peak of this protuberance exceeds significance level (Chapter 4.2.3). This means that the King's Palace, similar to the other languages, triggered a significant protuberance.

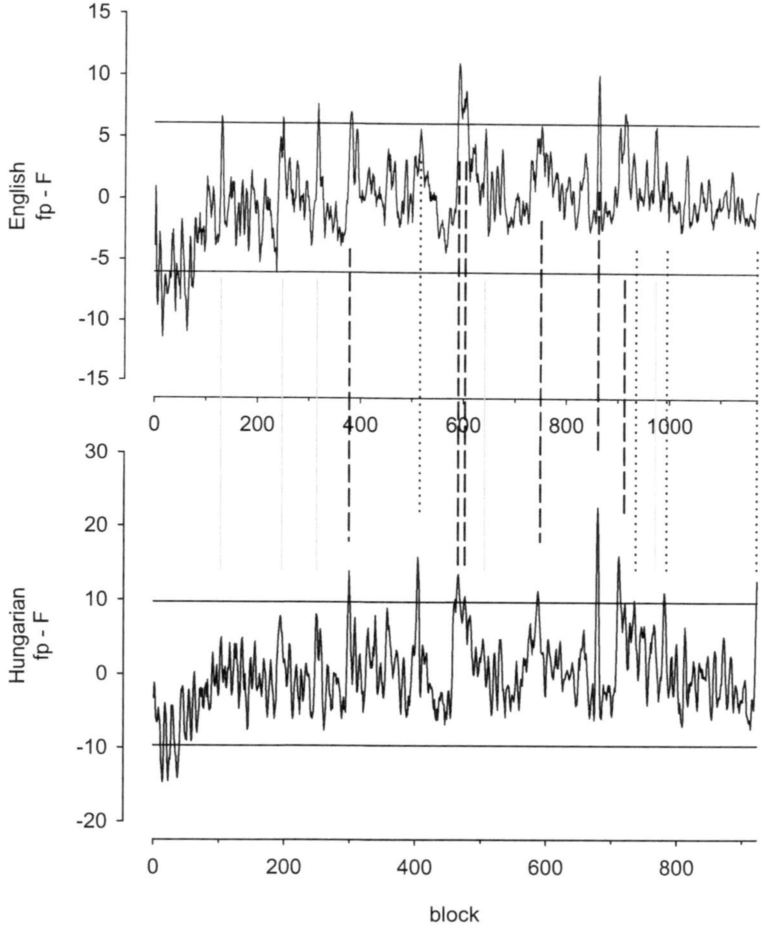

Figure 32. The detectable protuberances of the English (upper panel) and Hungarian (lower panel) THE JUNGLE BOOKS. The order of the Hungarian text is adjusted to the original English order. The domains of the two graphs are normalized to allow the corresponding lines between the protuberances of the two texts. The figure shows that the vocabulary rich text segments of the Hungarian translation follow those of the original text quite remarkably. There are only minor differences, which are mainly detectable in the intensity of the peaks.

The protuberance of *The White Seal* is clearly there (E[249] and H[194]), but does not reach significance level – while it does in the lemmatized text. The next clear peak just below significance level is a twin peak in the Hungarian text

(#3 in the English text, Figure 29), which is unique compared to the other texts. The reason is that the poem of *The White Seal*, *Lukkannon* (for the order of the stories see Table 8), triggered an 'almost' significant protuberance, which is followed as the second part of the twin peak by the introduction of Rikki-Tikki-Tavi – and this peak again reaches significance level in the lemmatized version (E[316–317] and H[249]).

As found with previously analyzed texts (Csernoch; 2006a, 2007b, 2007c) lemmatization does not necessarily clear up protuberances. However, it was also found that in the case of the morphologically rich Hungarian language, at the beginning of the texts some of the peaks might be forced below significance level, just as it happens in this case (Chapter 4.2.3). While is still true that the peaks are clearly there, they were just not able to reach significance level, which does not have any influence on this analysis.

These peaks are followed by a real protuberance of *Toomai of the Elephants* (E[379–382] and H[298–300]). After this peak the twin peaks of *The Miracle of Purun Bhagat* should appear, if the original English text is the yardstick. However, in the Hungarian text we have two 'almost' significant peaks – the introduction of an elephant herd in *Toomai of the Elephant* (H[339]), and Amir of Afghanistan in *Servants of the Queen* (H[357]) – and an extremely strong one at H[403–406]. The strong protuberance occurs with the poem of *Servants of the Queen*, *Parade-Song of the Camp-Animals*, whose peak in the English text was detectable, but stayed below significance level (E[516]).

The following twin peaks, as usual, stand for the descriptions from *The Miracle of Purun Bhagat* (E[588–607] and H[461–476]). Following the twin peaks of Purun Bhagat comes the significant peak of *The Undertakers* (E[750] and H[587–589]). After *The Undertakers* the peak of the *King's Ankus* appears (E[860–864] and H[677–681]). In the Hungarian translation this peak is extremely intensive, which must definitely influence the significance level.

The first peak of *Quiquern* is unique in the Hungarian text. If we take a closer look at the graphs of the English text (Figure 29, Figure 32, and Figure 33) and Haefs, 1987 (Figure 31 and Figure 33) texts, it is clear that this first peak of *Quiqern* is a twin peak, which is stronger in the second half than in the first. However, in the Hungarian text the first half of this twin peak is stronger and the second is weaker (Figure 32 and Figure 33). This strong first half stands for the poem preceding *Quiquern*, *The Song of the Little Hunter*, the poem of *The King's Ankus*. The second half of the twin peak just reaches significance level, but is still there and occurs with the description of the North Pole, similar to the other texts.

The next peak reaching significance level is unique to the Hungarian text, and describes a terrible winter (H[735]). However, peak #11 of the English text

(Table 9, Figure 32 E[973]) is way below significance level in the Hungarian graph.

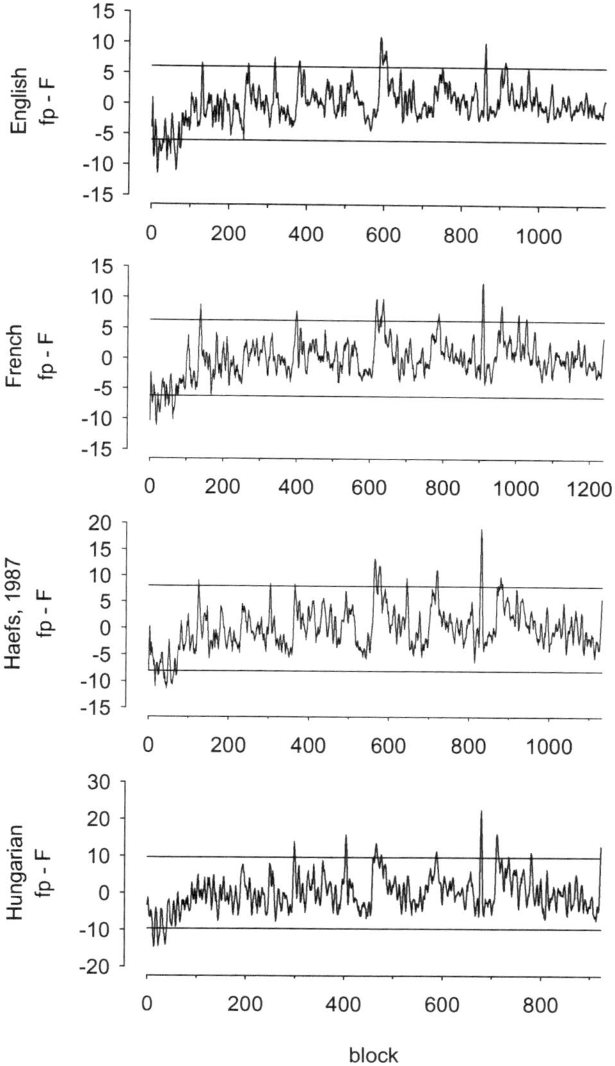

Figure 33. The protuberances in the four full-length texts of THE JUNGLE BOOKS.

At the end of the text there are, however, two more peaks, neither of which was there in the previously analyzed texts. They represent two poems. The first peak is the poem of *Quiquern, Angutivun Tania* (H[780–781]), then, at the very end, the poem of *The Spring Running, The Outsong,* generated the other peak (H[922]). This last peak is traceable in the French, Mikusch, 1951, and also in Haefs, 1987, but is remarkably small in the original English text.

The Hungarian translation thus has two remarkable characteristics. First of all, this translation followed quite well the original English text considering the changes in vocabulary. However, protuberances were found which were richer in the Hungarian text than in the English, and the text segments triggering these protuberances are mainly poems. I think that this is the straightforward consequence of the fact that the Hungarian text was translated by a writer and a poet (see Chapter 4.1.3.1.4), and the poet used richer and/or different vocabulary than either Kipling or the other Hungarian translator.

4.1.3.2.5. Mikusch, 1951 German edition

As mentioned in Chapter 4.1.3.1, the 1951 German edition (Kipling and Mikusch; 1951) – DAS DSCHUNGELBUCH and DAS NEUE DSCHUNGELBUCH – contains the stories of both of THE JUNGLE BOOK and THE SECOND JUNGLE BOOK, except for the story of *Servants of the Queen* and the connecting poem, *Parade-Song of the Camp-Animals*.

Due to the loss of *Servants of the Queen*, the analyses of the English, Haefs, 1987, and the French text had to be redone after cropping them. Similarly, later on the Hungarian text was also cropped to fit the Mikusch, 1951 edition. However, as we can see from Figure 29, neither the story nor the poem triggered any notable protuberances. Considering all these, it is not surprising that there are no significant differences between the protuberances of the full length and the cropped texts. Consequently, there was no need to include the graphs of the cropped English and French texts.

In the Mikusch, 1951 edition, as is clear from Figure 29 – Figure 34, the locations of the significant protuberances are different compared to all the other texts analyzed. The first protuberance from *Kaa's Hunting* is clearly present (E[130–131] and Mikusch[132–133]), but the following three in the English text (E[249], E[316–317], and E[379–382]) are missing. Similarly to the French text, the second and the third are completely lost (E[249] and E[316–317]), while in this German translation, unlike in the French, the fourth (E[379–382] and F[398–401]) does not reach significance level. It is traceable, but not as strong in intensity as it should be.

Similarly to the full length texts, the twin peaks of the story of *The Miracle of Purun Bhagat* are clearly there, occurring with the same text segments (Mikusch[532–551]).

The next significant protuberance, whose peak is clearly over significance level, shows a great resemblance to the French text, since in the English text it was just an 'almost' significant protuberance. This peak, again, represents the introductory section of *The Undertakers* along with the poem preceding *The Undertakers*, *Mowgli's Song Against People* (F[786–789] and Mikusch[679–686]).

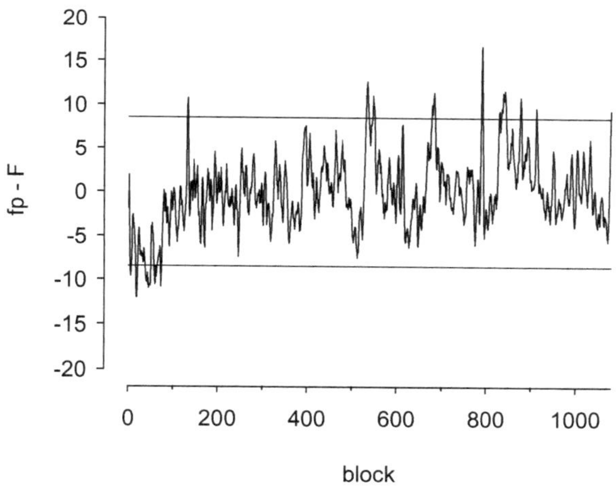

Figure 34. The protuberances in the Mikusch, 1951 German edition, DAS DSCHUNGELBUCH and DAS NEUE DSCHUNGELBUCH.

Following the protuberance of *The Undertakers* one finds the protuberance of *King's Ankus* triggered by the list of the treasures. This protuberance is so strong that it appears as significant in all of the texts.

In Mikusch, 1951, in the story of *Quiquern*, similarly to the French text, there are again three significant protuberances. Again, similarly to the French text, the first (E[912–916] and F[958–962]) and the third (E[973] and F[1027–1028]) represent the same text segments – peaks #7 and #11 in Figure 29 –, as the two of the English text do, and the second (Mikusch[877–879]) coincides with the second in the French text (F[1006–1007]), which is a description of the Northern Lights.

Altogether, Figure 29 – Figure 34 show that the French and the Mikusch, 1951 edition show a great resemblance, sharing more common features than they do with the English text.

4.1.3.2.6. *Harranth, 1987 German translation*

Unfortunately, the Harranth, 1987 (Kipling and Harranth; 2004) German translation contains only six of the stories, since only the first book was translated, and in addition, the text was truncated at *Servants of the Queen*. Since the whole second book is missing, and as we have seen from Figure 29 – Figure 34 the second part has considerable protuberances, which influences the significance level, the analyses of the already analyzed texts had to be repeated using the truncated texts.

In Figure 35 the newly introduced word types of the six-story-long English and German translations are mapped. In order of appearance, the first significant protuberance of the English text stands for the King's Palace in *Kaa's Hunting* (E[129–131]), the second is for the fights of Sea Catch for their territory (E[248–250]), the third is the introduction of Rikki-Tikki-Tavi (E[316–318]), while the fourth is for the story of Toomai (E[378–383]).

Table 10. The number of blocks (*n*), tokens in these blocks (*N*), different word types (*V*(*N*)), and hapax legomena (*V*(1,*N*)) in the original English, and in the analyzed three German translations. All the texts are truncated to the shortest, Harranth, 1987, thus containing the first six stories of THE JUNGLE BOOK.

	n	N	V(N)	V(1,N)
English	453	45300	4306	1911
Mikusch, 1951	464	46400	7638	4443
Harranth, 1987	463	46300	7247	4114
Haefs, 1987	433	43300	6423	3636

In Harranth, 1987 all four protuberances are present. However, in this translation new protuberances appeared. One appeared between the original first and second (Harranth[193]), and stands for the text segment in *Tiger-Tiger* when Mowgli goes to the village. The peak is not too wide, but it is clearly there. The other new protuberance is between the original second and third (Harranth[293–294] and represents the search for the Sea Cow in *The White Seal.* These two new protuberances mean that we were able to find text segments in this newer German translation which are richer in vocabulary than the original English text.

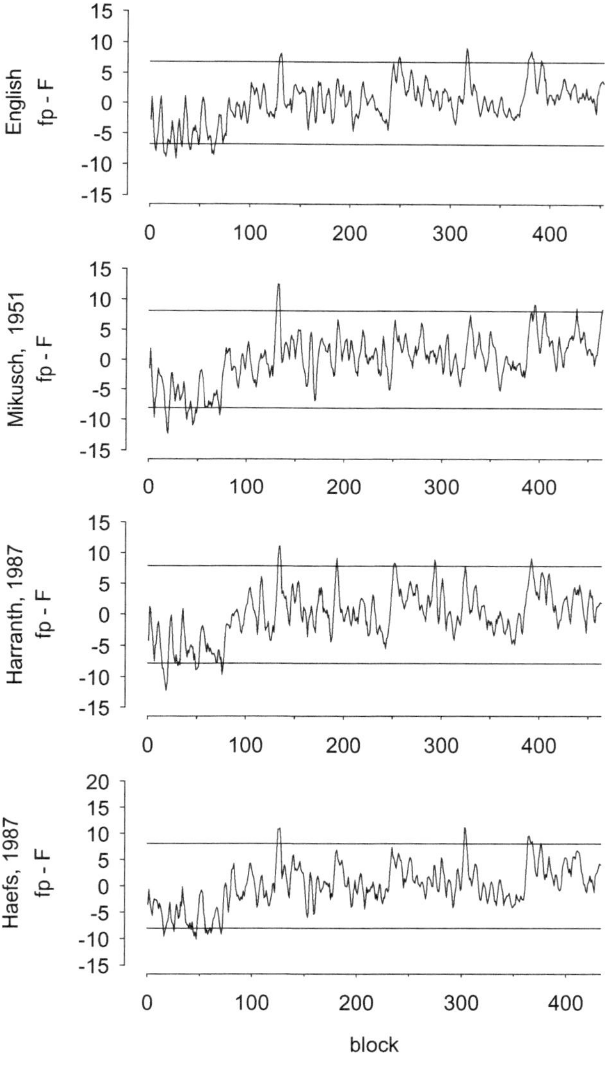

Figure 35. The comparison of the protuberances of the first six stories of the English and the three German translations: Mikusch, 1951, Harranth, 1987, and Haefs, 1987 of THE JUNGLE BOOK.

Haefs, 1987 has only three significant protuberances: at the description of the King's Palace (Haefs[125–127]), Rikki-Tikki-Tavi (Haefs[303–305], and

Toomai of the Elephants (Haefs[364–376]). However, a closer analysis reveals other remarkable similarities with the English text. The missing protuberance from *The White Seal* is clearly there, but its peak is just below significance level (Haefs[240]). Interestingly, the second peak of Harranth, 1987 is also detectable in this version.

Mikusch, 1951 seems to be the furthest away in vocabulary from the original English text. While the first peak for the King's Palace is clearly there (E[130–131] and Mikusch[131–133]), the next two, although detectable, did not reach significance level. Finally, the second of the text (Mikusch[395–396]) matches the fourth of the English text (E[379–382]). In addition to these, new peaks appeared which are unique to this translation: Kala Nag's rush (Mikusch[438]) and the song following the story, *Shiv and the Grasshopper* (Mikusch[464]).

In general, Mikusch, 1951 was found somewhat arbitrary compared to the original English text. The other two translations were able to reproduce the vocabulary rich text segments of the original text much better. Harranth, 1987 goes even further, for the translator generated more vocabulary rich text segments than were present in the original text. Overall, Haefs, 1987 seems to be the closest to the original English text.

The comparison of the number of the tokens and the word types to the number of newly introduced word types revealed another interesting feature. There is no difference in length between Mikusch, 1951 and Harranth, 1987, while Haefs, 1987 is 3000 tokens shorter than the other two texts (Table 4 and Table 10). Interestingly, the number of word types is the highest in Mikusch, 1951, and the lowest in Haefs, 1987 (Table 4 and Table 10).

We have seen in Figure 35 that Mikusch, 1951 does not follow the significant peaks of the English text. Thus we must address the question of where all the high number of word types come from. From the high number of word types of Mikusch, 1951 it follows that several of them cannot be found in either Haefs, 1987 or Harranth, 1987. Comparing those words in Mikusch, 1951 which are missing from the other two German translations to the word types of the English text it was found that Mikusch, 1951 is extended with words which have changed Kipling's original intention. Two examples from these words are 'sieges' and 'rasend'. Following the appearance of the different word types of these lemmas, it was found that their usage is rather arbitrary. The English text does not give reasons for the use of these provocative words or word chunks.

- Tongue – give tongue to it! Hark! O hark! (Kipling; 1961: 30)
- Bleckender Fang und rasender Lauf! (Kipling and Mikusch; 1951: 32)
- Laut – gib Laut jetzt! Hört! O hört! (Kipling and Haefs; 1987: 36)
- Mowgli's Song, Darzee's Chant (Kipling; 1961: 73, 110)

- Moglis Siegeslied, Darsies Siegesgesang (Kipling and Mikusch; 1951: 85, 131)
- Mowglis Gesang, Darzees Preislied (Kipling and Haefs; 1987: 91, 141)

In spite of the fact that Mikusch, 1951 used more word types than it was reasonable, these word types do not appear in the protuberances, they seem to appear more randomly in the text and as such, the text is closer to the first-order statistical model.

4.1.3.2.7. Comparison of the English and the Hungarian texts, using the Hungarian order of the stories

If we follow the order of the circled numbers (Figure 29 and Figure 36) we can see that all of the protuberances of the original English text with the original order are detectable, but only half of them are still significant, and only one new significant protuberance is gained (Table 11 peak #4, squared).

Table 11. The newly detectable – significant (solid square) and 'almost' significant (dashed square) – protuberances of the English text with the Hungarian order of the stories. These protuberances emerged after re-ordering the stories by placing the Mowgli stories before all the other stories.

	Title of the story	Text segment
1	Kaa's Hunting	poem, Road-Song of the Seeonee Pack
2	King's Ankus	poem, The Song of the Little Hunter
3	Letting in the Jungle	poem, song of the wolves
4	Letting in the Jungle	Hathi destroys the village
5	Red Dog	Little People
6	Red Dog	poem, Chil's Song
7	Servants of the Queen	Amir of Afghanistan

The comparison of the graphs in Figure 36 reveals some interesting characteristics of this collection of stories. In this order, the Mowgli stories – eight of them – are in the first half of the text and are followed by the other stories. First, it seems clear that the Mowgli stories use a more even vocabulary than the other stories. The beginning of a new story is not as clearly visible in the first half as it is in the second. On the other hand, it is also apparent that the other stories reuse the vocabulary items of the Mowgli stories. The only protuberances appearing in both orders are those which carry a high number of hapax legomena, and as such carry information which does not have any follow-up in the text.

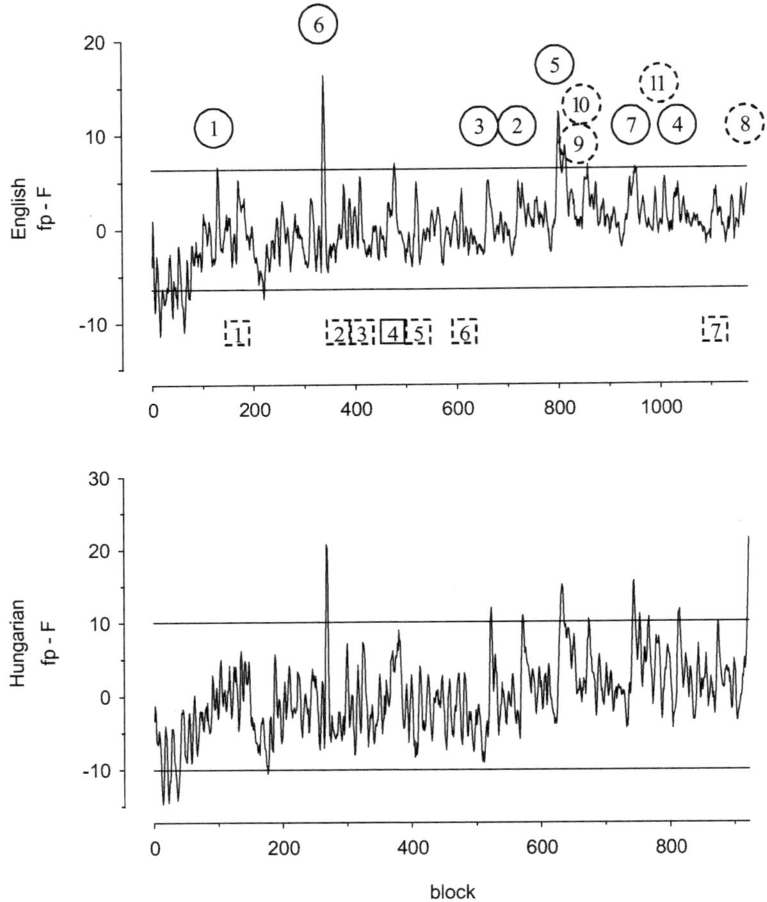

Figure 36. The protuberances of the re-ordered English text to fit the order of the Hungarian translation (upper panel) and the Hungarian translation (lower panel). The solid circles mark the significant, the dashed circles the 'almost' significant protuberances from Chapter 4.1.3.2.1, Figure 29. The numbers in the circles indicate the order of the protuberances of the original order of the text. The numbers in squares below the upper graph show those peaks, beyond those already marked by circles, which are clearly detectable. In Table 11 the text segments responsible for these peaks are listed.

There is one more noticeable difference between the two texts, which is marked with the squared numbers in Figure 36. Peaks – not significant but clearly detectable – which were not present with the original order of the stories appeared in the graph. Table 11 gives a list of the corresponding text segments. Interestingly, more poems than descriptions were revealed using this order. These poems with their relatively rich vocabulary are more emphasized in this order than they were in the original order. The only possible way to explain this observation is that the other stories 'used up' the vocabulary items of these poems.

The Hungarian poems seem so unique that the four which were significant with the original order remained significant, and only one is below significance level, and even this one is detectable. The three poems which stood out in both orders are the following: *Parade-Song of the Camp-Animals*, *Angutivun Taina*, and *The Outsong*, while the *Song of the Little Hunter* was below significance level.

Table 11 also reveals that the poems of the English text are somehow richer in vocabulary than the main body of the text, although still not as rich as the Hungarian poems. However, in the original order of the stories the richness of the vocabulary of the poems was hidden from the reader. With this new order of the stories, they are more emphasized than they were with the original order of the stories.

4.1.3.3. Conclusions of The Jungle Books project

In this analysis Rudyard Kipling's THE JUNGLE BOOKS and its five translations – French, Hungarian, and three German – were compared to the original English text, and, to some extent, to each other (Csernoch; 2010).

Already at the beginning of the analysis the different translations revealed obvious differences. They were different in terms of the number and order of the stories. The French translation and Haefs, 1987 followed both the number and the order of the stories the English text. Two of the German translations left out *Servants of the Queen*, and, unfortunately, the Harranth, 1987 translation contains only the first six stories. The Hungarian translation has all the stories, but their order is changed. In the first half of the text the Mowgli stories are listed and told, and they are followed by the other stories. Considering all these differences, which at first sight seem only technical, several normalizations had to be carried out to get comparable results.

The French and Mikusch, 1951 texts are very similar to each other. They share protuberances which are not in the English text and both of them miss strong protuberances in the English text. This result is not surprising if we consider the circumstances in which these translations came to life. In the 1951

German edition Mikusch only played the role of an editor. He did not translate the text, but simply re-edited the original German translation.

> Dieser Band enthält: 'Das Dschungelbuch' und 'Das neue Dschungelbuch' in der von Dagobert von Mikusch durchgesehenen Originalübersetzung (Kipling and Mikusch; 1951: 4).

All of this means that the French and this German translation are from the same era, the end of the 19th century.

The two 1987 German translations seem a lot closer to the original English text than the earlier translation. These translations were able to reproduce the significant protuberances of the original text. In Harranth, 1987, however, beyond these vocabulary rich text segments others were found which were richer in vocabulary than the original text. The translator of this German version gives a short summary of the preceding translations in the Nachwort of his book.

> Die erste deutsche Übersetzung, 1898, entstand nach dem säbelrasselnden Zeitgeschmack des Kaiserreichs und verdrehte ungeniert viele Aussagen Kiplings ins Gegenteil. Auch in der Folge wurde das Original radikal gekürzt und mit Erfindungen der Nach dichter gespickt. Als 1933 die Nationalsozialisten an die Mach kamen, verschwanden die Namen der jüdischen Übersetzer, und ein bewährter Faschist »bearbeitete« den Text ganz nach den ideologischen Zielsetzungen des Dritten Reichs. Diese Fassung erschien dann auch mach 1945 und bis in die jüngste Vergangenheit unverändert sowohl in der Bundesrepublik als auch in der DDR (Kipling and Harranth; 2004: 217, Appendix 6.5).

He interprets his translation as follows,

> Die hier vorliegende Ausgabe war bei ihrem Erscheinen 1987 nach fast 95 Jahren die erste, die sich bei den Erzählungen und Gedichten streng ans Original hielt, Kiplings Forderung an sich selbst zu achten versuchte kein Wort zu viel und keines zu wenig (Kipling and Harranth 2004: 218).

which is proved by the analysis. At one point, however, I have to disagree with him, since I found text segments which are richer than the original, so he added something to them. The other German translation from 1987 (Haefs, 1987) seems to be closer in vocabulary to the original because it is free from text segments which are richer than the original text.

These findings are in accordance with the review from Birgit Danken [13], where she states that while Haefs' translation follows the vocabulary of the original text faithfully, Harranth made changes to it.

Neue Übersetzungen sind oft preiswerter als der Kauf der Lizenzen alter Übertragungen. Neben der soeben veröffentlichten, dicht an Text und Orginalton gehaltenen, vorzüglichen Übersetzung von Gisbert Haefs im Hartmans Verlag legt Wolf Harranth in der neuen Klassiker-Reihe des Dressler-Verlages eine kindgemäße deutsche Fassung vor. Es fehlen Vorwort und Schlußgeschichte „Her Majesty's Servants". Die Ironie ist gemildert. Gedichte, Lieder und Gesänge vermeiden allzu aitißzielle und distanziert-intellektuelle Wendungen, bemühen sich aber – entgegen der weitgehend wörtlichen Übersetzung von Gisbert Haefs – um Reime und Versrhythmen. Weicher, gefälliger ist Harranths Übersetzung. Sie benutzt dem gegenwärtigen Sprachgebrauch entnommene Vokabeln, kommt der Aufnahmefähigkeit literarisch Ungeübter in zulässiger Weise entgegen« (Danken; 1987)

The Hungarian translation changed the order of the stories, and collected in the first half of the book the Mowgli stories, which are then followed by the other stories. The other characteristic of the Hungarian translation is that the poems are translated by a poet. The Hungarian translation followed the vocabulary rich text segments of the original text quite well throughout the whole text. However, this translation is somehow unique in this context. The presence of the poet, who translated the poems, is clear, since he uses richer and/or different vocabulary than any of the other writers. The primary translator also decided to change the text to some extent using a unique voice for Kaa. I found this change rather interesting, because it gave not only to Kaa, but to the whole Kaa stories, a unique voice.

Changing the order of the stories revealed only minor differences. These minor differences are mainly detectable in the English text, rather than in the Hungarian. In the English text the changes in the order provided only one new protuberance – quite weak in intensity –, but dissipated a couple of them. In addition, although the poems were not able to trigger significant protuberances, they appear more clearly than in the original order.

In general, the comparison of texts in different languages with this novel method is able to add information to that gained by the already well established methods.

One of the advantages of this statistical analysis is that it is independent of the fact that translators are free to use words, expressions, structures, and different kinds of techniques well known in translation studies. The only expectation here is that in a faithful translation the text segments in the target language should be as rich in vocabulary as they were in the original text compared to the main body of the texts.

4.1.4. Alice's Adventures in Wonderland and Through the Looking-Glass and What Alice Found There

4.1.4.1. The Hungarian translation of the Alice stories

The choice fell upon the ALICE stories (Carroll; 1866, Carroll; 1871) because Petőfi (1990) gave a detailed, though subjective, analysis of these works and their Hungarian translations. In his writing he compared the Hungarian translation of both stories (Carroll et al.; 1974, Carroll et al.; 1980) with the original English works. He does not say anything about his methods so I suppose his writing is based on his experiences. I was interested to see what can be added to his rather subjective statements, using a statistical analysis of the texts. Petőfi thought that the Hungarian translation neither followed the original text in vocabulary nor in visualization. Beyond this he found that in the English version there are connecting chapters where the transition between them is smoother than is usual between chapters and Carroll achieved this effect by an intentionally misusing punctuation. This punctuation was not applied in the Hungarian text and thus Petőfi thought that the transition between the chapters in the Hungarian translation is not as smooth as in the original English text.

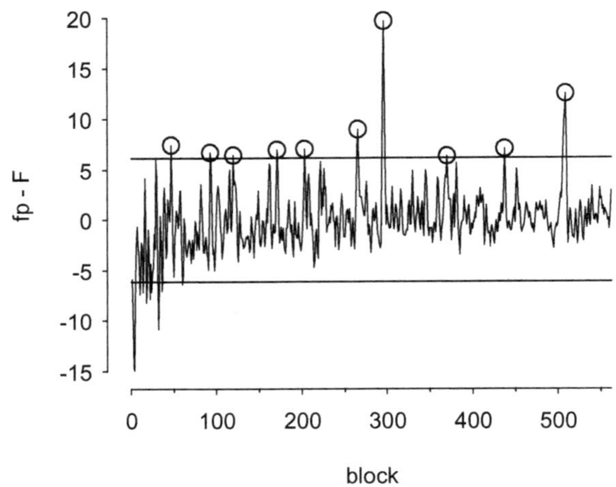

Figure 37. The protuberances in the concatenated ALICE stories. The protuberances of this text usually stand for short poems which require new vocabulary items. These words in many cases are lists of unusual objects. This can explain why these protuberances are narrow in length and low in their intensity, except the one in the middle and one more at the end of the text.

The original English ALICE stories carry a very interesting feature which was not present in the works previously analyzed (Figure 37). The length of the protuberances is unexpectedly short and, apart from two or three protuberances, their intensity is also weak. The Hungarian translation only followed the really strong protuberances (Figure 38). The small protuberances of the English text did not appear in the Hungarian translation. The question was whether this feature is due to the agglutinating character of the Hungarian language or the translation not being as rich in vocabulary as the original English text. Later the lemmatization of the texts was carried out so we were able to answer this question (Chapter 4.2.2).

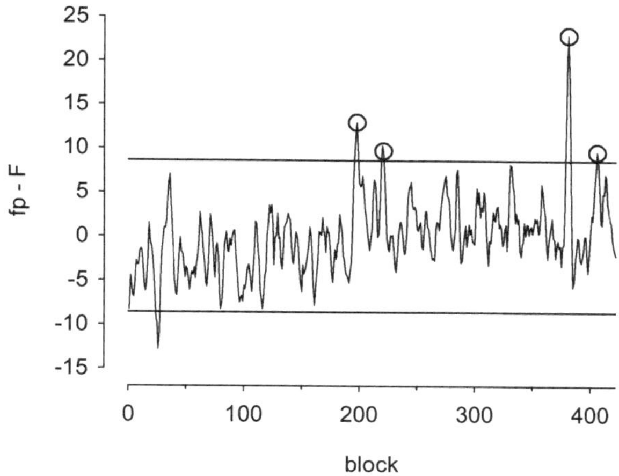

Figure 38. The protuberances of the Hungarian translation of the ALICE stories. The short protuberances found in the first half of the English text did not appear in the Hungarian translation. In the second half of the story the protuberances are detectable but their peaks do not reach the significance level.

However, we could not find any difference in the transitions between the connecting chapters. So the punctuation does not play any vital role in the number of newly introduced word types. The boundaries of the chapters, just by their existence, are not able to increase the number of newly introduced word types, as we have already seen with SORSTALANSÁG and its English translation (Chapter 4.1.2.3), and with THE JUNGLE BOOKS and their Hungarian translation (Chapters 4.1.3.2.4 and 4.1.3.2.7). If the author intentionally uses new vocabulary items even at the end of a chapter or at the end of the text the protuberances clearly appear on the graph; however, there is no straight connection between the start of a new chapter and the increase in the number of newly introduced word types.

4.1.4.2. *The French translation of the Alice stories*

The French translation (Carroll; 2004a, Carroll; 2004b) follows the unusual punctuation and transition between the chapters of the original text, but the chess-problem from the beginning of THROUGH THE LOOKING GLASS and the connecting poem are missing.

Figure 39 shows the significant protuberances in the French text. If we compare them to the protuberances in the English text (Figure 37) it is obvious that the major protuberances in the original text are present in the French translation, too. Both the significant and the detectable protuberances in the second story – from block 290 – follow the same pattern as the English text. The protuberances in the first story, however, are not as clearly present in the French translation as was expected. There are protuberances and they are stronger than in the English text, but except for the first and the last, their locations are different from the location of the protuberances in the English text.

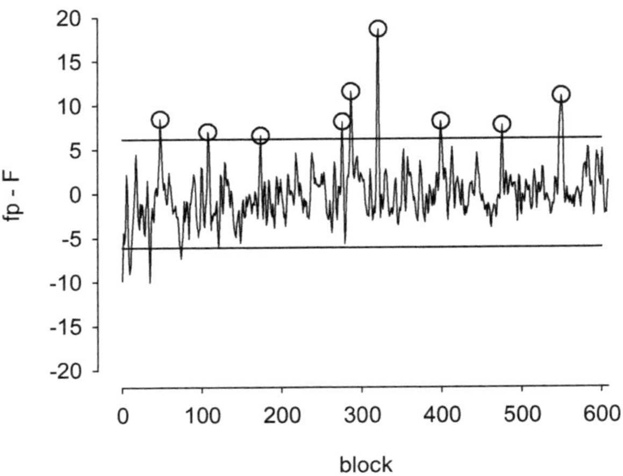

Figure 39. The protuberances in the French translation of the ALICE stories. This translation followed the changes in vocabulary remarkably well.

4.1.5. *The Da Vinci Code and its translations*

To take advantage of the relatively large number of different adaptations of "the most popular and controversial novel of our time" [11], Dan Brown's THE DA VINCI CODE was also selected for the analysis (Table 12, Csernoch; 2007c, 2008a).

Table 12. The different adaptations of Dan Brown's THE DA VINCI CODE analyzed in this study.

	full-length		condensed	
	non-lemmatized	lemmatized	non-lemmatized	lemmatized
English	+	+	+	+
Hungarian	+	+	+	+
French	+			
German	+			

When analyzing Dan Brown's novel it was interesting to see how changes in the vocabulary of the different translations follow that of the original. For this purpose the French, the Hungarian and the German translation of the novel were selected. The French translation was selected because French is the minor language in the story. Note, that in SORSTALANSÁG the minor language is German (Chapter 4.1.2.2). We found, through the comparison of the original Hungarian text and the German translation, that the German translation shows a great resemblance to the original text. The question was whether there is always a close connection between the original text and its translation to the language which is its minor language or not. Hungarian was selected to see what changes occur in translating a contemporary work from English into an agglutinating language. Finally, the German translation was selected because it was assumed to be neutral in respect of the above-mentioned criteria.

The practice of preparing condensed versions is the subject of an ongoing debate (see below), in which the present author does not wish to take sides. The condensed versions used in the present analysis are from *Reader's Digest* [14]. Unlike graded readers, condensed versions have no limit on vocabulary, i.e. there are no vocabulary bands. The inclusion of condensed versions in the analysis was designed to explore the effects of abridging the original text.

The analysis of newly introduced words was carried out on the level of both word types and lemmas.

4.1.5.1. *The original text of The Da Vinci Code*

To begin with and to set the paragon, first the original (English, non-lemmatized, full-length) text was analyzed (Brown; 2003). The length of the text was between 139,700 and 139,800 tokens, which was rounded off to 139,700, yielding 1,397 one-hundred-token-long blocks. As Figure 40 and Table 13 show, among the protuberances detected eleven were found to exceed significance level. These protuberances are different both in length and intensity. Eight of the eleven have lengths of five hundred tokens or less, and only three are longer (Table 14). All longer protuberances appear in the first one third of the novel (Figure 40 and Table 13). In addition, the intensity of the protuberances in the first half of the novel is greater than in the second half. These data indicate that towards the end of the story not too much is happening that would require rich vocabulary. The words that have already been introduced are reused.

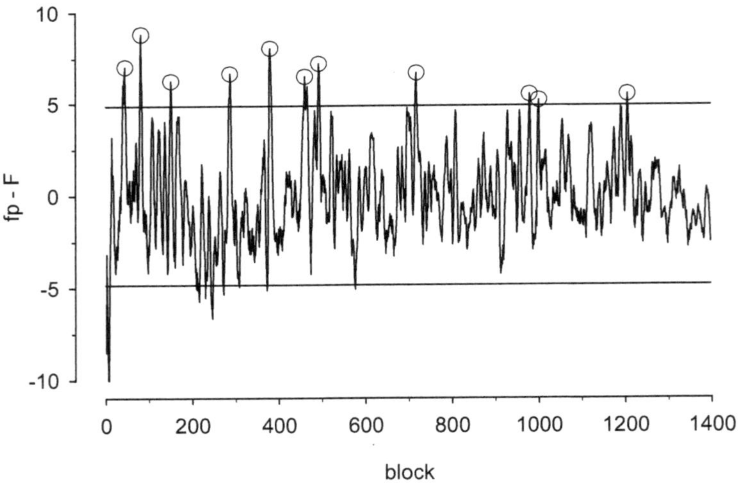

Figure 40. The difference between the original and artificial texts for the full-length English version of THE DA VINCI CODE. In this novel eleven significant text segments were found, positioned mainly in the first half of the novel. The protuberances occur in text segments which fall outside the main flow of the story; they represent historical or contemporary events, persons, places or substantial changes in style, or language.

In Table 13 those text segments which produced significant protuberances are listed in order of appearance. For easier identification, in the first column the number of the chapters in which these inlays appear are added, while the last two columns give the location of these significant protuberances.

Other data worth mentioning are the 2*SD* values (Chapter 3.1.3). The 2*SD* of a text is high if the intensity of the protuberances is high. With a higher 2*SD* we can expect a more varied vocabulary than with a shallow 2*SD*. In THE DA VINCI CODE the number of newly introduced word types was found to be relatively low, which is well demonstrated by the relatively low 2*SD* of the text.

Table 13. The location of significant protuberances in the original, non-lemmatized and lemmatized versions of the full-length THE DA VINCI CODE. The location of a protuberance is marked by the number of the blocks in which the protuberance begins and ends. In the non-lemmatized text the number of blocks (*n*) equals 1397, in the lemmatized 1415, while 2SD = 4.85 and 2SD = 4.4, respectively.

Chapter	Text segment	Position in text	
		non-lemmatized	lemmatized
3	Paris	40–46	37–47
5	Opus Dei	80–84	81–84
7	phone call to Sandrine		122–124
9	Sophie	150–152	152–153
20	nature of Phi	285–288	287+291
28	witch-hunting	378–383	383–387
34	Pope, Castel Gandolfo	458–467	463–470
36	Chase		486–488
37	Priory of Sion	491–495	497–499
54	Remy + Teabing's house		705
55	Jesus, Christianity	715–719	723–726
76	Baphomet, Hebrew alphabet	979–980	989–993
79	Grand Masters	1001	1011–1013
87	Hayloft		1132–1135
97	Westminster	1204–1206	

In Table 14, based on the data shown in Table 13, the significant protuberances are grouped according to their length. The first column shows the lengths of the protuberances (for the definition of the length of the protuberances see Chapter 3.1.3), according to the number of blocks where the protuberances are above the level of significance. The second column contains the number of the protuberances which have the corresponding length, while the third column contains the product of the first two columns of the same row.

Table 14. Length and cumulative length of the protuberances in the original English THE DA VINCI CODE.

length of protuberances (block)	number of same-length protuberances	cumulative length (block)
1	1	1
2	1	2
3	2	6
4	1	4
5	3	15
6	1	6
7	1	7
10	1	10
	11	**51**

4.1.5.2. The Hungarian translation of The Da Vinci Code

The protuberances in the original English text and those in the Hungarian translation (Brown and Bori; 2004) can be compared using the data in Table 13 and Table 17 and in Figure 40 and Figure 41. In general, the vocabulary of the Hungarian translation follows the original text remarkably well. As mentioned above, at the beginning of the text some of the protuberances might be lost due to the rich morphology of the Hungarian language. The description of Paris, and the appearance of Sophie do not produce significant protuberances in the non-lemmatized text, but both text segments carry so great a number of new vocabulary items that they were able to accelerate protuberances in the lemmatized text (Table 17). However, between the two segments the introduction of Opus Dei made such a strong protuberance that even in the non-lemmatized text it produced a protuberance (Table 17). The other protuberances of the English text are also present in the Hungarian, except for 'nature of Phi', the list of 'Grand Masters', and the description of 'Westminster' (Table 17). While 'nature of Phi' and the introduction of 'Westminster' are clearly detectable, since the peak of the corresponding protuberances are just slightly under the Hungarian significance level (H[251] and H[1034], respectively), the list of the names of the 'Grand Masters' is not recognizable.

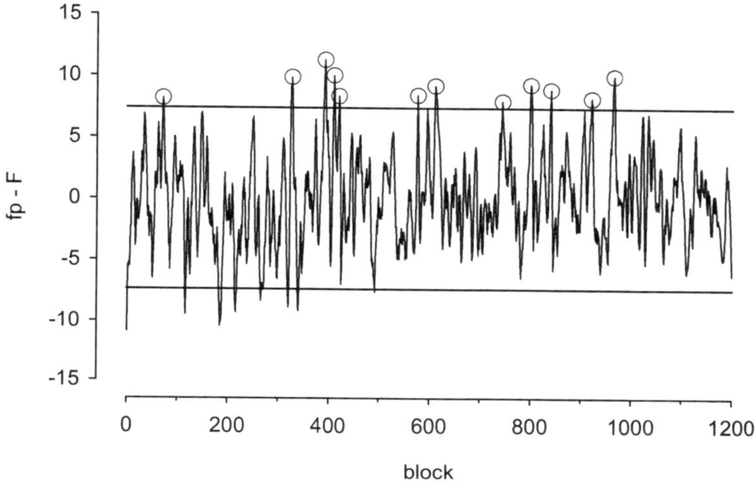

Figure 41. The protuberances in the Hungarian translation of THE DA VINCI CODE. The Hungarian translation followed the original text remarkably well considering the vocabulary rich segments. However, differences are also detectable. The Hungarian translation was found to be slightly richer in vocabulary than the original English text, especially towards the end of the novel.

On the other hand, the Hungarian text exhibits another surprising feature. Some of the text segments of the Hungarian translation were richer in newly introduced vocabulary items than the original text. These text segments produced significant protuberances in the Hungarian text which were not significant in the English text. These protuberances again represent 'longish' descriptions, so in this respect they behave in exactly the same way as other protuberances do. In order of appearance, the new significant protuberances occur in the following text segments: the description of the 'childhood of Silas', the 'chase through Paris', 'Teabing' and 'Remy', 'Teabing's house', the 'mirror-image poem', 'Remy lets Silas leave' (right before this is an 'almost' significant protuberance in the 'Temple Church'), and the 'search in the library' (Table 17). This finding indicates that in these text segments the Hungarian translation contains a richer vocabulary than the original English text. The mirror-image poem, however, is different in nature from the others. The Hungarian translation contains the poem both in English and Hungarian, followed closely by the details of the iambic pentameter. Including the poem in English is responsible for this protuberance.

4.1.5.3. The German translation of The Da Vinci Code

The first surprising finding about the German translation (Brown and Poll; 2004) was that it was the only book in the analysis whose title was not a literal translation of *The Da Vinci Code*, but *Sakrileg*. However, in the course of the analysis it became clear that there was no direct connection between the modified title and the vocabulary of the text.

The German translation retains all but one of the protuberances in the original English text. The missing text segment is in Chapter 76, the description of 'Baphomet' with the 'Hebrew alphabet'. The lack of this protuberance is surprising since it is present in all the other three full-length texts (Figure 42 and Table 15), and even in the condensed versions (Table 19).

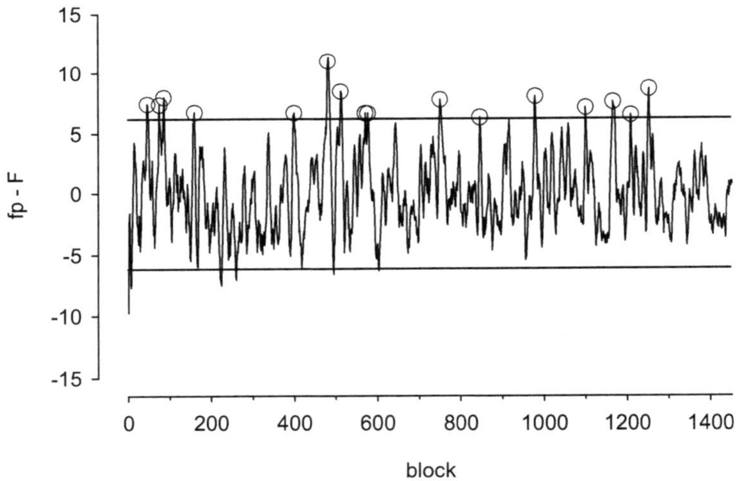

Figure 42. Protuberances in the German translation of THE DA VINCI CODE. The German translation replicates all but one of the significant protuberances in the original English text, and provides four more, which means that the corresponding text segments are richer in vocabulary than the original English text.

Similarly to the Hungarian translation, the German text also contains protuberances which were not present in the original English text. Again, these protuberances stand for vocabulary rich descriptions. At the beginning of the story, after the long drive through Paris, comes the introduction of the museum. The other three protuberances which do not occur in any of the other texts are the description of the 'Depository Bank of Zurich', 'Disney's influence on the world', and the architecture of the 'Temple Church'.

In general, on the basis of the vocabulary, the German translation was found to be a fairly good adaptation of the original text.

4.1.5.4. The French translation of The Da Vinci Code

The French translation (Brown and Roche; 2004) was included in the analysis for several reasons. Most of the events take place in France, French is the minor language of the novel and, finally, it was found earlier that the translation of a text into its minor language yielded a text whose changes in vocabulary followed the pattern of the original text (Csernoch; 2006a, Chapter 4.1.2.2). There was no proof, however, that the correlation between the two texts is due to the shared features of the novel.

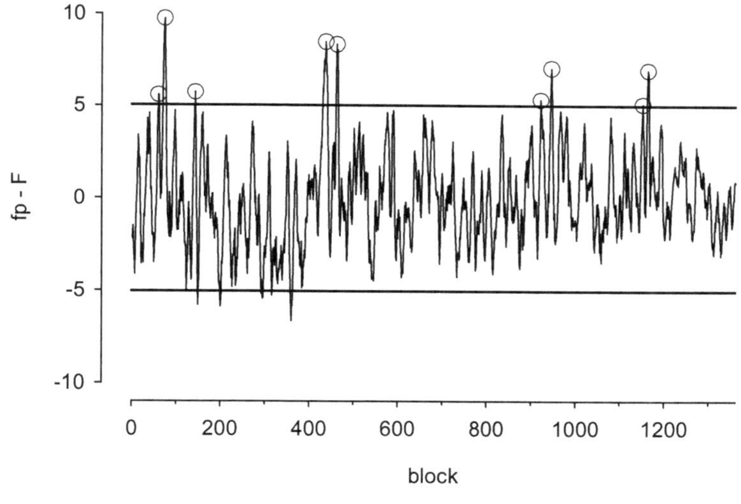

Figure 43. Protuberances in the French translation of THE DA VINCI CODE. There are only nine significant protuberances in the French text, all of them only one block long, and most of them weak in intensity.

At the very beginning of the novel, the description of Paris is missing from the translation, while it contains a short introduction of the museum, which the English text does not (Figure 43 and Table 15). It is easy to explain why the description of Paris is simplified in the French translation, compared to the original English text, but it is surprising that there are details on the museum, which must be equally familiar to French readers.

Table 15. The protuberances in the German and French translations of the full-length THE DA VINCI CODE. In the German translation the number of blocks (n) equals 1452, in the French 1361, while 2SD = 6.17 and 2SD = 5.04, respectively.

Chapter	Text segment	Position in text	
		German	French
3	Paris	45–47	—
4	Museum	75	60
5	Opus Dei	85–87	71
9	Sophie	159–160	141
20	nature of Phi	—	—
28	witch-hunting	397–400	—
34	Pope, Castel Gandolfo	479–486	430
37	Priory of Sion	511–515	461
42	entering the bank; bank	571; 577	
55	Jesus, Christianity	749–753	
61	Disney	846	
72	mirror-image poem	977–980	
74	Hieros Gamos		922
76	Baphomet, Hebrew alphabet		944
79	Grand Masters	—	—
84	Temple Church	1100	
87	Hayloft	1165–1171	
92	searching on the net	1209	
95	searching on the net		1152
97	Westminster	1251	1162

— text segments which caused significant protuberances in the English but not in the German or French translation

After the description of the museum eight more protuberances were found (Figure 43 and Table 15). 'Searching on the net' is a protuberance, which was also found in both the German and the Hungarian translations and was 'almost' significant in the non-lemmatized English and significant in the lemmatized English text. One protuberance was found which had no 'origin' in the English text. This protuberance related to 'Hieros Gamos' in Chapter 74, and occurred only in the French text. Similarly to 'museum', 'Hieros Gamos' made a significant protuberance because there is/are no preceding text segment(s) with which it could share its vocabulary. However, along with the nine significant protuberances, four protuberances were missing compared to the English text, which is more than expected.

From the above it follows that the nine protuberances in the French text are quite different in nature from the protuberances in the other texts, and in addition, unlike the other texts, all of these protuberances are only one block long, and their intensity is also surprisingly small. This means that even the detected protuberances do not stand out very much. Thus, there are hardly any concentrated, vocabulary rich text segments in the French text.

4.1.5.5. A comparison of the foreign language translations of The Da Vinci Code

Among the three translations it was the German text that followed the vocabulary changes of the original English text the most. The analysis of the Hungarian translation gave similar results concerning the vocabulary rich segments of the English text. All but two protuberances in the graph of the original text were also found significant in the Hungarian text. However, both in the Hungarian and the German translations several text segments were found which generated protuberances that were not present in the original text. This means that in these text segments the vocabularies of the translations were richer than in the English text. Two of the protuberances were shared by the Hungarian and the German versions. These protuberances occurred with the 'mirror-image poem', and later on with the 'search on the net'.

The mirror-image poem in English, along with the discovery of the pentameter in the poem generated a remarkable protuberance in both languages.

> An ancient word of wisdom frees this scroll … and helps us keep her scatter'd family whole … a headstone praised by templars is the key … and atbash will reveal the truth to thee.

The poem consists of thirty-two tokens and thirty word types altogether. This length would not be enough to produce a protuberance, since the smoothing of the graph suppresses single text segments (Chapter 3.2), but along with the pentameter they create a four-block-long protuberance in both languages.

If we want to demonstrate that a single vocabulary rich text segment on its own will not necessarily generate a protuberance, but a constellation of at least two such minor text segments is needed, we must compare the English and the French texts with the Hungarian and the German translations. The description of the pentameter is present in all of the texts, but neither the English, nor the

French text introduces new vocabulary here. Naturally enough, the English text here uses words that had previously been introduced, while the French text does not include the poem in English.

The French text was found to be the shallowest among the four, which is somewhat surprising. The translator, unable to take advantage of a shared culture and language, provided a leveled-out translation, without any remarkable changes in the vocabulary of the discourse, using a more restricted vocabulary than the other writers. It is not that he was unaware of the presence of French culture and France in the novel: the missing description of Paris shows otherwise. Another example of how he uses his background knowledge is found in Chapter 35 where the protagonists want to buy train tickets for the next train at Gare Saint-Lazare. In the English text the train they find is the 3:06 Lille – Rapide. They do the same in the German translation, but not in the Hungarian or the French text. In the Hungarian translation the departure time is left unchanged, but the destination is changed from Lille to Lyon. At first I thought that the translator confused Lille with Lyon, since in Chapter 54 the English text says "Remy is Lyonnais," while in the Hungarian it is changed to "Remy is from Lille". (I still have this feeling, because all the other texts retained the expression "Lyonnais",which in the case of a housekeeper might suggest a little more than someone being from Lyon; it might be a reference to his culinary professionalism.) In the French translation both the destination and the departure time are changed from Lille to Caen, and from 3:06 to 5:38. At this point I was confused, so I decided to check the train schedule from Gare Saint-Lazare [12]. It appeared that there is no train from Gare Saint-Lazare to Lille or Lyon, and definitely not at this time of the day, or more precisely, not at this time of the night. In general, the French translator's cultural awareness is clearly present, but he did not take advantage of this fact to make the vocabulary at least as rich as it is in the English text.

Finally, there is one protuberance, which has not yet been mentioned in the comparison of the foreign language translations. This protuberance is caused by the description of 'the nature of Phi' in the English text (Table 13). This text segment gives rise to a four-block-long protuberance, which is not too wide in length, but its intensity is quite remarkable (Figure 40), so I definitely think it is worth mentioning. Interestingly, none of the translators decided to share all the details of 'Phi' with their target-readers.

4.1.6. The Adventures of Tom Sawyer

At this point I do not want to give a detailed analysis of the original text of TOM SAWYER (Twain; 1876, Twain; 2006), because this was one of the texts which was involved from the very beginning of this project, and went through several phases. For results see Figure 4, Figure 5, Figure 6, Figure 44, Figure 57, Figure 59 – Figure 61, Figure 64, Figure 71 – Figure 74 and their connecting texts.

The digitized versions of the Hungarian (Twain, M. and Koroknay, I.; 1977) and the French translations (Twain; 2007) of TOM SAWYER were found in e-libraries. Unfortunately, the digitized version of the German translation was not available at the time of the analysis on the website from which texts were downloaded [7], while other sites were only offering trimmed versions. The text has recently become available so there is the opportunity to widen the range of the analyzed texts. Consequently, I was only able to use the Hungarian and the French translations in the comparison with the original English text.

In Figure 44 the protuberances of the English, French, and Hungarian texts are shown, respectively, from top to bottom. The English text carries an unusually high number of newly introduced word types at the beginning of the text. The other specialty of the text is that in the second half there is an extra long and extra intensive protuberance, the like of which was not detected in other analyzed texts. Apart from these peculiarities the text carries several well distinguishable protuberances, almost equally distributed through the text.

4.1.6.1. A comparison of the English, French and Hungarian texts of Tom Sawyer

Among the texts analyzed, TOM SAWYER is the only one where significant changes in the number of newly introduced word types were clearly for stylistic reasons. Usually, an increase in the number of newly introduced word types is due to a description. Among the text segments which triggered significant protuberances due to stylistic changes the most robust is the one, where the students present their writings for their school leaving exam. Here, a remarkable change in style is obvious and clearly caused an increase in the number of newly introduced word types (Csernoch; 2010).

The first section of the text, dense in vocabulary rich segments, ends around block 120 in the English text, which is around one seventh of the entire book. The corresponding sections are rich in vocabulary in both translations, but we should notice that they lack the first protuberance of the original text. This might be due to the character of the languages.

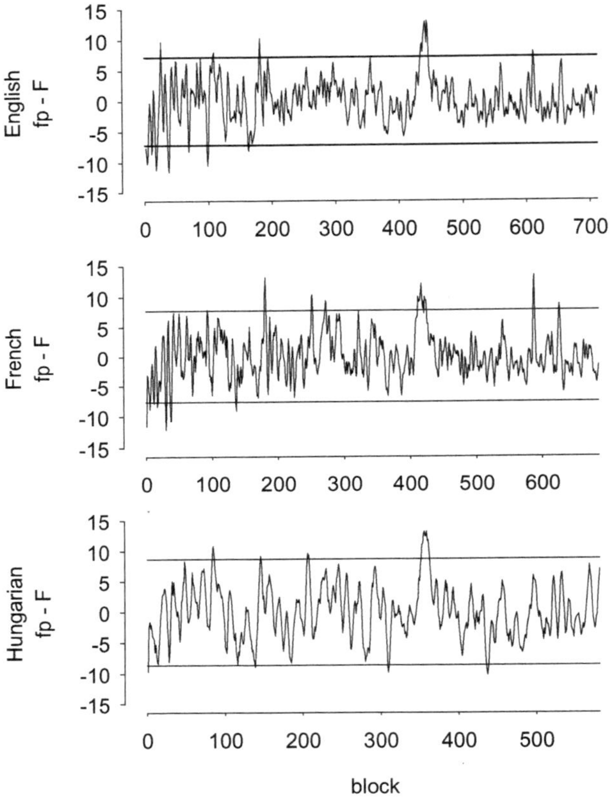

Figure 44. The English (upper panel), the French (middle panel), and the Hungarian (lower panel) versions of TOM SAWYER. The number of blocks (n) in these texts is 711, 685, and 581, respectively.

Beyond this vocabulary rich introductory segment there is another turning point in the text. Since the wide protuberance responsible for the stylistic change is equally represented in all three texts we can use the beginning and the end of this event as a divider. With these three virtual dividers the text can be divided into four sections. In the first and fourth sections the protuberances are almost equally distributed in all three texts. Differences can mainly be found in the intensity of the protuberances.

In the second part of the text – between the introductory part and the school-leaving exam – the translations seem richer than the original text, which is especially true for the French translation. In the Hungarian text – similarly to the English text – the protuberances are detectable; although their peaks do not reach significance level. In contrast, the protuberances in the French translation are closer to the significance level or above it.

In the fourth part of the text – following the school-leaving exam – the protuberances in the French text are the most intensive. They are followed in strength by the original English text, and finally the protuberances of the Hungarian text are the weakest. However, there is one noticeable protuberance in this section of the Hungarian translation. Namely, at the very end of the text we can find an extremely strong protuberance, which is unique to the Hungarian text. Neither of the other text carries this high number of newly introduced word types.

In general, the French translation followed the vocabulary rich segments of the original text remarkably well. However, in several cases the protuberances of the graph of the French translation are more intensive than those of the English text. Consequently, the text segments corresponding to these protuberances are richer in vocabulary in the French than in the English text. The Hungarian text produced a somewhat different pattern in the vocabulary rich descriptions. The difference is not that obvious in the first half of the text, before the school leaving examination. However, at the end the Hungarian text is not as rich in vocabulary as the original text, except for the last couple of blocks, where there is an unexpected increase in the number of newly introduced word types, which was not present either in the original English, or the translated French text.

4.2. Lemmatizated texts

After a comparison of the foreign language translations of texts the next question was whether the lemmatization of the texts might change the results gained by the analysis of the word types or not, especially with texts written in Hungarian. In this comparison two languages were involved, as mentioned above (Chapter 3.3), because we only had access to English and Hungarian lemmatizer programs (for details see Appendices 6.2 – 6.4).

4.2.1. Lemmatized Sorstalanság and Fateless

Table 16. The text segments which triggered significant protuberances in the non-lemmatized Hungarian, German, English, and the lemmatized Hungarian and English versions of SORSTALANSÁG. The table gives the position of the peaks of the protuberances.

Text segment	Hungarian non-lemm. (H)	Hungarian lemm. (HL)	German non-lemm. (G)	English non-lemm. (E)	English lemm. (EL)
Uncle Vili			45	43	
factory in Csepel		54	73	71	71
departure		118*	155	156	158
train's departure		148	209		
arriving at Auschwitz	170	170	222	215	215
in the shower					261
arriving at Buchenwald	262	262	337	329	329
Auschwitz vs. Buchenwald			345		
Weimar	270	270			345
mornings, factory	310	310	398	392	392
protagonist's mental state	354*	354*	453	447	447
protagonist's physical state	402*		518	511*	
hospital	429	429	552		
Pjetyka's cooking	459	459	587		
new transport	484*	484*		618	618
leaving camp	510	510	651	650*	653*

* text segments whose protuberances are slightly under significance level

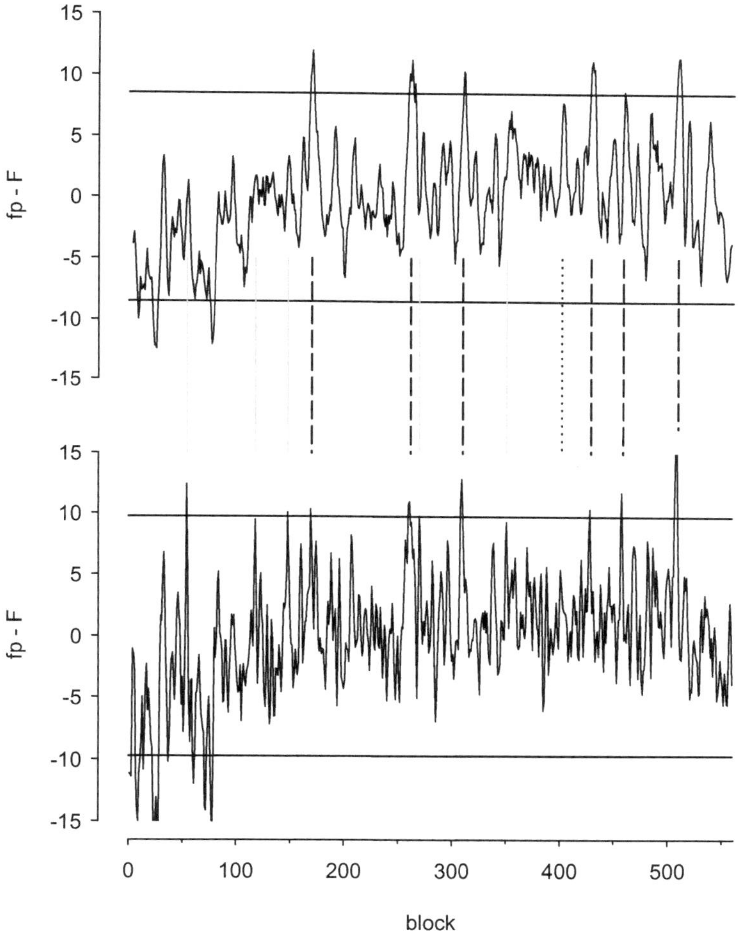

Figure 45. The protuberances of the non-lemmatized (upper panel) and lemmatized (lower panel) versions of SORSTALANSÁG. The dashed lines show the location of the protuberances which were detected in both versions. The continuous lines are for those protuberances which did not appear in the non-lemmatized version, only in the lemmatized one. Finally, the dotted line indicates the protuberance which is stronger in the non-lemmatized text than in the lemmatized.

In the lemmatized Hungarian SORSTALANSÁG nine and three 'almost' significant protuberances were found compared to the six significant and four 'almost' significant in the non-lemmatized version (Table 16, Figure 45). Two new protuberances (HL[54] and HL[148] – HL stands for Hungarian lemmatized), and one more between the two, which was only slightly under the significance level (HL[118]), appeared at the beginning of the story. The six significant protuberances of the original text are at same locations as detailed in Chapter 0 (Figure 25), and we can find two protuberances which are just below the significance level in both versions, but they are quite remarkable (H[354] and H[484] and HL[354] and [484]).

In addition to significant and 'almost' significant protuberances there is one, which is remarkable in the non-lemmatized version (H[402]), but lost in the lemmatized text (marked with the dotted line in Figure 45).

Further differences can be revealed in the intensity of the protuberances but in general the pattern which the two graphs follow shows a great resemblance (Figure 46). The pattern is demonstrated clearly on the graphs. Where there is a rise or a drop in the non-lemmatized version, similar ascending or descending intervals can be detected in the lemmatized version. This means that there might be differences in the intensity of the protuberances, but there is no difference in the tendency.

The missing protuberances in the Hungarian non-lemmatized text which were found at the beginning of the lemmatized text might suggest that this mismatch is due to the agglutinating character of the Hungarian language. As we will see in the coming chapters, in all non-lemmatized Hungarian texts there was a loss at the beginning, but later on there was no difference between the Hungarian and the English non-lemmatized and lemmatized texts.

This resemblance between the non-lemmatized and lemmatized texts has a great importance in our analysis because the significance level is sometimes responsible for the loss of minor protuberances which in a comparison might appear as a mismatch. However, if the pattern is the same we would still be able to identify the subtle differences by changing the significance level and re-evaluating the first, raw results. The data coming from the analyses of the word types and lemmas show clearly that to find reasons for the increases in the vocabulary there is no need for lemmatization (Figure 47).

Clearly, the analysis works on both levels of the words. The decision as to whether we need the lemmatization or not is highly dependent on the final goal of the analysis. However, if we want to find all of the protuberances, both the lemmatized and the non-lemmatized versions have to be taken into account. Let us now see those minor differences which can be found during the analyses.

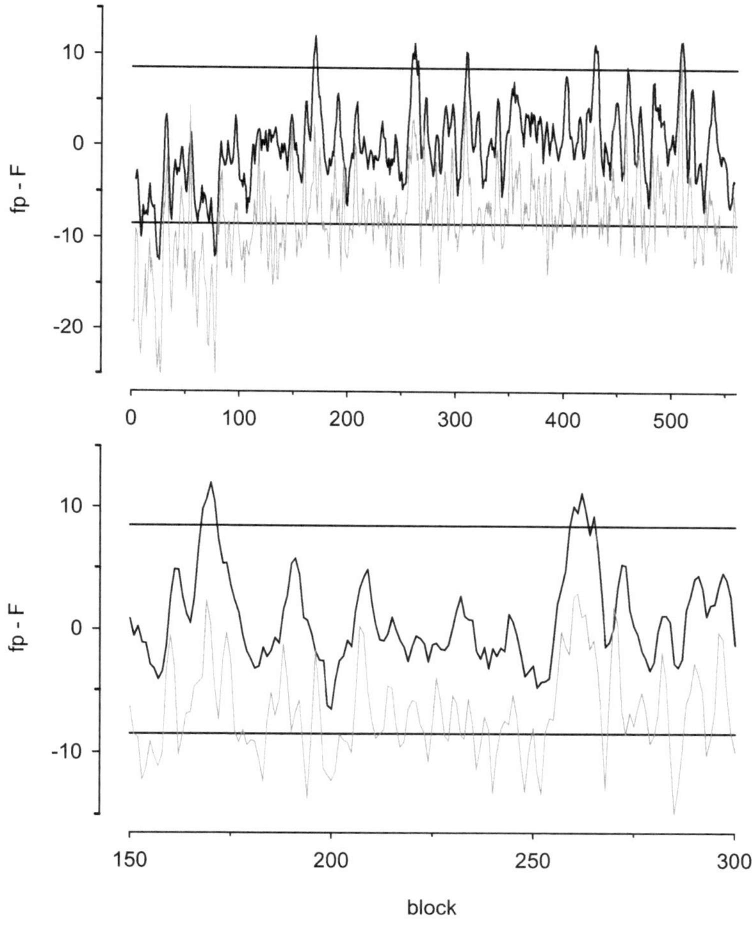

Figure 46. The pattern of the difference graphs of the observed and expected numbers of newly introduced words of non-lemmatized and lemmatized versions of SORSTALANSÁG. The lower graphs on both panels are for the non-lemmatized text, while the upper graphs are for the lemmatized one. To better visualize that the two graphs run parallel, the lemmatized graph is shifted down by 8 units. The two graphs follow a similar pattern. Where there is rise in one graph there is also a rise in the other and the same is true of falls. In the graphs in the lower panel the domain is truncated to the [150,300] interval to magnify the graphs and give a better view of the patterns.

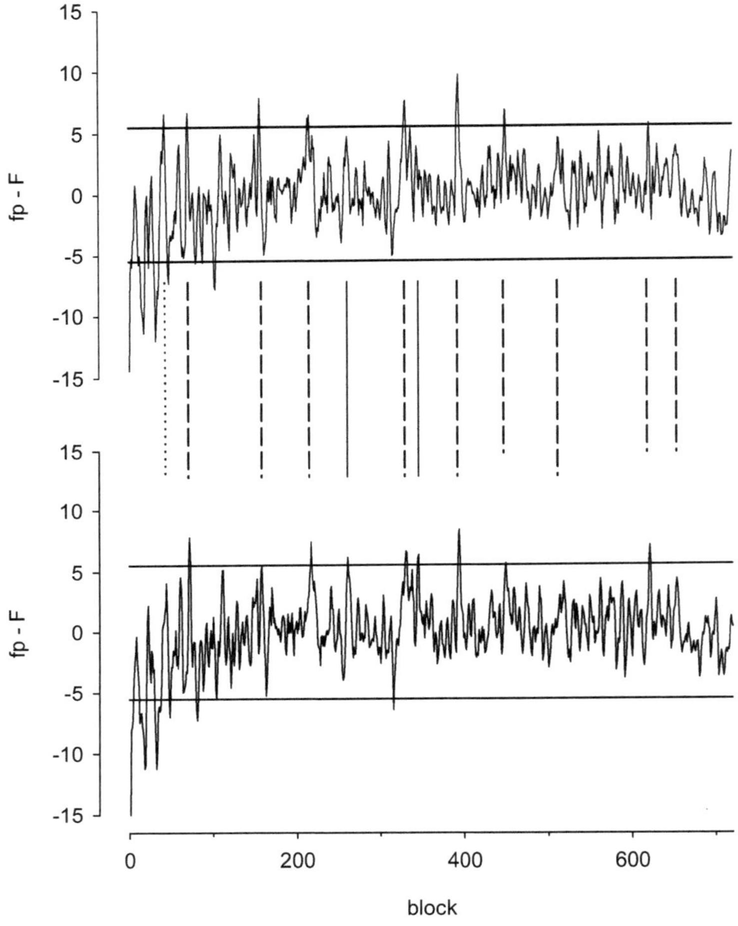

Figure 47. The protuberances of non-lemmatized (upper panel) and lemmatized (lower panel) versions of FATELESS. The dashed lines show the location of the protuberances which were detected in both versions. The continuous lines stand for the protuberances which did not appear in the non-lemmatized version, only in the lemmatized one. The dotted line is for a protuberance which is a significant in the non-lemmatized but whose peak is below the significance level in the lemmatized version.

4.2.2. Lemmatized Alice stories

In the English lemmatized ALICE stories all but two one-block-long protuberances of the non-lemmatized text were found (Figure 48 squared peaks). Their peaks were in the non-lemmatized text at blocks 123 and 171 (Figure 37 and Figure 48). Apart from these two short protuberances, the location of the protuberances in the lemmatized and non-lemmatized texts showed a perfect match.

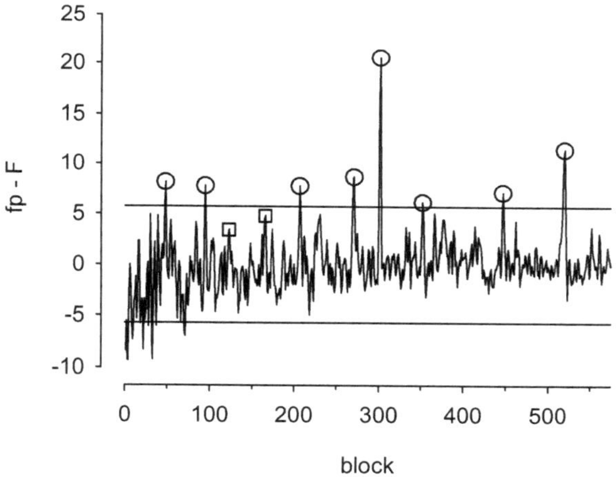

Figure 48. The lemmatized version of the English ALICE stories. The lemmatization diminished two significant protuberances which were found in the non-lemmatized version of the text (□). In these cases it was mainly the affixes which were responsible for the rise in vocabulary, as they carried information which was lost by lemmatization.

Similarly, the lemmatization of the Hungarian text did not produce major differences between the protuberances of the lemmatized and the non-lemmatized versions of the texts. As was mentioned in Chapter 4.1.4.1, the Hungarian translation of the ALICE stories did not produce as many protuberances as the English text. We were wondering if this was due to the incorrectness of the procedure applied to the text or to the translator using shallower vocabulary than the author of the original text.

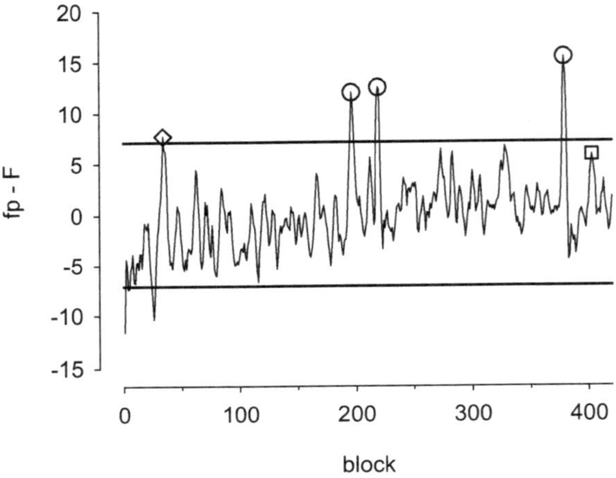

Figure 49. The lemmatized version of the Hungarian translation of the ALICE stories. The first protuberance appeared at the beginning of the text (◊), which was detectable, but slightly below the significance level in the non-lemmatized text. The lost protuberance of the non-lemmatized text is clearly present in the lemmatized text, but its peak is below significance level (□). Apart from these minor changes there was not much difference between the lemmatized and the non-lemmatized versions of the Hungarian text. These data clearly demonstrate that the protuberances of the English text, whether lemmatized or non-lemmatized, are lost in the first half of the Hungarian text, while in the second half they are there but even with lemmatization they stay below significance level.

As the analysis of the lemmatized text reveals, at the very beginning of the text one protuberance was lost at the analysis of word types (the peak marked with a diamond in Figure 49). It was detectable in the non-lemmatized text but slightly below significance level (H[36] in Figure 38). It seems, again that the high number of the highly inflected word types might swallow up real protuberances at the beginning of the text. However, it is not the word types that are responsible for the other missing protuberances in the first half of the Hungarian text. It can clearly be seen from the comparison of the graphs of Figure 38 and Figure 49 that neither the lemmatized, nor the non-lemmatized version produced as many protuberances as was expected from the English text. Note that most of the English protuberances were not strong, but they were detectable. The strong protuberances – remarkable both in length and intensity – appeared in both languages. On the other hand, the minor protuberances of the English text were lost in the first half, while they are detectable but not significant in the second half of the Hungarian text. At the end of the Hungarian non-lemmatized text a protuberance was found, which was not in the English text (H[406] in Figure 38). It is clearly there in the lemmatized English version, but its peak is way below the significance level. The peak of the protuberance remained below significance level in the Hungarian lemmatized version, too, but it is clearly there (squared peak in Figure 49). The peaks in the second half of the texts are detectable in all four texts. They are just below the significance level in the Hungarian versions, showing only minor differences to the English texts.

The pattern formed by the newly introduced word types and lemmas shows great similarities in both languages, similar to the other analyzed texts – SORSTALANSÁG (Chapter 4.2.1), THE JUNGLE BOOK (Chapter 4.2.3), and THE DA VINCI CODE (4.2.4). There might be detectable differences between the length and intensity of the protuberances, but in general, the protuberances triggered both in the lemmatized and non-lemmatized texts are at the same locations. The only difference found between the English and the Hungarian texts was that at the beginning of the Hungarian non-lemmatized texts the word types might hide significant protuberances by forcing their peaks below significance level.

Apart from the obvious differences between the original and translated texts of the ALICE stories, found by Petőfi (1990) and strengthened by this statistical analysis the major changes in the vocabulary are detectable in all four texts. These major changes in the vocabulary are also present in both the non-lemmatized and lemmatized versions of the texts, while the minor vocabulary rich segments of the English text are lost in the Hungarian translation. The lemmatization of the ALICE stories, however, clearly shows that it is not the word types that are responsible for these losses of the protuberances in the first half of the Hungarian text, rather the translator, who worked with shallower vocabulary than the author of the original text.

4.2.3. Lemmatized versions of The Jungle Book

In THE JUNGLE BOOK the lemmatization gave rise to only minor differences compared to the non-lemmatized texts, both in the English and the Hungarian texts (Figure 50 and Figure 51).

As we have seen in the Hungarian translations, at the beginning of the texts the first protuberance(s) appeared later than in other languages. Our suspicion was that the agglutinating character of the language might be responsible for this delay. After lemmatizing the texts it was clear that the lemmatized Hungarian texts produced the first protuberance(s) earlier than the non-lemmatized texts. However, it is not always the word types that are responsible for this delay. As we have seen in connection with the ALICE stories, the translator might also be responsible for loss of protuberances.

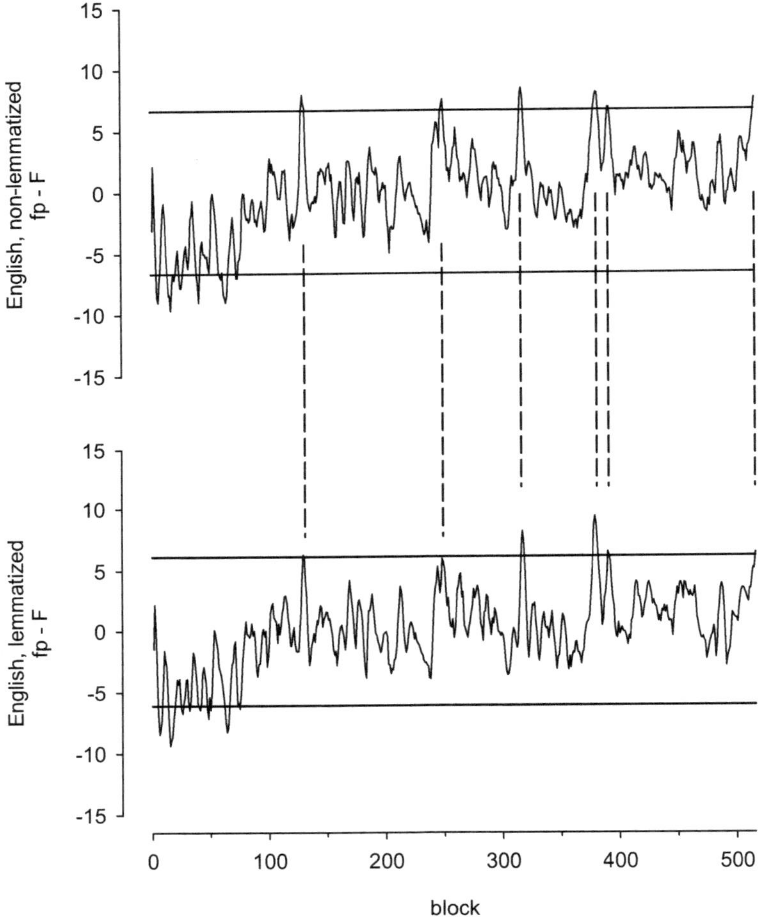

Figure 50. The non-lemmatized (upper panel) and lemmatized (lower panel) versions of THE JUNGLE BOOK. In this analysis BOOK I of THE JUNGLE BOOKS was involved, using the original order of the stories. The dashed lines start from the protuberances of the non-lemmatized text towards the peak of the protuberances of the lemmatized text. Following the lines, it is obvious that the lemmatization did not change the position of the protuberances. There are only differences between the length and the intensity of the protuberances.

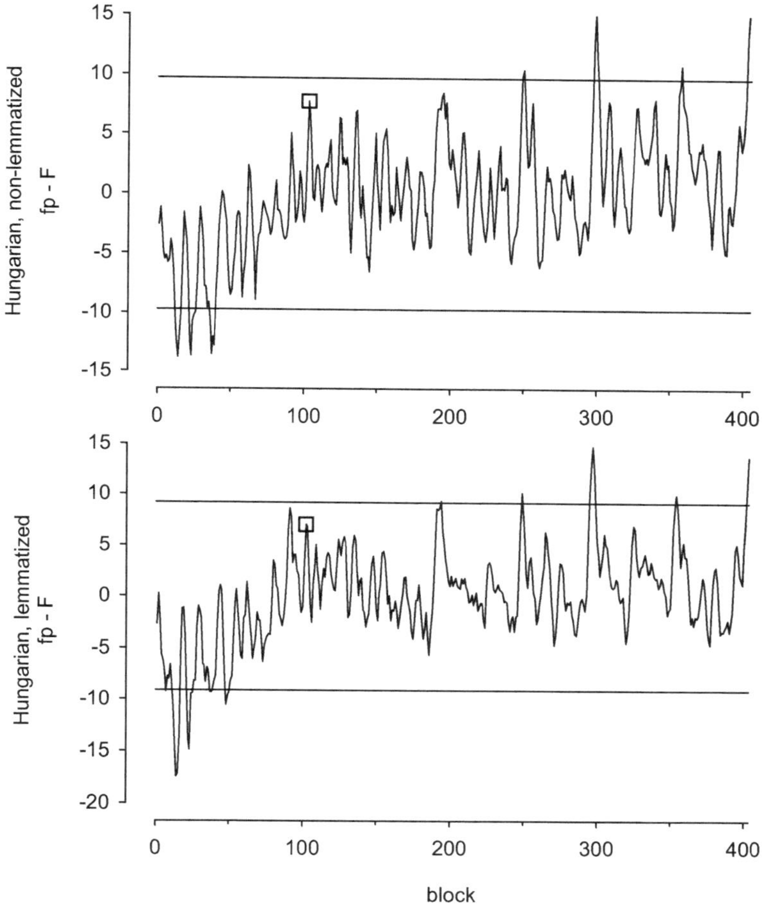

Figure 51. The non-lemmatized (upper panel) and lemmatized (lower panel) versions of the Hungarian translation of THE JUNGLE BOOK, A DZSUNGEL KÖNYVE. In this analysis BOOK I of THE JUNGLE BOOKS was involved using the original order of the stories. The text segment in the Hungarian translation which corresponds to the first protuberance of the English text does not reach the significance level, either in the lemmatized or in the non-lemmatized version (squared peaks).

The first protuberance is almost lost both in the non-lemmatized and lemmatized A DZSUNGEL KÖNYVE (Figure 51), since it is detectable, but below significance level. This could be due to at least three reasons. One is obvious: in this segment of the text the translator used shallower vocabulary than the original author. The other is that the immediate context of this text segment is richer in the translated texts than in the original, and consequently these words swallowed up this protuberance. This is not the case, however, with THE JUNGLE BOOK. As we have seen in Chapter 4.1.3.2.4 the voice of the Hungarian Kaa increased the number of word types in the text segments around King's Palace. The lemmatization cleared up this extremely rich segment, producing an 'almost' significant peak earlier than King's Palace, but the peak of King's Palace, even in the lemmatized version stayed below significance level; consequently this second explanation is ruled out. The explanation should thus be found elsewhere. As it was demonstrated in Chapter 2.3.2 (Figure 5), even assuming the hypergeometrical distribution of words within a text, there is always an overestimation of the original text at the beginning. The overestimation of the measured values at the beginning of the text might be due to two reasons. If the overestimation is relatively small, it indicates that either the beginning is rich in vocabulary or the text is closer to a random selection. However, if we compare the very beginning of the texts preceding H[40], it is obvious that the overestimation of the Hungarian text is greater than that of the English text.

In the comparison of the lemmatized and non-lemmatized texts minor differences can be detected. More precisely, protuberances might be lost by lemmatization and new ones might appear. These minor differences are the reason why it is worth analyzing both versions of the text if one wants to find all of the protuberances.

What is definite is that lemmatization might be responsible for the loss of protuberance(s). Again, Genette's other suggestion – that there might be text segments in a text where the affixes carry information – seems to be confirmed (Genette; 1995). These pieces of information, however, are lost by the lemmatization of the texts. This is the case when the author, instead of introducing new vocabulary items, preferred to use the available affixes of the already introduced lemmas. This can be detected when a new character appears in the text, whose style is different from the other characters previously introduced. Lemmatization diminishes these differences between the word usage of these characters.

On the other hand, lemmatization might reveal new protuberances, as happened at the beginning of the Hungarian texts. Although it does not occur too often, a protuberance which was not found in the non-lemmatized text might appear anywhere in the lemmatized versions of the texts. These protuberances, however, are detectable in the non-lemmatized text; they are there, but just did not reach the significance level.

4.2.4. Lemmatized The Da Vinci Code

When comparing the non-lemmatized and lemmatized THE DA VINCI CODE only minor differences can be found between the two texts (Figure 40, Figure 52, and Table 13).

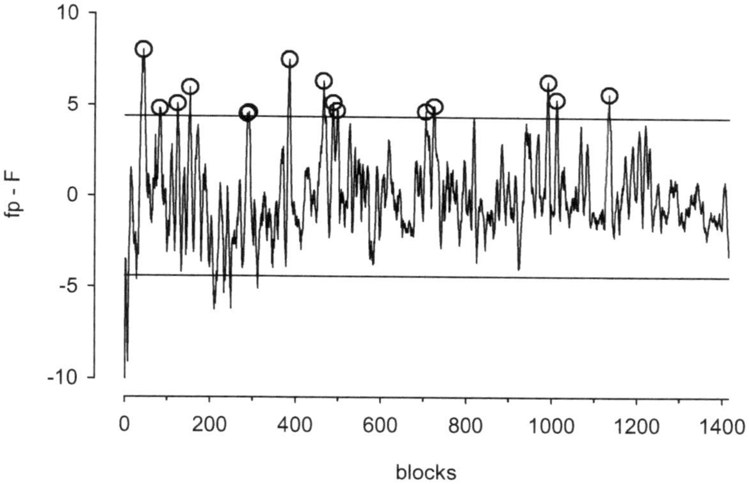

Figure 52. The protuberances of the lemmatized English THE DA VINCI CODE. There are only minor differences between the protuberances of the lemmatized and non-lemmatized versions of the novel.

In the lemmatized text four new significant protuberances appear ('phone call to Sandrine, 'chase', 'Remy + Teabing's house', 'hayloft') and one was lost ('Westminster'). However, these so called new protuberances were detectable in the non-lemmatized version too; their peaks just did not reach significance level. In contrast, while the peak of 'Westminster' exceeded significance level in the non-lemmatized version, the peak of the corresponding protuberance in the lemmatized version was just below significance level. The other ten protuberances are present both in the original and the lemmatized versions. The corresponding protuberances differ in length and intensity, similar to the new and lost protuberances.

The appearance of new protuberances in the lemmatized text means that affixes must be responsible for this loss. On the other hand, protuberances can also be lost through lemmatization. In this case the affixes carry the information.

Table 17. The locations of text segments responsible for the protuberances in the non-lemmatized and lemmatized versions of the full-length Hungarian texts. In the non-lemmatized text the number of blocks (n) equals 1199, in the lemmatized 1189, while $2SD = 7.36$ and 5.99, respectively.

Chapter	Text segment	Position in text	
		non-lemmatized	lemmatized
3	Paris		33–36
5	Opus Dei	71	69–73
7	phone call to Sandrine	—	—
9	Sophie	133*	132
12	Silas' childhood	148*	146–150
20	nature of Phi	—	—
28	witch-hunting	325–328	321–326
34	Pope, Castel Gandolfo	390–394	387–391
36	Chase	409–411	
37	Priory of Sion	420	
51	Teabing	576	
54	Remy + Teabing's house		590
55	Jesus, Christianity	610–614	608
66	search in Teabing's house	744–745	
72	mirror-image poem, iambic pentameter	799–802	791–796
76	Baphomet, Hebrew alphabet	839–840	830–834
79	Grand Masters	—	—
84	Remy lets Silas leave	920–921	
87	Hayloft	963–966	
95	searching on the net	1023*	1013–1014
97	Westminster	—	—

— text segments which caused significant protuberances in the English but not in the Hungarian text
* text segments whose protuberances are slightly under significance level

In agreement with previous results (Chapter 4.2.1 – 4.2.3 and Csernoch; 2006a), the lemmatized and non-lemmatized versions of the Hungarian translation of THE DA VINCI CODE do not show major differences. However, due to the agglutinating character of the Hungarian language, two remarkable features appear in all the earlier analyzed lemmatized / non-lemmatized text pairs. At the beginning of the text the affixes swallow up weak protuberances. Only the extremely strong protuberances are detectable in the first hundred blocks of the non-lemmatized text. In the non-lemmatized Hungarian THE DA

VINCI CODE one protuberance is completely lost (Paris), two are diminished ('Sophie' and 'Silas' childhood'), and there is one, which is small both in length and intensity, but reaches the significance level ('Opus Dei') (Table 17). Another difference due to the morphological richness of Hungarian, as compared to English, is that there are several protuberances which are present in the non-lemmatized version, but not in the lemmatized one. This means that affixes carry information and introduce vocabulary items, and this is lost through lemmatization.

As we have seen during the analysis of the four novels, the lemmatization of a text does not provide major differences in the number of newly introduced words. The decision as to whether we need lemmatization or not always depends on the aim of the analysis. For analyses designed to find out why the protuberances appear in the graph there is no need for lemmatization. To find all the protuberances, and along with them the vocabulary rich segments of a text, the analysis of both the lemmatized and the non-lemmatized versions might be needed.

4.3. Condensed versions of literary works

In this analysis the condensed books published by Reader's Digest were digitized both in English and Hungarian. The existence of these condensed versions causes continuous and heated debates as to their values and intended audience. The noble aim which brought to life the condensed books was to reach out to those who for one reason or another cannot or will not read the original texts, or do not have access to them. Instead of forcing the full-text version on them a somewhat lightened version is offered. However, the condensation of literature has to deal with substantial losses, and indeed the first question to arise in this connection is whether what we get is a piece of literature at all if the text has been severely curtailed. Another question to consider is whether the abridged versions are read by their intended audience: other people, who could read the original versions, might find them more convenient to read and might switch to reading the condensed versions instead of the originals.

4.3.1. Condensed English The Da Vinci Code

Table 18. Number of one-hundred-token-long blocks, word types and lemmas in the English and the Hungarian full-length and condensed THE DA VINCI CODE.

language	length	block		word type		lemma	
English	full-length	1397	46%	11442	64%	10300	64%
	Condensed	645		7333		6584	
Hungarian	full-length	1199	45%	25394	55%	13888	61%
	Condensed	543		14041		8414	

The condensed English text is 46% of the original THE DA VINCI CODE in length. This represents a severe curtailment of the text; more than half of the tokens are lost. However, if we compare the number of word types and lemmas, the loss is found to be less pronounced (Table 18).

My goal was to analyze the changes in the vocabulary, so again using DyMoCASAT, and based on this model, artificial texts were created to match the condensed versions and the same method was applied (Chapter 3.1 – 3.3).

In the condensed non-lemmatized English text six protuberances were found, while the lemmatized text contained one more (at the very beginning, one-block-long). Thus, the number of protuberances dropped to half of that in the original text. It was not only the number of the protuberances that was reduced;

their length also decreased, although their intensity was not necessarily smaller (Table 19, Figure 40 and Figure 53). Among the remaining text segments four are clearly historical, and three are contemporary events or a mixture of the two.

Another comparable parameter of the texts in the same language is the cumulative length of the protuberances (Table 14 and Table 20). In the original full-length text the cumulative length of protuberances was 3.65%, while in the condensed version this value was 4.19%. In this respect there is no loss compared to the full-length text.

The 2*SD* of the condensed version compared to the same parameter of the original text does not show a significant drop, either; in fact, there is a slight increase (see Table 13 and Table 19). These two parameters show that despite the decrease in the number of protuberances, their intensity may increase the 2*SD*. All this means that there must be a serious drop in vocabulary in the rest of the text – in those parts where protuberances do not appear. This further indicates that the condensed version – by eliminating some of the protuberances – is closer to a random selection of words than the original work.

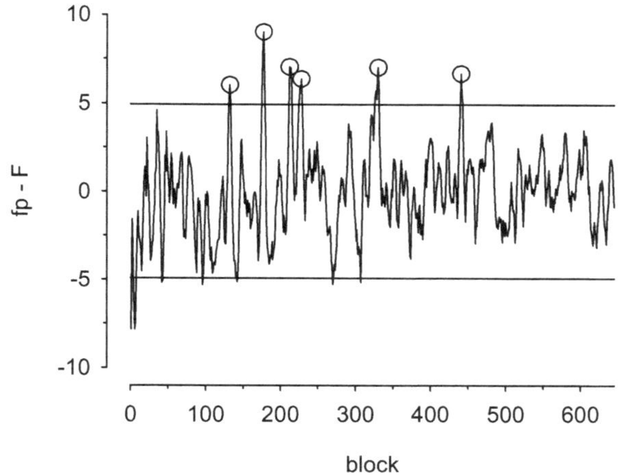

Figure 53. The difference between the original and artificial texts for the condensed version of the English THE DA VINCI CODE. Note the lower number of blocks and the decreased number of protuberances as compared to the original full-length version.

4.3.2. *A comparison of the English and the Hungarian condensed versions of The Da Vinci Code*

Both the English and the Hungarian condensed versions are divided into fourteen chapters, as compared to the original one hundred and five. Since the protuberances are related to the same events in both the original and the condensed texts, this again proves that the chapter-boundaries do not automatically generate an increase in the number of newly introduced words.

In the Hungarian condensed text the description of Sophie and Baphomet is not present; on the other hand, Aringarosa collecting the bonds provided a protuberance (Table 19, Figure 53, and Figure 54). Interestingly, this protuberance was found only in the condensed Hungarian text (both in the non-lemmatized and the lemmatized versions).

Table 19. Protuberances in the condensed English and Hungarian versions of THE DA VINCI CODE. In the non-lemmatized English text the number of blocks (n) equals 645, in the lemmatized English text 654, in the non-lemmatized Hungarian text 543, in the lemmatized Hungarian text 538, while $2SD$ = 4.93, 4.62, 7.28, and 5.79, respectively.

Text segment	Position in text			
	English		Hungarian	
	non-lemmatized	lemmatized	non-lemmatized	lemmatized
Paris		21		
Sophie	131–133	132–134		
witch-hunting	175–179	177–181	147–148	145–147
Pope, Castel Gandolfo	212–215	214–217	214–217	175–177
Priory of Sion	225–229	227–229	186–191	186–188
Aringarosa			207–208	206–206
Jesus, Christianity	326–331	329–334	275–278	272–275
Baphomet, Hebrew alphabet	440–443			

It was also interesting to see whether the method of analyzing the number of newly introduced words could provide a means of determining the source of the condensed Hungarian version; was it an abridgement of the Hungarian translation or a translation of the condensed English text? Since both the Hungarian translation and the condensed English version are adaptations of the original text, information losses and similarities may provide clues.

Table 20. Length and cumulative length of protuberances in the condensed English THE DA VINCI CODE.

length of protuberances	number of same-length protuberances	cumulative length
3	1	3
4	2	8
5	2	10
6	1	6
	6	27

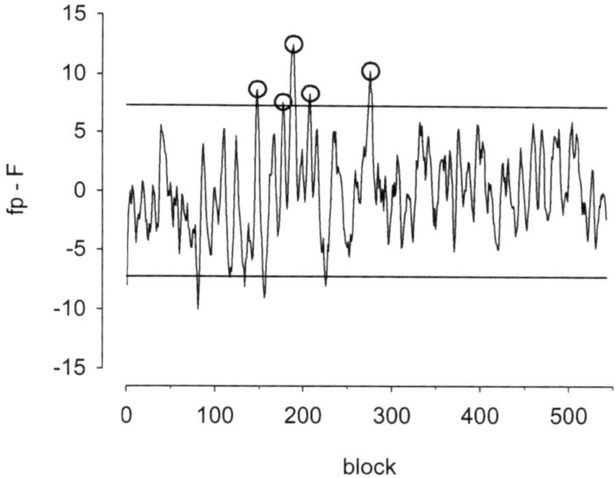

Figure 54. Protuberances of the condensed Hungarian THE DA VINCI CODE. By the comparison of the full-length English and Hungarian and the condensed English and Hungarian texts we were able to tell whether the condensed Hungarian text is the direct adaptation of the full-length Hungarian or the condensed English text.

There are three events that can be found – marked by significant or 'almost' significant protuberances – in both of the long texts, but which are missing from the condensed versions ('Opus Dei', 'hayloft' and 'Westminster'; see Table 13, Table 17, and Table 19). On the other hand, there is one text segment which is hardly recognizable in the full-length Hungarian translation, but has a strong presence in both condensed versions. This text segment is the introduction and description of the Priory of Sion. Furthermore, none of the text segments unique to the Hungarian translation appears in the condensed Hungarian text.

As a result, the comparison of the protuberances was indeed sufficient to identify the condensed English version as the direct source of the condensed Hungarian version. Further evidence was supplied by minor changes in the text, one of them already mentioned above (Chapter 4.1.5.5); the protagonists wanted to buy tickets to Lille in the English full-length version, to Lyon in the Hungarian full-length version, and to Lille in both the condensed versions.

4.3.3. A comparison of the full-length and the condensed texts of The Scarlet Pimpernel

Dan Brown's THE DA VINCI CODE and Baroness Orczy's THE SCARLET PIMPERNEL share many common features both in the structure of the novels and in their reception. I do not want to go into details regarding the structure of the two novels because it is far beyond the scope of this project but the similarities are so obvious that we cannot pretend not to see them. All I would like to give is a short list of the obvious similarities:

- the story starts in Paris with a chase
- a male protagonist whose mother tongue is English
- a beautiful, interesting, but odd female protagonist
- traveling between France and England
- lethal chase(s)
- French police who want to hunt down the protagonist(s)
- conspiracy
- romance
- film adaptation

Not only in the structure but in the reception of the novels we can find striking similarities. As mentioned in Chapter 4.1.5, THE DA VINCI CODE was "the most popular and controversial novel of our time" [11]. THE SCARLET PIMPERNEL was similarly acclaimed despite of the distance in time between the first publications. Baroness Orczy gained fame in 1903 with the stage version of THE SCARLET PIMPERNEL, but regardless of the success on stage the book was rejected by a dozen publishers (Hoppenstand; 2000). After all these shared features, it was really interesting to reveal the changes in the vocabulary of the two novels and how the condensation of the texts was carried out.

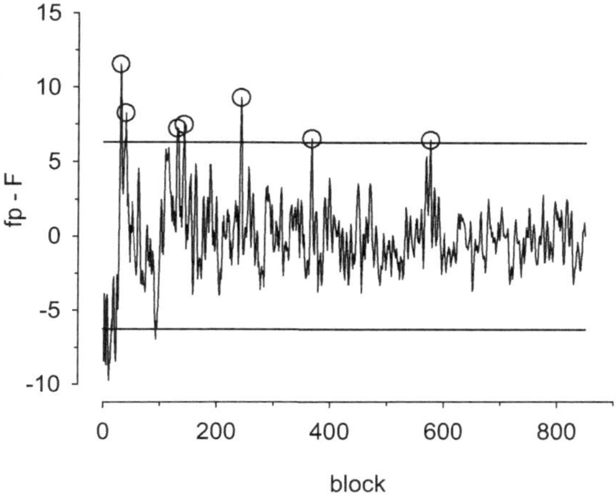

Figure 55. The protuberances of Baroness Orczy's THE SCARLET PIMPERNEL. All but one of the major protuberances appear in the first half of the text, representing descriptions of characters and places.

As can be seen in Figure 55, similarly to THE DA VINCI CODE the significant protuberances mostly appear in the first half of the novel. However, neither of them is related to historical events, all of them are descriptions of either characters in the novel or places where the events take place. Most of the characters and locations are introduced at the beginning of the story. Towards the end of the story, in the last 200 blocks, there are hardly any new vocabulary items. Exactly the same was found in THE DA VINCI CODE. By comparing the two graphs of the newly introduced word types (Figure 40 and Figure 55) it can be seen that the number of the protuberances is in direct proportion to the length of the texts.

The two other parameters I would like to mention are the repetition rate ($N/V(N)$) and the significance level ($2SD$) of the two texts. Based on the data in Table 13 and Table 21 the repetition rate for the full length THE DA VINCI CODE is higher than for the full length THE SCARLET PIMPERNEL. The $2SD$ for THE DA VINCI CODE is 4.85 (Table 13) and 6.3 for THE SCARLET PIMPERNEL. This parameter indicates that the vocabulary of THE SCARLET PIMPERNEL is more varied than that of THE DA VINCI CODE.

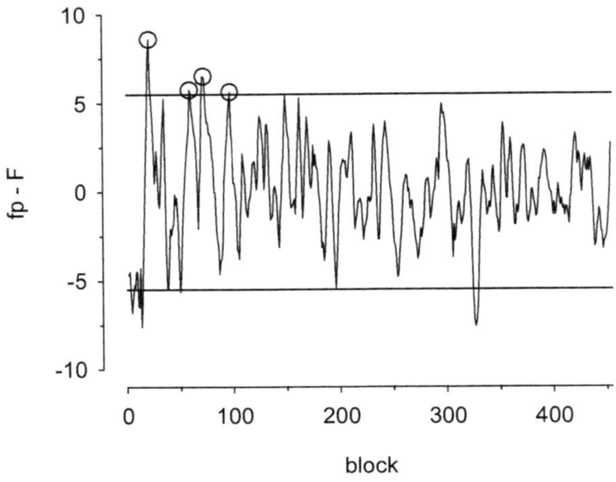

Figure 56. The protuberances of the condensed version of Baroness Orczy's THE SCARLET PIMPERNEL. The protuberances of the original text are remarkably well repeated in the condensed version.

Table 21. A comparison of the number of one-hundred-token-long blocks, word types, hapax legomena, and the repetition rate of three novels and their condensed versions.

	n	V(N)	V(1,N)	N/V(N)
		The Da Vinci Code		
full-length	1397	11442	4899	12.2
condensed	645	7333	3424	8.8
		The Scarlet Pimpernel		
full-length	849	7267	3041	11.7
condensed	452	5117	2301	8.8
		The Adventures of Tom Sawyer		
full-length	711	7331	3556	9.7
condensed	455	5618	2819	8.1

The condensed version of THE SCARLET PIMPERNEL (Figure 56) is 53% of the full-length text, somewhat longer than the condensed version of THE DA VINCI CODE (Table 22). However, the percentage of the word types remains noticeably higher in THE SCARLET PIMPERNEL than in THE DA VINCI CODE (Table 21 and Table 22). Similarly, the percentage of hapax legomena kept in the condensed version of THE SCARLET PIMPERNEL is higher than in THE DA

VINCI CODE (Table 21 and Table 22). These last two parameters again indicate that the text of THE SCARLET PIMPERNEL is reduced to half of the length of the original text but word types and hapax legomena are not as severely damaged.

Table 22. Number of one-hundred-token-long blocks, word types, and hapax legomena in THE SCARLET PIMPERNEL, THE ADVENTURES OF TOM SAWYER, and THE DA VINCI CODE full-length and condensed texts. Next to the absolute numbers the percentage of the data from the condensed texts in relation to the full-length texts is also given.

	length	blocks		word type		hapax legomena	
The Scarlet Pimpernel	full-length	849	53%	7267	70%	3041	76%
	condensed	452		5117		2301	
Tom Sawyer	full-length	711	64%	7331	77%	3556	79%
	condensed	455		5618		2819	
The Da Vinci Code	full-length	1397	46%	11442	64%	4899	70%
	condensed	645		7333		3424	

Finally, the protuberances of the condensed THE SCARLET PIMPERNEL and the text segments which triggered these protuberances were examined. From the seven protuberances of the original text four are left in the condensed version. All but one are descriptions of a character or characters in the story. The text segments belonging to the protuberances were trimmed in a different way than in THE DA VINCI CODE. In this case many of the descriptions of the original text are kept but pulled closer to each other, so in two of the four the text segments contain two descriptions. Considering this fact and the parameters given above in this chapter, it can be established that the characteristics of THE SCARLET PIMPERNEL were not damaged as crudely as happened with THE DA VINCI CODE. From THE SCARLET PIMPERNEL some of the minor events were left out instead of the valuable descriptions of the major characters.

4.3.4. A comparison of the full-length and the condensed texts of The Adventures of Tom Sawyer

Mark Twain's TOM SAWYER is different from the two novels discussed above because it was well received from the very beginning and has never given rise any serious debate considering the values which it stands for.

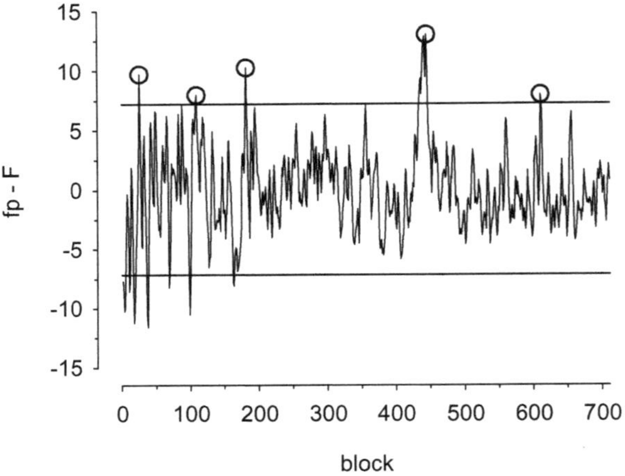

Figure 57. The protuberances of the full-length text of Mark Twain's THE ADVENTURES OF TOM SAWYER applying a 7-point smoothing algorithm.

The protuberances of the original text of TOM SAWYER showed a great variety in the nature of the text segments corresponding to the increase in the number of new words. These text segments, unlike in the other two stories, mainly represent changes in style and only the first and last occur with descriptions. The changes in style are so decisive that they were able to suppress protuberances of descriptions below significance level. The largest protuberance, both in length and intensity, represents a school leaving exam where the students have to read their own poems or stories (Chapter 4.1.6 and Figure 57).

TOM SAWYER is the least condensed among the three novels (Table 21, Table 22, and Figure 58). 64% of the original text is kept, as well as 77% of the word types and 79% of the hapax legomena. From these data we could have assumed that the condensed version of TOM SAWYER is the closest to the original text.

After comparing the pure numbers gained from the text, in the next step we considered the protuberances and the text segments which triggered them. The number of the protuberances did not drop seriously but, surprisingly, their locations are different from the locations of the original protuberances and they are different in nature as well. The dense vocabulary at the beginning of the text is somewhat damaged, since none of the protuberances of the condensed version reached significance level. In the second and the fourth sections of the text (for the definition of sections see Chapter 4.1.6.1) the protuberances which did not reach significance level in the full-length text did so in the condensed version, and the other way around. Consequently, significant protuberances were lost in the condensation. The change in style is only detectable at the school leaving examination section but nowhere else. The other significant protuberances in the condensed version are for descriptions and only the last one represents the text segment which is also found to be significant in the full-length text.

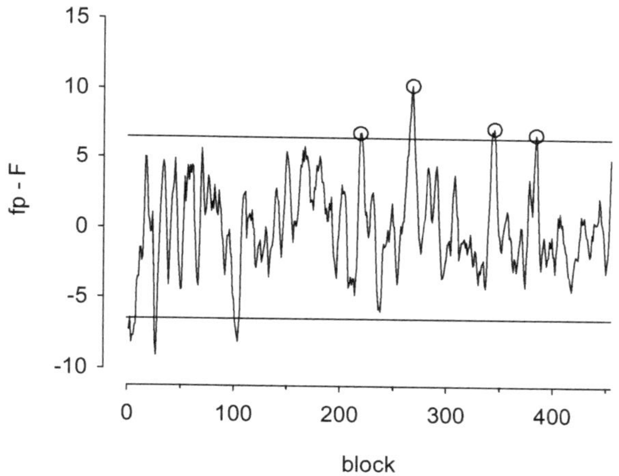

Figure 58. The protuberances of the condensed version of THE ADVENTURES OF TOM SAWYER. The condensation caused serious damage to the vocabulary rich segments of the text.

Summing up the results of the statistical analysis aiming at describing the vocabulary richness of the full-length and condensed versions of TOM SAWYER it was found that despite of the fact that TOM SAWYER was the least condensed among the three novels in terms of text length, this novel endured the most serious damage in vocabulary richness.

5. Hapax legomena and newly introduced words

As detailed in the previous chapters, the protuberances occurred on the *fp* – *F* graph when either a 'longish' description or an unexpected list of words, such as names, was inserted into the text or a severe change in style or language occurred (Chapter 4.1 – 4.3). However, Genette went further, claiming that the text segments containing descriptions, lists of unexpected words, and changes in style are 'functionally useless' (Genette; 1995), which means that if we leave these text segments out of the text or change them back to the style of the story, the text would still be understandable and compact. If he is right, the significant protuberances on the graph of newly introduced word types should, with a high probability, appear where the number of hapax legomena is also high. To test this suggestion, I decided to check the number of hapax legomena, using a similar method which was applied to word types and lemmas.

5.1. Hapax legomena in the texts

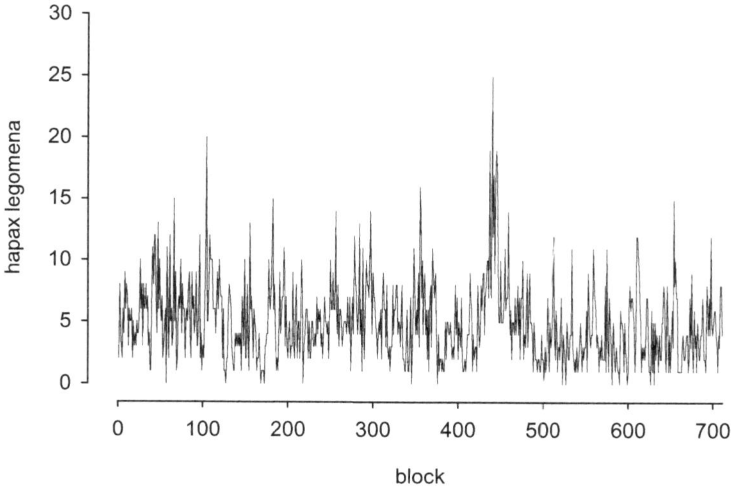

Figure 59. The number of hapax legomena in each block in TOM SAWYER, where the text is divided into one-hundred-token-long blocks.

In this context hapax legomena are understood, similarly to newly introduced words, within the scope of the analyzed text, which can either be a complete work or a concatenated text of several works. That is, the hapax legomena are those words which occur only once in the text analyzed.

5.1.1. The appearance of hapax legomena

The text, again, similar to the analyses of the newly introduced words, was divided into *h*-token long blocks (*h* is usually set to one-hundred), and the number of the hapax legomena was counted in each block ($h(i)$, $i = 1, \ldots, n$, Figure 59). For the whole text the following equations hold true considering the number of newly introduced word types and the number of hapax legomena ($f(i)$, $h(i)$ respectively, where $i = 1, \ldots, n$).

$$\sum_{i=1}^{n} f(i) = V(N) \qquad \textbf{(17)}$$

$$\sum_{i=1}^{n} h(i) = V(1, N) \qquad \textbf{(18)}$$

Equation 17 means that the sum of the newly introduced word types in each block equals the number of different word types of the analyzed text ($V(N)$). Equation 18 means that the sum of the hapax legomena in each block is the number of hapax legomena of the analyzed text ($V(1,N)$).

As was mentioned in Chapter 2.3.4, in general the graph of the newly introduced word types follows a monotonic decay as we advance through the text and the deviances in these graphs suggest the vocabulary rich segments of the texts analyzed.

Unlike the number of newly introduced word types, we cannot draw general conclusions concerning the number of hapax legomena in these blocks. There is definitely no monotonic decay as is well represented in Figure 59. Rather, there might be a slight rise towards the end of the text. The reason for this slight increase in the number of hapax legomena in the last couple of blocks is contained in the definition of hapax legomena, since a word appearing for the first time towards the end of the text has a greater chance of becoming a hapax legomenon than a word which is encountered at the beginning of the text.

To be able to expand our knowledge in connection with the vocabulary rich segments of the text, the number of hapax legomena and the number of newly introduced word types have to be compared. These two sets of numbers are mapped on the same graph in Figure 60. The two plots, especially at the beginning of the text, do not seem comparable, due to their different behavior. To get comparable results, the absolute numbers of newly introduced word types are replaced by the difference to the model-based values as detailed in Chapter 3.1.3 and Figure 21. With this method the protuberances of the plot clearly show the location of the vocabulary rich segments of the text. This plot and the plot of the hapax legomena in each block are comparable and are the source for further analysis (Figure 61 and Figure 62).

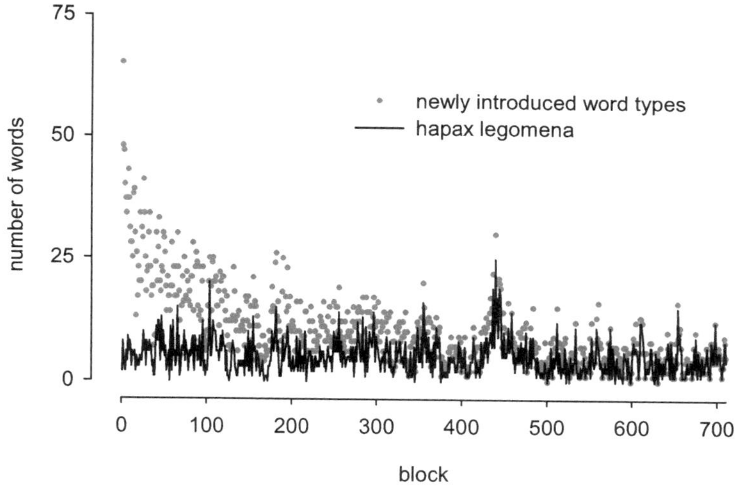

Figure 60. The number of hapax legomena and the number of the newly introduced word types in each block in TOM SAWYER.

The visualization of the two plots of Figure 61 and Figure 62 suggests that in general there is a high correlation between the number of the newly introduced word types and the number of hapax legomena in each block. This means that those segments of the text which carry a high number of newly introduced word types are also loaded with hapax legomena. To prove this hypothesis Student's t-test was applied, so the correlation coefficient (r) of the two sets of values should be calculated. To calculate r, $h(i)$ and $d(i)$ should be used. $h(i)$ stands for the hapax legomena and $d(i)$ for the newly introduced word types. However, instead of the absolute number of the newly introduced word types ($f(i)$), the differences of $fp(i) - F(i)$ should be used, which is shortened as $d(i)$, in Equation 19.

$$r=\frac{\sum_{i=1}^{n}\left(d(i)-\overline{d(i)}\right)\cdot\left(h(i)-\overline{h(i)}\right)}{\sqrt{\sum_{i=1}^{n}\left(d(i)-\overline{d(i)}\right)^{2}\cdot\sum_{i=1}^{n}\left(h(i)-\overline{h(i)}\right)^{2}}} \quad \textbf{(19)}$$

In the given example (Figure 61) the correlation coefficient of TOM SAWYER was calculated. In TOM SAWYER the number of blocks (n) equals 711, and r is 0.6612. To decide whether this correlation coefficient actually represents a correlation between the two sets of values, a new variable, t (Equation 20) is introduced, which follows the Student's t-distribution.

$$t=\frac{r}{\sqrt{\frac{1-r^{2}}{n-2}}} \quad \textbf{(20)}$$

Application of this formula to any particular observed value of r will accordingly test the null hypothesis, that the two populations are not correlated. We can check the t values in tables which list the upper critical values of the t-distribution for a $df = n - 2$ degrees of freedom. If the absolute value of the test statistic (t) is greater than the upper critical value, then we reject the null hypothesis.

For TOM SAWYER the calculated value of t is 13.208. The critical value for the probability $\alpha = 0.01$ is $t = 2.581$ with $df = 1000$. This means that with a probability of 99%, there is correlation between the two sets of values. The same was found true of the other analyzed texts (Table 23).

The fact that there is a strong correlation between the two sets of values visually means that if there is a rise or a decrease on one of the graphs, there is a rise or a decrease, respectively, on the other graph, too. However, there might be segments which carry a high number of newly introduced word types and fewer hapax legomena. These words are naturally reused in a later section of the text, and using Genette's expression, are less 'useless'. They have a function in the text but their special feature is that they were introduced in that particular segment. Those segments which carry both a high number of newly introduced word types and hapax legomena are the real 'useless' segments of the text.

On both Figure 61 and Figure 62 we can find blocks where the number of hapax legomena seems greater than the number of the newly introduced word types. This seems impossible because of the definitions of the two notions (Chapter 2.1.2 and Chapter 5). The appearance of such blocks on the graph is the straightforward consequence of the smoothing process (Chapter 3.2 and Figure 22).

Table 23. The values of r and t with the $n-2$ degree of freedom (df) for four English and two Hungarian texts. All t-values exceed the critical value of $t = 2.581$ for $\alpha = 0.01$ probability.

	n	r	t
Tom Sawyer	711	0.661	13.208
Robinson Crusoe	1214	0.356	11.593
The Da Vinci Code	1397	0.516	16.511
The Jungle Books	1171	0.513	15.059
Sorstalanság (Hungarian)	561	0.561	10.989
A Da Vinci-kód (Hungarian)	1199	0.583	16.393

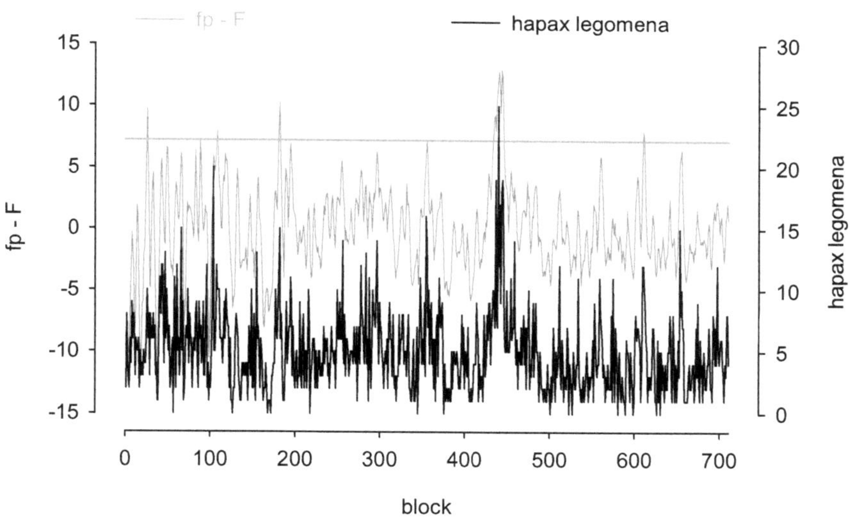

Figure 61. The protuberances of newly introduced word types (upper graph) and hapax legomena (lower graph) in TOM SAWYER. The two plots show remarkable similarities.

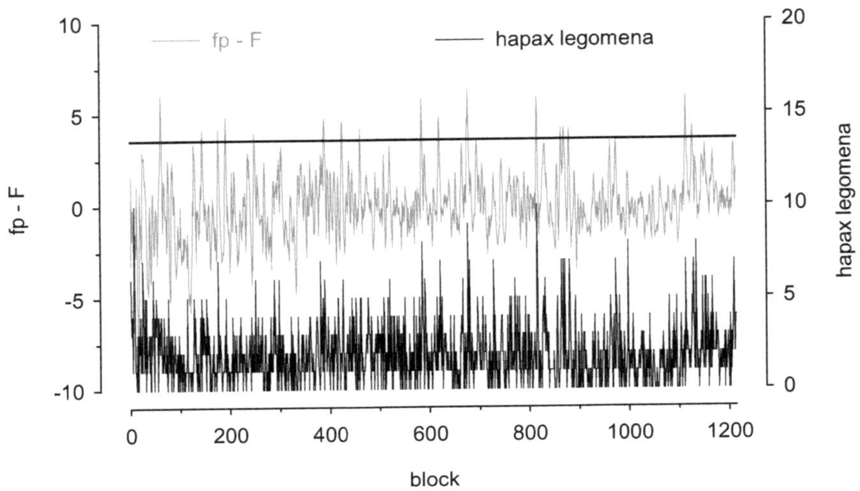

Figure 62. The newly introduced word types (upper graph) and hapax legomena (lower graph) of ROBINSON CRUSOE. The graphs show that the significant protuberances of the *fp* – *F* plot are weak in both intensity and length. This is a clear consequence of the fact that the introduction of newly introduced word types is close to a random selection of word types (see Figure 20). Similarly, the peaks in the plots of hapax legomena are weak both in intensity and length.

5.1.2. The distribution of hapax legomena

In the following phase of the analysis the number of hapax legomena in blocks were grouped. I counted how many blocks carry zero, one, etc. hapax legomena. If $h(i)$, $i = 1, \ldots, n$ marks the number of the hapax legomena in each b_i block we are able to tell the number of blocks where the number of hapax legomena is k, if the length of the blocks is h. In this case k runs from $minh$ (usually 0) to $maxh$, where $minh = \min(h(i))$ and $maxh = \max(h(i))$.
Let

$hap(0, h)$ denote the number of those blocks which carry 0 hapax legomena,

$hap(1, h)$, which carry 1 hapax legomenon,

…

$hap(k, h)$, which carry k hapax legomena,

… and finally,

$hap(maxh, h)$, which carry the greatest number of hapax legomena in the text analyzed, when the length of the blocks is h.

With these definitions the following equations hold true:

$$hap(k, h) = \sum_{i=1}^{n} I_{[h(i)=k]} \tag{21}$$

$$V(1, N) = \sum_{j=minh}^{maxh} hap(j, h) \tag{22}$$

Finally, let *mfreq* denote the most frequent number of hapax legomena in a block (that is the value of *k* where *hap*(*k*, *h*) reaches its maximum).

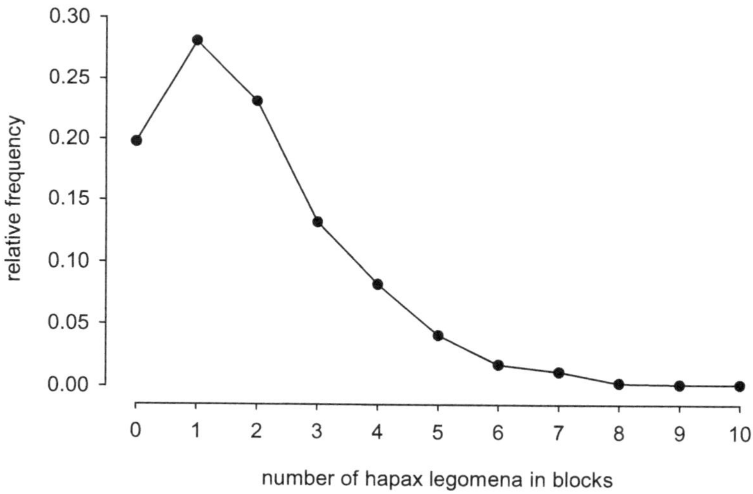

Figure 63. The distribution of hapax legomena in Daniel Defoe's ROBINSON CRUSOE. The greatest number of hapax legomena is 10 (*maxh* = 10), while the most frequent number of hapax legomena in a block is 1 (*mfreq* = 1).

In Figure 63 and Figure 64 we can compare the distribution of hapax legomena in two English novels: Daniel Defoe's ROBINSON CRUSOE (Figure 63) and Mark Twain's TOM SAWYER (Figure 64). The blocks which do not carry hapax legomena at all in ROBINSON CRUSOE are approximately ten times more frequent than in TOM SAWYER. The most frequent number of hapax legomena in blocks is 1 in ROBINSON CRUSOE, and 4 in TOM SAWYER. The greatest number of hapax legomena in a block in ROBINSON CRUSOE is 10, and in TOM SAWYER 25. These numbers clearly indicate, as was already suggested by the analysis of newly introduced word types, that the vocabulary of TOM SAWYER (Figure 44 and Figure 57) is more varied than that of ROBINSON CRUSOE (Figure 62). When analyzing the newly introduced word types it was found that the vocabulary of ROBINSON CRUSOE is closer to a random selection than the vocabulary of TOM SAWYER, since ROBINSON CRUSOE has only minor protuberances on the graph of newly introduced word types, and these protuberances are weak both in intensity and length (Figure 62). On the other hand, in TOM SAWYER we were able to find text segments which are richer in vocabulary than the main body of the text (Figure 44 and Figure 57).

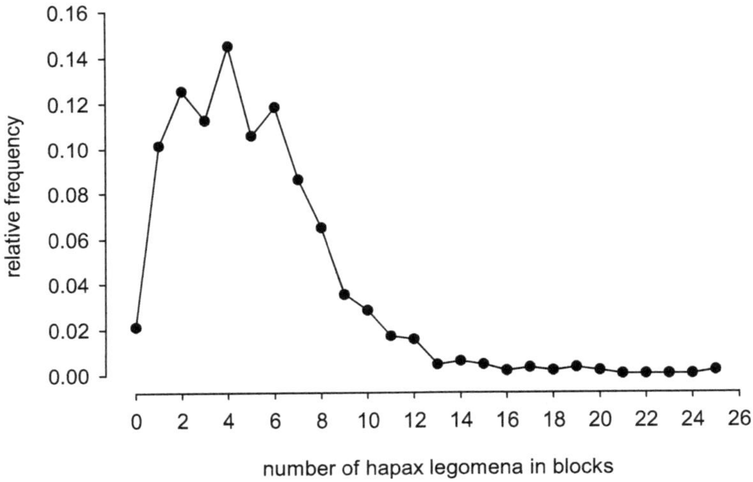

Figure 64. The distribution of hapax legomena in Mark Twain's TOM SAWYER. The greatest number of hapax legomena in a block is 25 (*maxh* = 25), while the most frequent number of hapax legomena in a block is 4 (*mfreq* = 4).

If we compare the distribution of hapax legomena in the English TOM SAWYER (Figure 64) and in its Hungarian translation (Figure 65) we find a similar pattern, however there are clear differences in the absolute values. It is obvious from the visual comparison that the graph of the distribution of hapax legomena of the Hungarian text is much broader and shallower. This is reflected in the fact that in the Hungarian translation we cannot find blocks with $k = 0, \ldots, 4$ hapax legomena (with an exception at $k = 1$), that is, although *minh* = 1, blocks usually carry many hapax legomena. Similarly, *maxh* is also greater than in the English text. Since the change in *maxh* is greater then in *minh*, *mfreq* is greater, while the relative frequency at *mfreq* is lower than in the English text. The latter result is a straightforward consequence of the longer domain of the Hungarian graph. This is all due to the agglutinating character of the language.

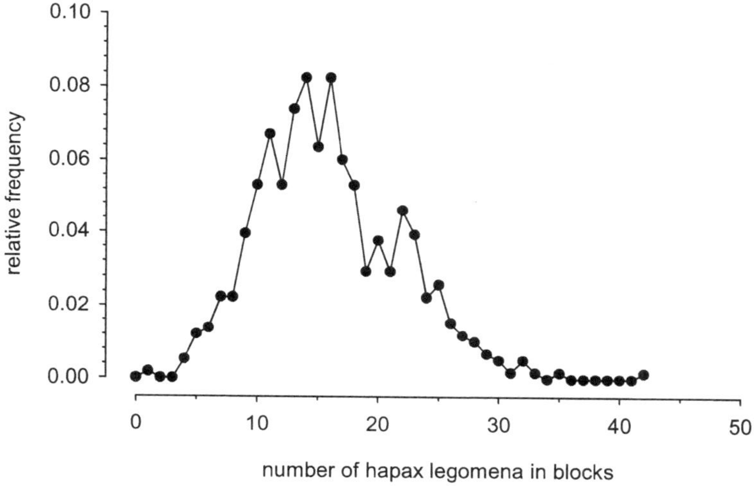

Figure 65. The distribution of hapax legomena in the Hungarian translation of Mark Twain's TOM SAWYER. The greatest number of hapax legomena is 42 (*maxh* = 42), while the most frequent number of hapax legomena in a block is 14 and 16 (*mfreq* = {14;16}).

To further the comparison of newly introduced word types in Hungarian and English texts, I have introduced their lemmatization since this reduces the difference arising from the agglutinating character of the Hungarian language (Chapter 1.1). As shown in Figure 66, the lemmatization of the Hungarian text eliminated or decreased the number of those blocks which carry low numbers of hapax legomena and high numbers of hapax legomena. Consequently, the domains of the lemmatized texts are shorter than of the non-lemmatized texts and, in addition, the relative frequencies at *mfreq* are greater in the lemmatized than in the non-lemmatized texts (Figure 66).

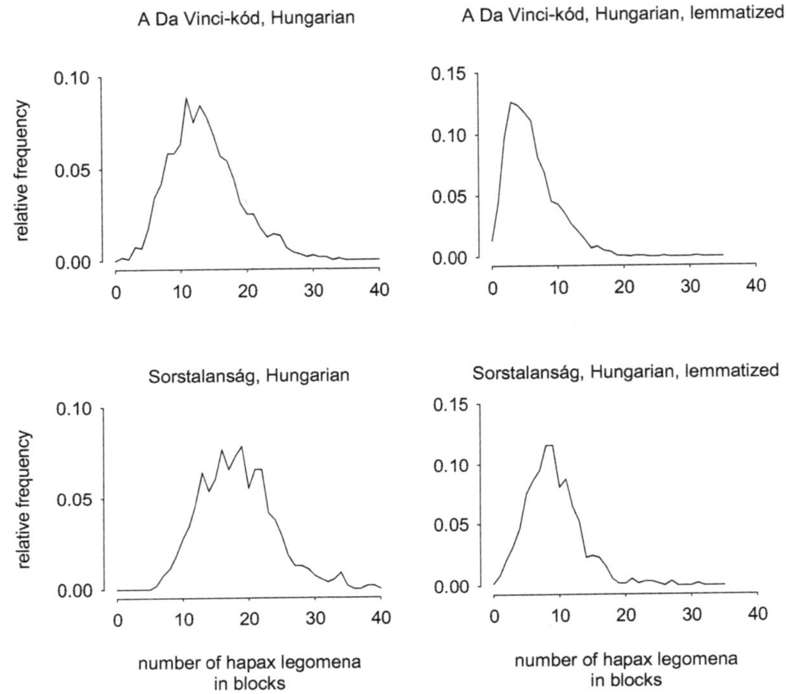

Figure 66. The distribution of hapax legomena in the Hungarian translation of Dan Brown's THE DA VINCI CODE (A Da Vinci-kód, upper panels), and in the original Hungarian text of Imre Kertész's SORSTALANSÁG (lower panels). The left-hand graphs map the data of the non-lemmatized texts, the right-hand those of the lemmatized texts.

If we draw a vertical axis to the graphs of $hap(k, h)$ at $k = mfreq$ and check how lemmatization of the Hungarian texts changes this location we find that the tails of the distributions are shortened less than their beginnings. This means that the lemmatization reduces the number of those blocks which carry low numbers of hapax legomena more than those which carry high numbers of hapax legomena.

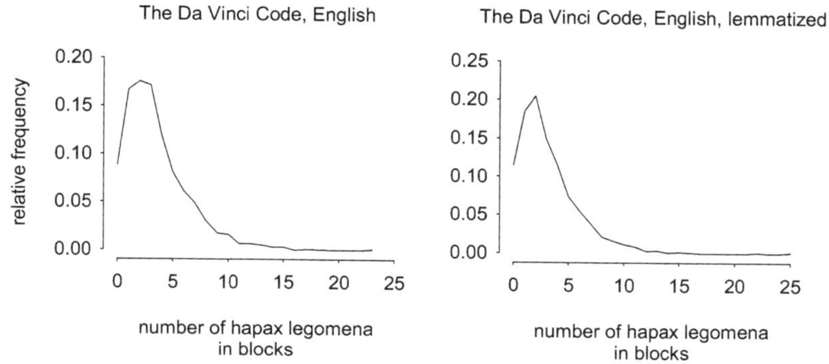

Figure 67. The distribution of hapax legomena in the non-lemmatized and lemmatized English texts of THE DA VINCI CODE.

In the English texts, as detailed in Chapter 1.1, there is no significant difference between the appearance of newly introduced words of the non-lemmatized and lemmatized versions. The same was found true for the hapax legomena as is demonstrated in Figure 67. The peak around *mfreq* is somewhat wider, consequently the relative frequency of the hapax legomena is lower in the original text than in the lemmatized one. However, the two distributions look alike.

5.2. Distribution of hapax legomena

Similarly to the analysis of the distribution of newly introduced word types, the distribution of hapax legomena can also be examined with the application of first-order statistical models. When building models for the distribution of hapax legomena three alternatives seemed reasonable:

- the application of the urn model
  - the assumption of a binomial distribution of words,
  - the assumption of a hypergeometrical distribution of words,
- the distribution of hapax legomena of an artificial text.

5.2.1. *First order statistical models*

5.2.1.1. *Binomial distribution of hapax legomena*

As detailed in Chapter 2.3.1 and 2.3.2, the urn model for word frequency distributions is commonly applied in connection with first-order statistical models. Here, for the distribution of hapax legomena we consider an urn containing marbles of two colors. One color corresponds to the hapax legomena, the other color to the other words, the non-hapax legomena of the text. Assuming the binomial distribution of the words we randomly draw N marbles from the urn in sets of h words (h is usually set to one-hundred, as it is in the analysis of the distributions of newly introduced word types). After each draw we examine the color of each marble, whether it is a hapax legomenon or not, and put it back into the urn (Hajtman; 1971, Meszéna and Ziermann; 1981, Solt; 1971, Baayen; 1996a, 1996b, 2001). Under these conditions the probability that among h words there are k hapax legomena is

$$P(\xi = k) = \binom{h}{k}\left(\frac{V(1,N)}{N}\right)^{k}\left(1-\frac{V(1,N)}{N}\right)^{h-k} \tag{23}$$

5.2.1.2. *Hypergeometrical distribution of hapax legomena*

Assuming the hypergeometrical distribution of words means that after examining the color of the marbles they are not returned into the urn. Consequently, the major difference between the binomial and the hypergeometrical distribution is that with the binomial distribution there is no guarantee that the number of word types equals their number in the original text.

On the other hand, with the hypergeometrical distribution the number of word types and the number of hapax legomena after N draws is the same in the original text. Assuming the hypergeometrical distribution of word, the probability that among h words there are k hapax legomena is

$$P(\xi = k) = \frac{\binom{V(1,N)}{k}\binom{N - V(1,N)}{h-k}}{\binom{N}{h}} \quad \textbf{(24)}$$

5.2.1.3. Hapax legomena of an artificial text

The third method for creating a model for the distribution of hapax legomena is to create an artificial text as is detailed in Chapter 3.1.2. The artificial text is then divided up, similar to any natural language text, into one-hundred-token-long intervals, blocks (for details see Chapter 2.3.3 and Figure 8), the number of hapax legomena in each block is counted.

5.2.1.4. Comparison of the models

Unlike the models for newly introduced word types there is no significant difference between the three applied models for the distribution of hapax legomena, which is the straightforward consequence of the nature of the urn model when the number of the colored marbles is small compared to the size of the urn (Johnson et al.; 1992, Bertsekas and Tsitsiklis; 2008, see Figure 68). As a result, either of them can be used, ideally the one that is the most accessible for the user.

Similar to texts in natural languages, the number of blocks which carry the same number of hapax legomena can be counted. In this context, if $eh(i)$ ($i = 1, \ldots, n$) marks the number of the hapax legomena to each drawing set (using one of the urn models) or b_i block (using the artificial text) than we are able to tell the number of blocks where the number of hapax legomena is k, if the length of the blocks is h. According to this let $eh(i)$ denote the expected value of hapax legomena in each drawing set or b_i block ($i = 1, \ldots, n$), and $ehap(0, h)$, $ehap(1, h), \ldots, ehap(emaxh, h)$ the number of those blocks which carry 0, 1, …, $emaxh$ number of hapax legomena in the model where $emaxh$ denotes the maximal value of $eh(i)$.

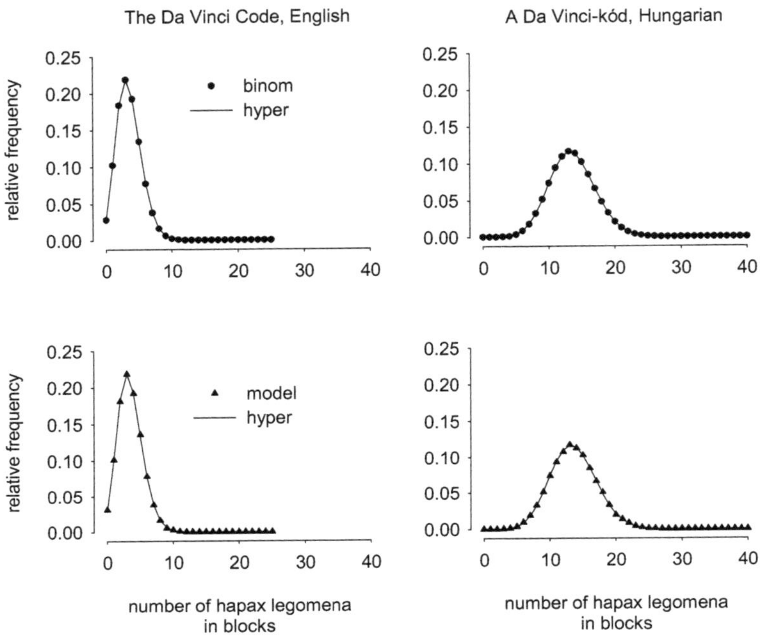

Figure 68. The distribution of hapax legomena in the models of Dan Brown's THE DA VINCI CODE for the original English text (left panels) and for the Hungarian translation (right panel) The graphs clearly show that there is no significant difference between the three methods applied to modeling the distribution of hapax legomena. The upper graphs show the result of the comparison of the binomial and the hypergeometrical distribution of words, while the lower graphs the comparison of the hypergeometrical and artificial-text-based distribution.

5.2.2. The comparison of the distribution of hapax legomena in English texts and in their models

For modeling the distribution of hapax legomena a unique model should be built for each text in all of the languages tested, both for the lemmatized and the non-lemmatized versions. In the next phase of the analysis these model-based results were compared to the original data.

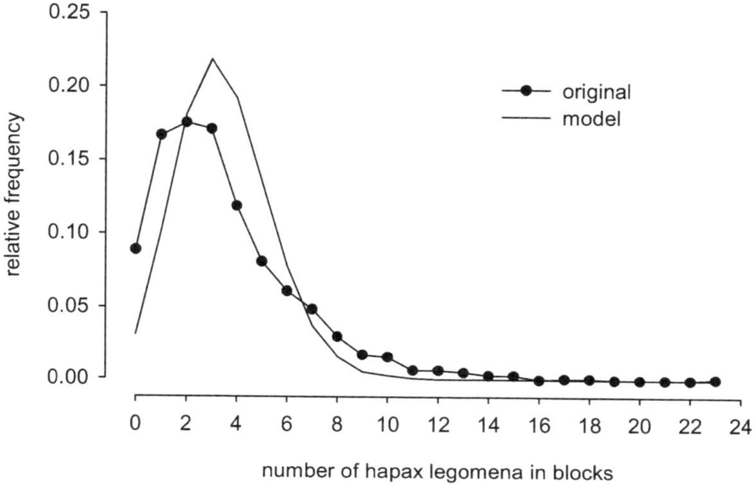

Figure 69. The distribution of hapax legomena in the original text and the model of Dan Brown's THE DA VINCI CODE. The values are presented as relative frequencies (a discrete probability distribution), meaning that the sum of all values equals 1.

When comparing the plots of the original and the model-based data of THE DA VINCI CODE, it is clear that the model is not able to reproduce the values from the two ends of the distribution (Figure 69). It is a remarkable difference that the domain of the model is shorter than that of the original text, *maxh* > *emaxh* (Figure 70). This means that the model was not able to reproduce the number of those blocks which carry a high number of hapax legomena. The other difference is that at the beginning of the domain the number of blocks, and thus their relative frequency as well, with a low number of hapax legomena is underestimated, *hap*(0,100) > *ehap*(0,100). Consequently, the relative frequency at *mfreq* is greater in the model than in the original text of THE DA VINCI CODE *hap*(*mfreq*,100) < *ehap*(*emfreq*,100). In addition, even *mfreq* has changed its location, that is, in this text *mfreq* < *emfreq*. These observations, i.e. that both *mfreq* and the relative frequency of hapax legomena at *mfreq* are greater in the model than in the original text, was found true for most of the analyzed texts (see later Figure 71 and Figure 73).

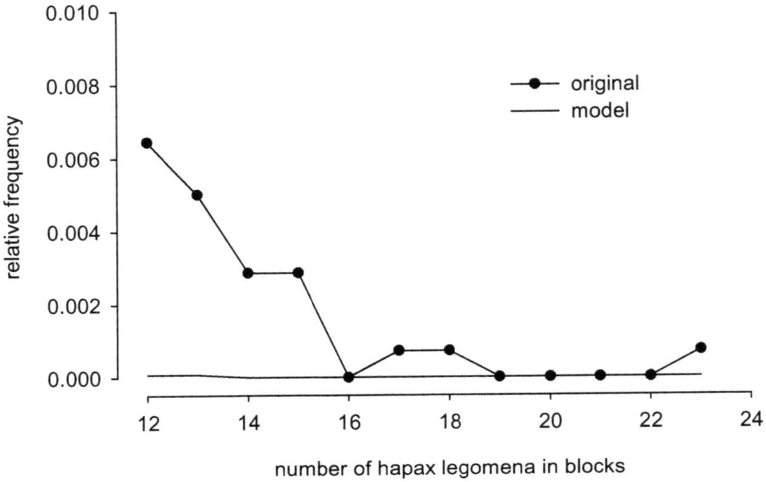

Figure 70. The end of the domain, the [12,23] interval, of the graph of the distribution of hapax legomena in the original text and in the model of Dan Brown's THE DA VINCI CODE.

However, the comparison of these distributions reveals other hidden characteristics of the texts. At first sight THE DA VINCI CODE seems rich in hapax legomena, since its *maxh* = 23. However, the fact that *mfreq* is only 2 and the relative frequency at *mfreq* is high suggests otherwise. The enlarged tail of the graph clears up this ambiguity (Figure 70). There is no block with 16, 19, 20, 21, and 22 hapax legomena (*hap*(16,100) = *hap*(19,100) = *hap*(20,100) = *hap*(21,100) = 0), and there is only one block with 17, 18, and 23 hapax legomena (*hap*(17,100) = *hap*(18,100) = *hap*(23,100) = 1), giving rise to a 'false tail' in the graph. Consequently, more realistically, the value of *maxh* should be 15 (*hap*(15,100) = 4), and it is also true that *hap*(14,100) = 4. Blocks containing 17 (b_{468}), 18 (b_{980}), and 23 (b_{1001}) hapax legomena are isolated, they all are one-block-long text segments with a high number of hapax legomena. Blocks b_{468} and b_{980} are the opening paragraphs of a new chapter. b_{468} is the 'inside of Gare Saint-Lazare', whose vocabulary is different from the main body of the text. b_{980} is a list of the names of the Hebrew characters, words which are again rare in this context. Finally, b_{1001}, which is different from the other two in the sense that it is not an opening paragraph of a chapter, is again a list of words, the names of the Grand Masters. All three blocks contain words which do not have any follow-up, since they do not have any close connection with the story. The story is understandable and complete without these blocks of words; they seem 'functionally useless'. These blocks are obviously not reproduced by the model.

The two graphs of Figure 69 have two intersections (*minhi*, *maxhi*). *Minhi* ∈ [1,2], close to $k = 2$, Maxhi ∈ [6,7]. Consequently, the following equations are true: (*hap*(1,100) > *ehap*(1,100) and (*hap*(2,100) < *ehap*(2,100) while, *hap*(6,100) < *ehap*(6,100) and *hap*(7,100) > *ehap*(7,100), when the model again falls under the measured values.

Since the sum of the relative frequencies equals 1, due to the underestimation of the values of *hap*(*k*,100) at the beginning (around *minh*) and at the end of the domain (around *maxh*), there is an overestimation around *mfreq*. The location of the maximum (*mfreq* and *emfreq*) and their values (*hap*(*mfreq*,100) and *ehap*(*emfreq*,100), respectively) are also different for the two functions, so are the values in the environment of *mfreq*.

Naturally, the distribution of hapax legomena is different for different texts, and so also for their models. In Figure 71 the distribution of hapax legomena of four original English texts and their corresponding models are mapped. In general, what is learned from THE DA VINCI CODE is also true for the other texts. The domain of the model is shorter than that of the original text d[*minh*,*maxh*] > d[*eminh*,*emaxh*] (tails are enlarged in Figure 72), which means that the number of hapax legomena, and their relative frequency is underestimated at large *k* values. Similarly, at the beginning of the domain, at small *k* values, the relative frequency of the hapax legomena is also underestimated. Consequently, the model consistently overestimates the values around *mfreq* or, in other words, there is always an environment characterized by *min_freq* and *max_freq*. It should be noted here that a text is the closer to a random selection of words the smaller the above mentioned under- and overestimations are.

The distribution of hapax legomena of THE JUNGLE BOOKS shows a similar pattern to that of THE DA VINCI CODE, except that THE JUNGLE BOOKS do not have a 'false tail' (Figure 72). The distribution of the hapax legomena of ROBINSON CRUSOE is the closest to the model. It does not have a long tail, which means that there are hardly any blocks with a high number of hapax legomena (*hap*(10,100) = *hap*(9,100) = 2 and *hap*(8,100) = 3). The hapax legomena are much more evenly distributed in the text than in either THE DA VINCI CODE or THE JUNGLE BOOKS.

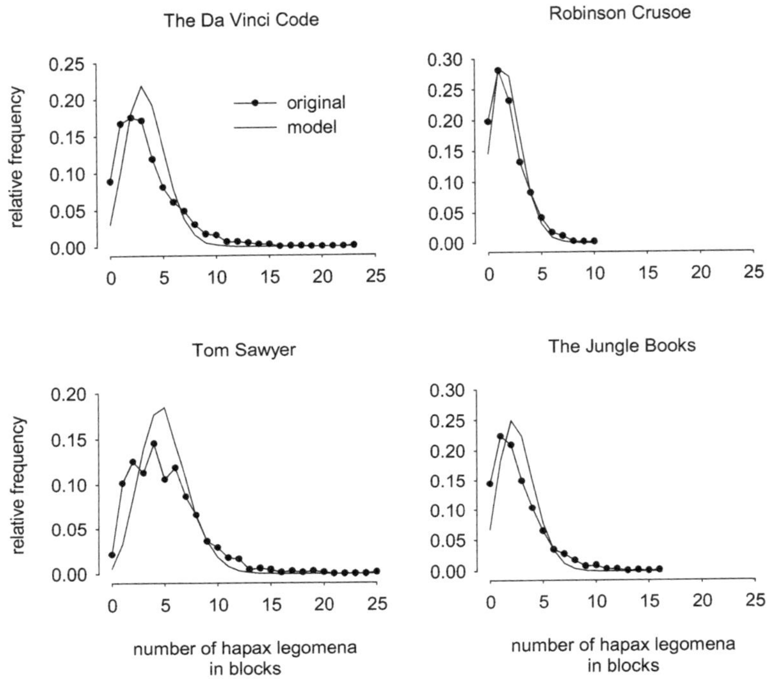

Figure 71. The distribution of hapax legomena of four English novels and their models.

TOM SAWYER is, in this respect, the richest in vocabulary among the four texts. It also has a 'false tail', but definitely shorter than that of THE DA VINCI CODE. If we eliminate this 'false tail', it is still *maxh* = 20, the highest among the selected texts. The other indication of the rich vocabulary is that the most frequent number of hapax legomena in a block is 4 (*mfreq* = 4). On the graph of the distribution of hapax legomena (Figure 71 and Figure 73 lower left panel) this is represented by the highest peak. The graph also tells us that in TOM SAWYER not only 4 but 2 or 3 hapax legomena in a block is also more common than in the other analyzed texts. Carrying more hapax legomena in a block in TOM SAWYER than in the other texts results in a wider segment around the peak of the graph.

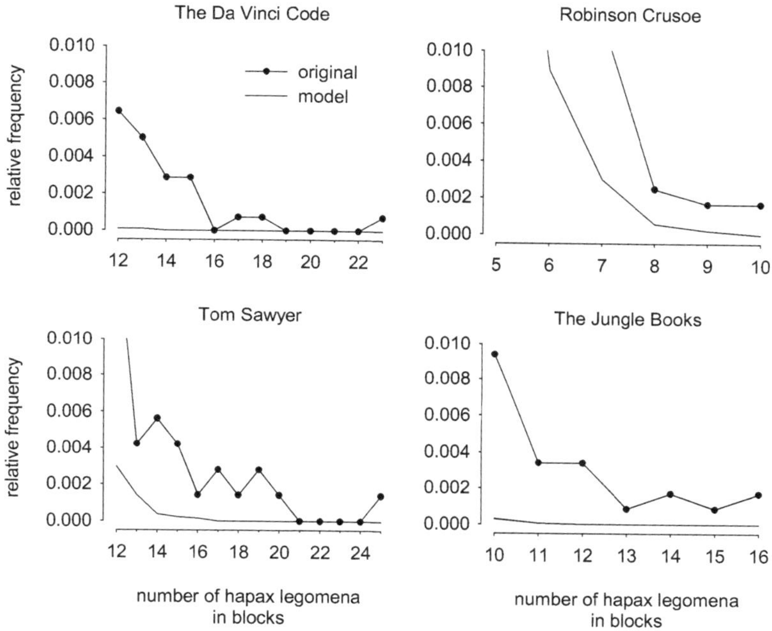

Figure 72. The enlarged tails of the graphs of the distribution of hapax legomena in four English novels.

After discussing the specialties of THE DA VINCI Code and TOM SAWYER we can draw general conclusions considering the under- and overestimation of hapax legomena. In general, *hap*(*k*,100) and *ehap*(*k*,100) have two intersections:

$$hap(k,100) \cap ehap(k, 100) = \{minhi, maxhi\}. \qquad \textbf{(25)}$$

Advancing from *minh* to *minhi* the measured values are greater than the expected values. The two graphs first meet at *minhi*, which is usually around *mfreq*. From *minhi* the expected values of *ehap*(*k*,100) are greater than the measured (*hap*(*k*,100)) until the next intersection of the two graphs (*maxhi*). This means that in the interval of [*minhi*,*maxhi*] the values of *hap*(*k*,100) are less than those of *ehap*(*k*,100).

$$\begin{cases} hap(k,100) > ehap(k,100), \text{ if } k \in [minh, minhi] \\ hap(k,100) < ehap(k,100), \text{ if } k \in [minhi, maxhi] \\ hap(k,100) > ehap(k,100), \text{ if } k \in [maxhi, maxh] \end{cases} \quad \textbf{(26)}$$

In three of the four texts not only the values but the location of the peak changes – *mfreq* ≠ *emfreq*. Among the analyzed texts ROBINSON CRUSOE is the only exception, here *mfreq* = *emfreq*. Consequently, ROBINSON CRUSOE is the only text where the expected values never exceed the measured values in the [*mfreq*,*emfreq*] interval. This finding further strengthens the suggestion (see Figure 62) that ROBINSON CRUSOE is closer to random selection than the other three texts.

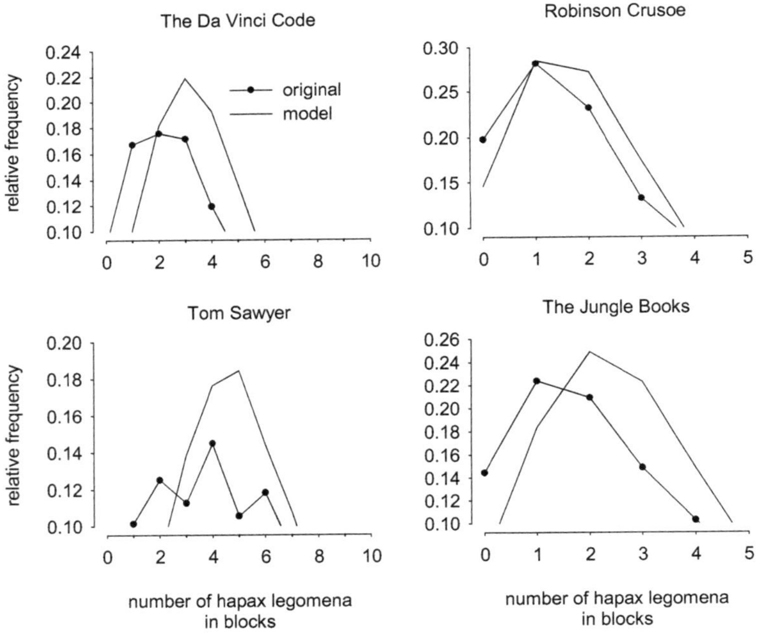

Figure 73. The enlarged surroundings of the maximum of the graphs of the distribution of hapax legomena (*hap*(*k*,*h*)) in four English novels. *k* = *mfreq* is the value where *hap*(*k*,*h*) function reaches its maximum. The most frequent number of hapax legomena in a block is 1 in ROBINSON CRUSOE and THE JUNGLE BOOKS (*mfreq* = 1), 2 in THE DA VINCI CODE (*mfreq* = 2), and 4 in TOM SAWYER (*mfreq* = 4).

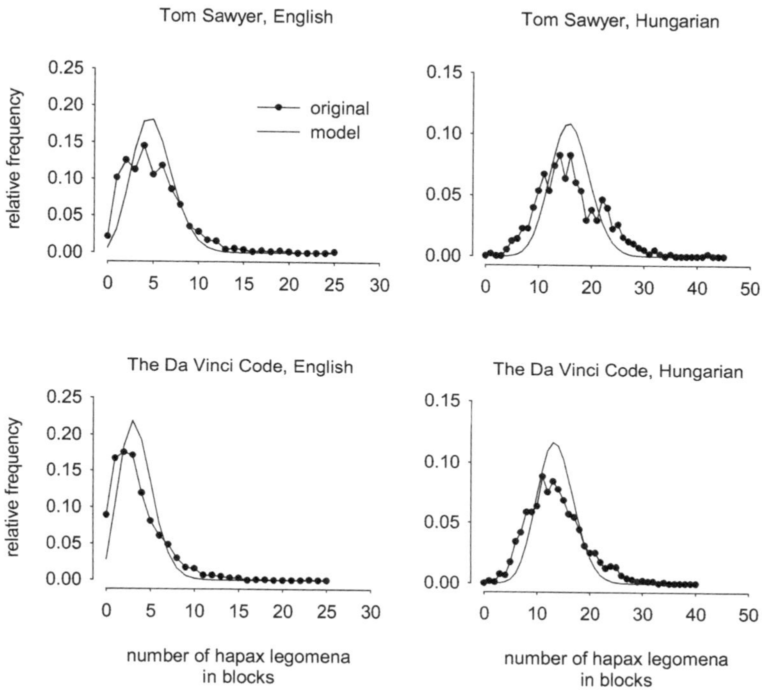

Figure 74. Comparison of two non-lemmatized English texts (left panels) and their Hungarian translations (right panels).

5.2.3. Hapax legomena of the Hungarian texts and their models

Similarly to the English texts, models are unique to each Hungarian text regardless of the high number of hapax legomena (compare Figure 68, Figure 74, Figure 75, and Figure 76). To see whether the distribution of hapax legomena is influenced by lemmatization or not, models were built both for the lemmatized and non-lemmatized Hungarian texts (compare Figure 64 and Figure 65). The Hungarian non-lemmatized texts carry hardly blocks with a low number of hapax legomena (Figure 74 – Figure 76), unlike what was found for the English texts. The fact that $minh > 0$ means that there are no blocks with 0, 1, …, $minh - 1$ in the analyzed Hungarian texts.

The models of the non-lemmatized Hungarian texts also start with blocks carrying no hapax legomena. However, similar to the models of the English texts, underestimations of the original distribution are also present. First of all, an underestimation is realized in the value of *minh*. Here *hap*(*minh*,100) is greater for the model than for the original text (Figure 74, *hap*(*minh*,100) < *ehap*(*minh*,100)). Another underestimation is present at the tails of the graphs. In compensation for these underestimations there has to be an overestimation somewhere, similar to the English texts (Chapter 5.2.2 and Figure 69). The overestimation is detected in the neighborhood of *mfreq*. This means that *hap*(*mfreq*,100) < *ehap*(*emfreq*,100) and, if $k \in$ [*minhi*,*maxhi*] *hap*(*k*,100) < *ehap*(*k*,100). The length of this interval is unique to each text, to the Hungarian translation of THE DA VINCI CODE $k \in$ d[10,19] and to TOM SAWYER $k \in$ d[12,21].

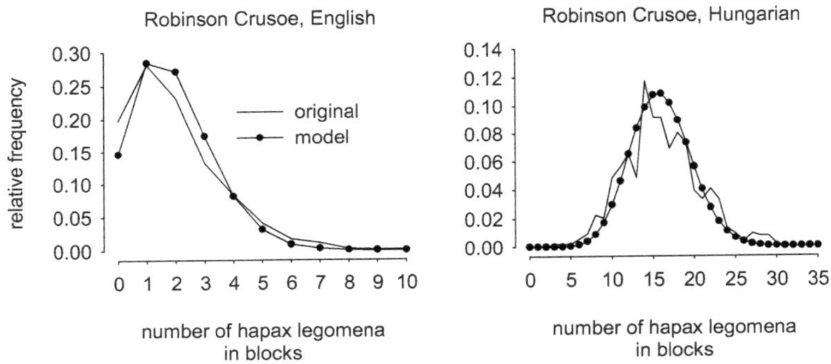

Figure 75. The comparison of the distribution of hapax legomena in the English and Hungarian ROBINSON CRUSOE. Both for the distribution of the original text and the Hungarian translation we find that the model is closer to a text written in a natural language than in THE DA VINCI CODE and TOM SAWYER.

The comparison of the distribution of hapax legomena in the lemmatized and non-lemmatized English texts shows that the absence of lemmatization does not influence the relationship between the original and the model-based artificial texts (Figure 66 and Figure 67).

Models built for Hungarian texts can also be used to test how random the selection of hapax legomena in the text is. For example, similarly to ROBINSON CRUSOE (Figure 75), the distribution of hapax legomena in EGRI CSILLAGOK is relatively close to the model, while it is further away in SORSTALANSÁG (Figure 76). In EGRI CSILLAGOK there is a relatively small underestimation at the beginning and at the end of the domain. Consequently, there is only a slight overestimation at and around *mfreq*. In contrast, in SORSTALANSÁG the underestimation on both extremes of the domain is more pronounced, as is the overestimation at *mfreq*.

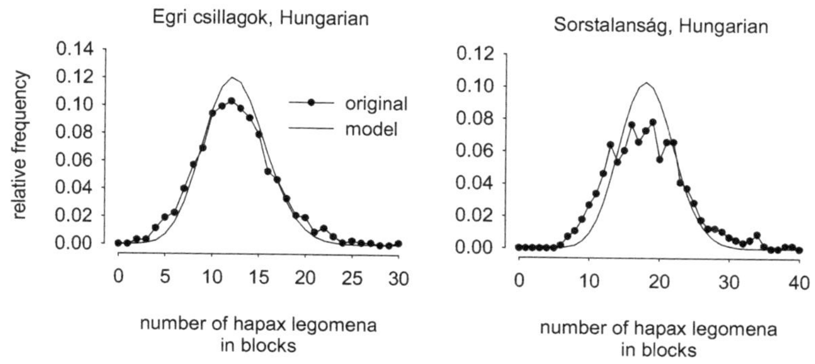

Figure 76. The comparison of the number of hapax legomena in blocks in two Hungarian novels, Gárdonyi Géza's EGRI CSILLAGOK (left panel) and Kertész Imre's SORSTALANSÁG (right panel).

In general, it was found that the appearance of newly introduced words and hapax legomena follow a similar pattern, in other words, there is a strong correlation between these two parameters. That is, the vocabulary rich segments of the texts were also found to be rich in hapax legomena. Note that these are the segments which make a text more varied.

It should also be stressed that those texts which carry a high number of vocabulary rich segments are further away from a random selection of words than those which have only a few or no remarkable vocabulary rich segments. The same result was found when modeling the distribution of hapax legomena. Texts carrying only weak protuberances on the graph of newly introduced word types, that is, which have hardly any recognizable vocabulary rich segments, have distributions of hapax legomena close to a random selection.

6. Appendix

6.1. Frequency lists of The Gold Bug

Frequency list in the order of the frequency of the words

word	f(i, N)
the	881
of	464
and	359
i	333
to	332
a	330
in	236
it	207
you	162
was	135
that	128
as	113
for	113
with	113
at	108
had	108
he	102
but	98
this	98
we	98
by	91
my	91
is	90
which	84
his	82
upon	81
de	73
be	71
me	71
have	69
from	65
what	63
him	62
no	62
not	59
all	57
or	50

word	f(i, N)
legrand	46
now	46
when	46
been	45
one	44
jupiter	42
so	42
about	41
some	41
are	40
us	40
will	40
very	39
there	38
an	37
bug	37
well	37
your	37
were	36
massa	35
said	35
any	34

year	2
'tis	2
'twas	2
abandon	1
aberration	1

youth	1
z	1
zaffre	1
zeal	1

Frequency list in the order of frequency classes

V(m, N)	f(i, N)
1	1543
2	421
3	209
4	131
5	61
6	45
7	39
8	23
9	27
10	17
11	19
12	13
13	12
14	7
15	11
16	10
17	7
18	9
19	2
20	5
21	2
22	3
23	2
24	3
25	1
26	1
27	3
28	0
29	1
30	3
31	0
32	3
33	2
34	1
35	2
36	1
37	4
38	1

V(m, N)	f(i, N)
39	1
40	3
41	2
42	2
43	0
44	1
45	1
46	3
47	0
48	0
49	0
50	1
51	0
52	0
53	0
54	0
55	0
56	0

878	0
879	0
880	0
881	1

6.2. Editing the lemmatized texts

The English texts were lemmatized by Paul Rayson from Lancaster University (Rayson; 2003, 2005), while the Hungarian texts by Csaba Oravecz from the Research Institute for Linguistics of the Hungarian Academy of Science (Oravecz and Dienes; 2002a, 2002b).

The POS tagged and lemmatized versions of the texts arrived with unknown extensions to the programs available on my computer. The English texts arrived with *.pl*, while the Hungarian texts with *.ana* extensions. The size of the file of the full-length novels is around 6–10 MB, sometimes more, regardless of the language. Fortunately, both data types can be opened in Microsoft (MS) Word. After realizing that Notebook could not open them MS Word was a great relief. Still, I had to deal with the problem that the number of characters was so high in these files that the files had to be broken into smaller segments to obtain a size which could be opened in a relatively short time.

Both the English and the Hungarian lemmatized texts came back in a vertical format (Appendices 6.3.2 and 6.4.2, respectively). The English lemmatized texts contained five columns of constant width separated by space characters (Appendix 6.3.2), while the Hungarian lemmatized texts had six columns of different widths separated by the Tab character (Appendix 6.4.2).

The differences between the two formats required different deleting processes. These deleting process had a vital role because all the unnecessary information had to be removed, since both the English and the Hungarian lemmatized texts contained pieces of information which were unnecessary or, occasionally, redundant. These had to be eliminated. All that was kept for the analyses was the lemma derived from the original word type along with the POS tag of the lemma (see Figure 23 and Figure 24).

6.3. Lemmatization of the English texts

6.3.1. Cleaning the English lemmatized files

The English lemmatized texts had a *.pl* extension containing five columns separated by an unknown number of Space characters (Appendix 6.3.2). Since the texts were arranged into vertical format, the original text was broken into lines. Each line contained a token of the text, numbers, and information about the structure of the sentence. The first two columns contained the numbers, first the number of the sentence, then the number of the recognized part of the sentence in the order of appearance. The third column had the POS tag of the word types, data which was crucial because for the analysis the tags of the lemmas were needed, instead of the tags of the word types. Had the tags of the word types been kept the whole lemmatization process would have been a waste of time. Keeping the tags of the word types along with the lemmas does not make any difference to the original word types. Replacing the word type with the corresponding lemma and the POS tag of the word type will not cause any loss of information, although the readability of the text will suffer somewhat.

The fourth column contained the word types, while the fifth the lemmas. From these data, the POS tags and the lemmas had to be kept, the other columns had to be deleted.

Before carrying out the deletion of the unused columns of data it seemed worth removing those lines from the file which did not contain tokens (Appendix 6.3.3). This process resulted in a serious reduction in the number of lines and the size of the file. Both were crucial for the success of the following steps. The reduction in the size of the file speeded up the whole process, while the number of the lines had to be kept fewer than 2^{16} because MS Excel 2003 was not able to work with more rows. The deletion was carried out with MS Word macros written in MS VisualBasic (Appendix 6.3.3). To delete the unnecessary columns MS Excel seemed a good choice, since it is able to open text files and recognize the columns based on the fixed number of Spaces as separator characters (Appendix 6.3.6).

In Excel the unnecessary columns, Column A, B, and D, were deleted and two columns were left (Appendix 6.3.7). In this new table the first column contained the POS tags and the second the lemmas (Appendix 6.3.8). It seemed reasonable to switch the two columns, in order to move the POS tags after the lemmas (Appendix 6.3.5). After changing the order of the columns the text was moved back to MS Word with two columns of data separated by the Tab character. After several runs of the *Replace* command and some of the macros developed for the project (Appendix 6.3.10) that part of the POS tags was removed which was unique and referred to the affixes of the original word types (Appendix 6.3.9). Finally, the Tab character was removed from each line to concatenate the lemma with its POS tag. The result is shown in Figure 23, where the 'end of paragraph' characters were eliminated by DyMoCASAT.

6.3.2. Raw lemmatized English text

```
0000001 002  -----          -----                 PUNC
0000002 010  NP1            Louvre                louvre
0000002 020  NN1            Museum                museum
0000002 021  ,              ,                     PUNC
0000002 030  NP1            Paris                 paris
0000003 010  MC             10:46                 10:46
0000003 020  RA             P.M.                  p.m.
0000004 010  JJ             Renowned              renowned
0000004 020  NN1            curator               curator
0000004 030  NP1            Jacques               jacques
0000004 040  NP1            Sauniere              sauniere
0000004 050  VVD            staggered             stagger
0000004 060  II             through               through
0000004 070  AT             the                   the
0000004 080  JJ             vaulted               vaulted
0000004 090  NN1            archway               archway
0000004 100  IO             of                    of
0000004 110  AT             the                   the
0000004 120  NN1            museum                museum
0000004 121  GE             's                    's
0000004 130  JJ             Grand                 grand
0000004 140  NN1            Gallery               gallery
0000004 141  .              .                     PUNC
0000004 142  -----          -----                 PUNC
0000004 150  PPHS1          He                    he
0000004 160  VVD            lunged                lunge
0000004 170  IF             for                   for
0000004 180  AT             the                   the
0000004 190  JJT            nearest               near
0000004 200  NN1            painting              painting
0000004 210  PPHS1          he                    he
0000004 220  VM             could                 could
0000004 230  VVI            see                   see
0000004 231  ,              ,                     PUNC
0000004 240  AT1            a                     a
0000004 250  NN1@           Caravaggio            caravaggio
0000004 251  .              .                     PUNC
0000004 252  -----          -----                 PUNC
0000004 260  VVG            Grabbing              grab
0000004 270  AT             the                   the
0000004 280  JJ             gilded                gilded
0000004 290  NN1            frame                 frame
0000004 291  ,              ,                     PUNC
0000004 300  AT             the                   the
0000004 310  JJ             seventy-six-year-old  seventy-six-
year-old
0000004 320  NN1            man                   man
0000004 330  VVD            heaved                heave
0000004 340  AT             the                   the
0000004 350  NN1            masterpiece           masterpiece
```

0000004	360	II	toward	toward
0000004	370	PPX1	himself	himself
0000004	380	CS	until	until
0000004	390	PPH1	it	it
0000004	400	VVD	tore	tear
0000004	410	II	from	from
0000004	420	AT	the	the
0000004	430	NN1	wall	wall
0000004	440	CC	and	and
0000004	450	NP1	Sauniere	sauniere
0000004	460	VVD	collapsed	collapse
0000004	470	RL	backward	backward
0000004	480	II	in	in
0000004	490	AT1	a	a
0000004	500	NN1	heap	heap
0000004	510	II	beneath	beneath
0000004	520	AT	the	the
0000004	530	NN1	canvas	canvas
0000004	531	.	.	PUNC
0000005	001	-----	-----	PUNC
0000005	010	CSA	As	as
0000005	020	PPHS1	he	he
0000005	030	VHD	had	have
0000005	040	VVN	anticipated	anticipate
0000005	041	,	,	PUNC
0000005	050	AT1	a	a
0000005	060	JJ@	thundering	thundering
0000005	070	NN1	iron	iron
0000005	080	NN1	gate	gate
0000005	090	VVD	fell	fall
0000005	100	RL	nearby	nearby
0000005	101	,	,	PUNC
0000005	110	VVG	barricading	barricade
0000005	120	AT	the	the
0000005	130	NN1	entrance	entrance
0000005	140	II	to	to
0000005	150	AT	the	the
0000005	160	NN1	suite	suite
0000005	161	.	.	PUNC
0000005	162	-----	-----	PUNC
0000005	170	AT	The	the
0000005	180	NN1	parquet	parquet
0000005	190	NN1	floor	floor
0000005	200	VVD	shook	shake
0000005	201	.	.	PUNC

6.3.3. Procedure to delete the non-token rows from the raw lemmatized English text

```
Sub angol()
Dim betu As String
Do
   Selection.Find.ClearFormatting
   With Selection.Find
      .Text = "PUNC"
      .Replacement.Text = ""
      .Forward = True
      .Wrap = wdFindContinue
      .Format = False
      .MatchCase = False
      .MatchWholeWord = False
      .MatchKashida = False
      .MatchDiacritics = False
      .MatchAlefHamza = False
      .MatchControl = False
      .MatchWildcards = False
      .MatchSoundsLike = False
      .MatchAllWordForms = False
   End With
   Selection.Find.Execute
   Selection.HomeKey Unit:=wdLine
   Selection.EndKey Unit:=wdLine, Extend:=wdExtend
   Selection.Delete Unit:=wdCharacter, Count:=1
   Selection.HomeKey Unit:=wdLine
      Selection.MoveRight Unit:=wdCharacter, Count:=1, Extend:=wdExtend
      betu = Selection.Text
      Selection.MoveLeft Unit:=wdCharacter, Count:=1
Loop Until betu = "@"
End Sub
```

6.3.4. *Rows of non-tokens cleaned from the lemmatized English text*

0000002	010	NP1	Louvre	louvre
0000002	020	NN1	Museum	museum
0000002	030	NP1	Paris	paris
0000003	010	MC	10:46	10:46
0000003	020	RA	P.M.	p.m.
0000004	010	JJ	Renowned	renowned
0000004	020	NN1	curator	curator
0000004	030	NP1	Jacques	jacques
0000004	040	NP1	Sauniere	sauniere
0000004	050	VVD	staggered	stagger
0000004	060	II	through	through
0000004	070	AT	the	the
0000004	080	JJ	vaulted	vaulted
0000004	090	NN1	archway	archway
0000004	100	IO	of	of
0000004	110	AT	the	the
0000004	120	NN1	museum	museum
0000004	121	GE	's	's
0000004	130	JJ	Grand	grand
0000004	140	NN1	Gallery	gallery
0000004	150	PPHS1	He	he
0000004	160	VVD	lunged	lunge
0000004	170	IF	for	for
0000004	180	AT	the	the
0000004	190	JJT	nearest	near
0000004	200	NN1	painting	painting
0000004	210	PPHS1	he	he
0000004	220	VM	could	could
0000004	230	VVI	see	see
0000004	240	AT1	a	a
0000004	250	NN1	Caravaggio	caravaggio
0000004	260	VVG	Grabbing	grab
0000004	270	AT	the	the
0000004	280	JJ	gilded	gilded
0000004	290	NN1	frame	frame
0000004	300	AT	the	the
0000004	310	JJ	seventy-six-year-old	seventy-six-year-old
0000004	320	NN1	man	man
0000004	330	VVD	heaved	heave
0000004	340	AT	the	the
0000004	350	NN1	masterpiece	masterpiece
0000004	360	II	toward	toward
0000004	370	PPX1	himself	himself
0000004	380	CS	until	until
0000004	390	PPH1	it	it
0000004	400	VVD	tore	tear
0000004	410	II	from	from

0000004	420	AT	the	the
0000004	430	NN1	wall	wall
0000004	440	CC	and	and
0000004	450	NP1	Sauniere	sauniere
0000004	460	VVD	collapsed	collapse
0000004	470	RL	backward	backward
0000004	480	II	in	in
0000004	490	AT1	a	a
0000004	500	NN1	heap	heap
0000004	510	II	beneath	beneath
0000004	520	AT	the	the
0000004	530	NN1	canvas	canvas
0000005	010	CSA	As	as
0000005	020	PPHS1	he	he
0000005	030	VHD	had	have
0000005	040	VVN	anticipated	anticipate
0000005	050	AT1	a	a
0000005	060	JJ	thundering	thundering
0000005	070	NN1	iron	iron
0000005	080	NN1	gate	gate
0000005	090	VVD	fell	fall
0000005	100	RL	nearby	nearby
0000005	110	VVG	barricading	barricade
0000005	120	AT	the	the
0000005	130	NN1	entrance	entrance
0000005	140	II	to	to
0000005	150	AT	the	the
0000005	160	NN1	suite	suite
0000005	170	AT	The	the
0000005	180	NN1	parquet	parquet
0000005	190	NN1	floor	floor
0000005	200	VVD	shook	shake
0000005	210	JJ21	Far	far
0000005	220	JJ22	off	off
0000005	230	AT1	an	an
0000005	240	NN1	alarm	alarm
0000005	250	VVD	began	begin
0000005	260	TO	to	to
0000005	270	VVI	ring	ring
0000006	010	AT	The	the
0000006	020	NN1	curator	curator
0000006	030	VVD	lay	lie
0000006	040	AT1	a	a
0000006	050	NN1	moment	moment
0000006	060	VVG	gasping	gasp
0000006	070	IF	for	for
0000006	080	NN1	breath	breath
0000006	090	VVG	taking	take
0000006	100	NN1	stock	stock
0000006	110	PPIS1	I	i
0000006	120	VBM	am	be
0000006	130	RR	still	still

6.3.5. Lemmas with the tags of the word types

louvre	NP
museum	NN
paris	NP
p.m.	RA
renowned	JJ
curator	NN
jacques	NP
sauniere	NP
stagger	VVD
through	II
the	AT
vaulted	JJ
archway	NN
of	IO
the	AT
museum	NN
's	GE
grand	JJ
gallery	NN
he	PPHS
lunge	VVD
for	IF
the	AT
near	JJT
painting	NN
he	PPHS
could	VM
see	VVI
a	AT
caravaggio	NN
grab	VVG
the	AT
gilded	JJ
frame	NN
the	AT
seventy-six-year-old	JJ
man	NN
heave	VVD
the	AT
masterpiece	NN
toward	II
himself	PPX
until	CS
it	PPH
tear	VVD
from	II
the	AT
wall	NN

and	CC
sauniere	NP
collapse	VVD
backward	RL
in	II
a	AT
heap	NN
beneath	II
the	AT
canvas	NN
as	CSA
he	PPHS
have	VHD
anticipate	VVN
a	AT
thundering	JJ
iron	NN
gate	NN
fall	VVD
nearby	RL
barricade	VVG
the	AT
entrance	NN
to	II
the	AT
suite	NN
the	AT
parquet	NN
floor	NN
shake	VVD
far	JJ
off	JJ
an	AT
alarm	NN
begin	VVD
to	TO
ring	VVI
the	AT
curator	NN
lie	VVD
a	AT
moment	NN
gasp	VVG
for	IF
breath	NN
take	VVG
stock	NN
i	PPIS

6.3.6. *Importing the lemmatized text into an Excel spreadsheet*

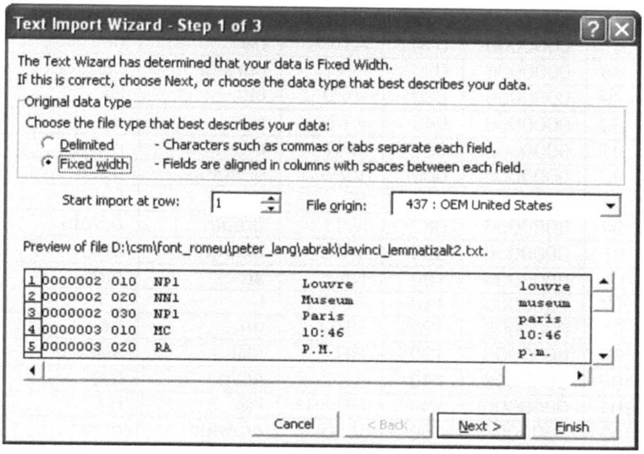

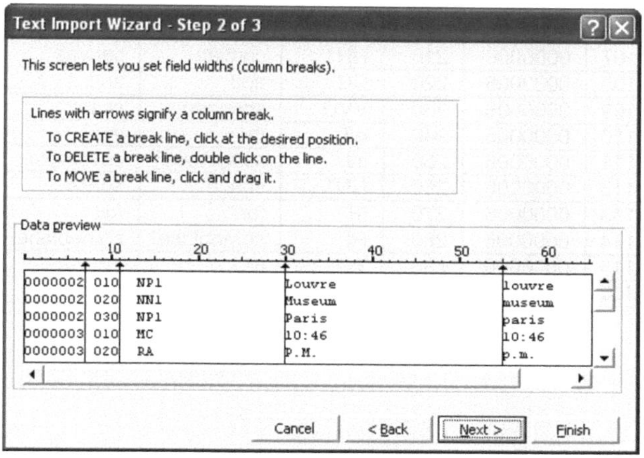

6.3.7. Deleting the uninformative columns

	A	B	C	D	E
87	0000006	010	AT	he	he
88	0000006	020	NN1	curator	curator
89	0000006	030	VVD	lay	lie
90	0000006	040	AT1	a	a
91	0000006	050	NN1	moment	moment
92	0000006	060	VVG	gasping	gasp
93	0000006	070	IF	for	for
94	0000006	080	NN1	breath	breath
95	0000006	090	VVG	taking	take
96	0000006	100	NN1	stock	stock
97	0000006	110	PPIS1	I	i
98	0000006	120	VBM	am	be
99	0000006	130	RR	still	still
100	0000006	140	JJ	alive	live
101	0000006	150	PPHS1	He	he
102	0000006	160	VVD	crawled	crawl
103	0000006	170	RP	out	out
104	0000006	180	II	from	from
105	0000006	190	II	under	under
106	0000006	200	AT	the	the
107	0000006	210	NN1	canvas	canvas
108	0000006	220	CC	and	and
109	0000006	230	VVD	scanned	scan
110	0000006	240	AT	the	the
111	0000006	250	JJ	cavernous	cavernous
112	0000006	260	NN1	space	space
113	0000006	270	IF	for	for
114	0000006	280	RL	someplace	someplace
115	0000006	290	TO	to	to
116	0000006	300	VVI	hide	hide

6.3.8. *Changing the order of the columns*

	A	B
87	AT	he
88	NN1	curator
89	VVD	lie
90	AT1	a
91	NN1	moment
92	VVG	gasp
93	IF	for
94	NN1	breath
95	VVG	take
96	NN1	stock
97	PPIS1	i
98	VBM	be
99	RR	still
100	JJ	live
101	PPHS1	he
102	VVD	crawl
103	RP	out
104	II	from
105	II	under
106	AT	the
107	NN1	canvas
108	CC	and
109	VVD	scan
110	AT	the
111	JJ	cavernous
112	NN1	space
113	IF	for
114	RL	someplace
115	TO	to
116	VVI	hide

	A	B
87	he	AT
88	curator	NN1
89	lie	VVD
90	a	AT1
91	moment	NN1
92	gasp	VVG
93	for	IF
94	breath	NN1
95	take	VVG
96	stock	NN1
97	i	PPIS1
98	be	VBM
99	still	RR
100	live	JJ
101	he	PPHS1
102	crawl	VVD
103	out	RP
104	from	II
105	under	II
106	the	AT
107	canvas	NN1
108	and	CC
109	scan	VVD
110	the	AT
111	cavernous	JJ
112	space	NN1
113	for	IF
114	someplace	RL
115	to	TO
116	hide	VVI

6.3.9. Lemmas and their tags separated by Tab

```
louvre	NP
museum	NN
paris	NP
pm	RA
renowned	JJ
curator	NN
jacques	NP
sauniere	NP
stagger	VV
through	II
the	AT
vaulted	JJ
archway	NN
of	IO
the	AT
museum	NN
's	GE
grand	JJ
gallery	NN
he	PP
lunge	VV
for	IF
the	AT
near	JJ
painting	NN
he	PP
could	VM
see	VV
a	AT
caravaggio	NN
grab	VV
the	AT
gilded	JJ
frame	NN
the	AT
seventysixyearold	JJ
man	NN
heave	VV
the	AT
masterpiece	NN
toward	II
himself	PPX
until	CS
it	PP
tear	VV
from	II
the	AT
wall	NN
and	CC
sauniere	NP
collapse	VV
backward	RL
in	II
a	AT
heap	NN
beneath	II
the	AT
canvas	NN
as	CSA
he	PP
have	VH
anticipate	VV
a	AT
thundering	JJ
iron	NN
gate	NN
fall	VV
nearby	RL
barricade	VV
the	AT
entrance	NN
to	II
the	AT
suite	NN
the	AT
parquet	NN
floor	NN
shake	VV
far	JJ
off	JJ
an	AT
alarm	NN
begin	VV
to	TO
ring	VV
the	AT
curator	NN
lie	VV
a	AT
moment	NN
gasp	VV
for	IF
breath	NN
take	VV
stock	NN
i	PP
be	VB
still	RR
```

6.3.10. Procedure to retrieve the tags of the lemmas

```
Selection.Find.Execute Replace:=wdReplaceAll
With Selection.Find
    .Text = "VBDR"
    .Replacement.Text = "VB"
    .Forward = True
    .Wrap = wdFindContinue
    .Format = False
    .MatchCase = False
    .MatchWholeWord = True
    .MatchKashida = False
    .MatchDiacritics = False
    .MatchAlefHamza = False
    .MatchControl = False
    .MatchWildcards = False
    .MatchSoundsLike = False
    .MatchAllWordForms = False
End With
Selection.Find.Execute Replace:=wdReplaceAll
With Selection.Find
    .Text = "VBDZ"
    .Replacement.Text = "VB"
    .Forward = True
    .Wrap = wdFindContinue
    .Format = False
    .MatchCase = False
```

6.4. Lemmatization of the Hungarian texts

6.4.1. Cleaning the Hungarian lemmatized files

Similar to the English lemmatized texts, the Hungarian lemmatized texts came back in vertical format, but containing six columns of data (Appendix 6.4.2). The column separator character was also different, instead of the fixed number of Space characters a single Tab character was used to separate the columns (Appendix 6.4.2).

- The first column is for an ID number or for the # character (marking the sentence boundaries),
- the second refers to the type of the token (e.g. TOK for token, DIG for number, PUNC for punctuation marks),
- the third contains the original word types as they were found in the text,
- the fourth column marks the beginning (BOS) and end (EOS) of the sentence or is left empty if the token is between the first and last word of the sentence,
- the fifth column contains all the possible interpretations of the word type separated by the | character, and each interpretation is divided into three additional segments
  - in the first segment the lemma appears, followed by the POS tag of the word type, and these two are separated by a \ character,
- finally, in the sixth column, after the disambiguating process, comes the correct lemma followed by the \ character, and the corresponding POS tag.

Since the structure of the Hungarian lemmatized texts was different from the English lemmatized texts, another cleaning process had to be applied.

At first sight the Hungarian lemmatized texts seemed more chaotic than the English lemmatized texts, because of the different widths of the columns (Appendix 6.4.2). However, this arrangement of the text was easier to handle because there was only one character between the columns and this was the Tab character, which is not a valid character in the Hungarian alphabet, unlike the Space character.

By deleting the #, DIG, and PUNC lines with a VisualBasic macro (Appendix 6.4.3) from the text the number of lines and the size of the file was reduced to a reasonable size (Appendix 6.4.4).

Relying on the Tab character, the first five columns could easily be removed and the necessary sixth column kept (Appendix 6.4.5). Both the unique Tab positions with the Alt + selection in MS Word or the selection of columns in

Excel could be used to select and delete the unnecessary columns, but in several cases the manual Search command and re-reading and then manual correction was the only solution.

In the Hungarian text the word types tagged with the '\UNKNOWNTAG' tag had to be tagged manually. This means that the affixes along with '\UNKNOWNTAG' had to be deleted. The major part of this process was carried out again with a suitable VisualBasic macro (Appendices 6.4.6 and 6.4.7).

Finally, parts of the POS tags which refer to the time, person etc. and make the word types unique were removed (Appendices 6.4.8 and 6.4.9). The result is shown in Appendix 6.4.10 and Figure 24.

Neither of the lemmatizer programs work with 100% accuracy, so further manual assistance was needed to correct their mistakes. These included many repeated mistakes, so in many cases the pattern had to be found and then either the Search or the Replace commands or a unique macro were of great help.

The Hungarian lemmatizer program was not able to handle correctly the verbs with their affixes. When the affix was attached to the verb, it was tagged as [Pre][V] (Figure 24 Line 1 and 15, e.g. Appendix 6.4.4 Line 4\41). However, when the affix followed the verb and was separated from the verb, the verb was tagged with the [V] tag and the affix was tagged with [Pre] tag (Figure 24 Line 6, Appendix 6.4.4 Line 3\52 and 3\58).

6.4.2. *Raw lemmatized Hungarian text*

```
#                   [CHUNK    <DIV FROM="1">
#                   (PAR      <P FROM="2">
#                   (SENT     <S>
2\1       TOK       LOUVRE    BOS       LOUVRE\UNKNOWNTAG   LOUVRE\UNKNOWNTAG
2\7       PUNCT     ,                   ,\WPUNCT  ,\WPUNCT
2\9       TOK       PÁRIZS              Párizs\[N][NOM]     Párizs\[N][NOM]
2\16      DIG       22                  22\DIG    22\DIG
2\18      PUNCT     :                   :\WPUNCT  :\WPUNCT
2\19      DIG       46                  46\DIG    46\DIG
3\1       TOK       Jacques             Jacques\UNKNOWNTAG Jacques\UNKNOWNTAG
3\9       TOK       Sauniere            Sauniere\UNKNOWNTAG Sauniere\UNKNOWNTAG
3\17      PUNCT     ,                   ,\WPUNCT  ,\WPUNCT
3\19      TOK       a                   a\[Det]   a\[Det]
3\21      TOK       neves               neves\[A][NOM]      neves\[A][NOM]
3\27      TOK       kurátor             kurátor\[N][NOM]    kurátor\[N][NOM]
3\35      TOK       rogyadozó           rogyadozó\[MIF][NOM]          rogyadozó\[MIF][NOM]
3\45      TOK       lábbal              láb\[N][INS]        láb\[N][INS]
3\52      TOK       esett               esett\[A][NOM]|esett\[MIB][NOM]|esik\[V][Me3]
          esik\[V][Me3]
3\58      TOK       be                  be\[Pre]  be\[Pre]
3\61      TOK       a                   a\[Det]   a\[Det]
3\63      TOK       múzeum              múzeum\[N][NOM]     múzeum\[N][NOM]
3\70      TOK       Nagy                nagy\[A][NOM]|Nagy\[N][NOM]   nagy\[A][NOM]
4\1       TOK       Galériába           galéria\[N][ILL]    galéria\[N][ILL]
4\11      TOK       a                   a\[Det]   a\[Det]
4\13      TOK       boltíves            boltíves\[A][NOM]   boltíves\[A][NOM]
4\22      TOK       bejárón
          bejáró\[A][SUP]|bejáró\[MIF][SUP]|bejárón\[Adv]|bejáró\[N][SUP]
          bejáró\[N][SUP]
4\30      TOK       keresztül
          keresztül\[NU]|kereszt\[N][ESS]|keresztül\[Adv]|keresztül\[Pre]
          keresztül\[NU]
4\39      PTERM_P   .         EOS       .\SPUNCT  .\SPUNCT
#                   )SENT     </S>
#                   (SENT     <S>
4\41      TOK       Rávetette BOS       Rávetet\[Pre][V][TMe3]|Rávet\[Pre][V][TMe3]
          Rávetet\[Pre][V][TMe3]
4\51      TOK       magát               maga\[Pro][ACC]     maga\[Pro][ACC]
4\57      TOK       a                   a\[Det]   a\[Det]
4\59      TOK       legközelebb                   közel\[FF][A][FOK][NOM]
          közel\[FF][A][FOK][NOM]
4\71      TOK       eső                 eső\[A][NOM]|eső\[MIF][NOM]|eső\[N][NOM]
          eső\[MIF][NOM]
5\1       TOK       festményre                    festmény\[N][SUB]   festmény\[N][SUB]
5\11      PUNCT     ,                   ,\WPUNCT  ,\WPUNCT
5\13      TOK       egy                 egy\[Num][NOM]      egy\[Num][NOM]
5\17      TOK       Caravaggióra                  Caravaggióra\UNKNOWNTAG
          Caravaggióra\UNKNOWNTAG
5\29      PTERM_P   .         EOS       .\SPUNCT  .\SPUNCT
#                   )SENT     </S>
#                   (SENT     <S>
5\31      TOK       A         BOS       a\[Det]   a\[Det]
5\33      TOK       hetvenhat           hetvenhat\[Num][NOM]          hetvenhat\[Num][NOM]
5\43      TOK       éves                éves\[A][NOM]       éves\[A][NOM]
5\48      TOK       férfi               férfi\[N][NOM]      férfi\[N][NOM]
5\54      TOK       az                  az\[Det]|az\[Pro][NOM]        az\[Det]
5\57      TOK       aranyozott                    aranyozott\[MIB][NOM]|aranyoz\[V][Me3]
          aranyozott\[MIB][NOM]
5\68      TOK       keretnél            keret\[N][ADE]      keret\[N][ADE]
6\1       TOK       fogva               fogva\[NU]|fog\[V][HIN]       fogva\[NU]
6\7       TOK       maga                maga\[Pro][NOM]     maga\[Pro][NOM]
6\12      TOK       felé                felé\[Adv]|felé\[NU]|fel\[N][POS][NOM]|ő_felé\[NU]
          felé\[Adv]
6\17      TOK       rántotta            rántotta\[N][NOM]|ránt\[V][TMe3]
          ránt\[V][TMe3]
6\26      TOK       a                   a\[Det]   a\[Det]
6\28      TOK       műremeket           műremek\[N][ACC]    műremek\[N][ACC]
```

```
6\37    PUNCT   ,               ,\WPUNCT  ,\WPUNCT
6\39    TOK     letépte         letép\[Pre][V][TMe3]          letép\[Pre][V][TMe3]
6\47    TOK     a               a\[Det]   a\[Det]
6\49    TOK     falról          fal\[N][DEL]          fal\[N][DEL]
6\55    PUNCT   ,               ,\WPUNCT  ,\WPUNCT
6\57    TOK     és              és\[Con]  és\[Con]
6\60    TOK     hátrazuhanva              hátrazuhan\[Pre][V][HIN]
        hátrazuhan\[Pre][V][HIN]
7\1     TOK     elterült        elterül\[Pre][V][Me3]|elterült\[MIB][NOM]
        elterül\[Pre][V][Me3]
7\10    TOK     a               a\[Det]   a\[Det]
7\12    TOK     földön          föld\[N][SUP]         föld\[N][SUP]
7\19    TOK     a               a\[Det]   a\[Det]
7\21    TOK     vászon          vászon\[N][NOM]       vászon\[N][NOM]
7\28    TOK     alatt           alatt\[Adv]|alatt\[NU]        alatt\[NU]
7\33    PTERM_P .       EOS     .\SPUNCT  .\SPUNCT
#               )SENT   </S>
#               (SENT   <S>
8\1     TOK     Pontosan BOS    Pontosan\[Adv]        Pontosan\[Adv]
8\10    TOK     az              az\[Det]|az\[Pro][NOM]        az\[Pro][NOM]
8\13    TOK     történt         történik\[V][Me3]|történt\[MIB][NOM]
        történik\[V][Me3]
8\20    PUNCT   ,               ,\WPUNCT  ,\WPUNCT
8\22    TOK     amire           ami\[Pro][SUB]|amire\[Con]    amire\[Con]
8\28    TOK     Sauniere        Sauniere\UNKNOWNTAG Sauniere\UNKNOWNTAG
8\37    TOK     számított       számított\[MIB][NOM]|számít\[V][Me3]
        számít\[V][Me3]
8\46    PUNCT   :               :\WPUNCT  :\WPUNCT
8\48    TOK     a               a\[Det]   a\[Det]
8\50    TOK     közelben        közelben\[Adv]        közelben\[Adv]
8\59    TOK     mennydörögve              mennydörög\[V][HIN] mennydörög\[V][HIN]
9\1     TOK     lecsapódott
        lecsapódik\[Pre][V][Me3]|lecsapódott\[MIB][NOM]|lecsapód\[Pre][V][Me3]
        lecsapódik\[Pre][V][Me3]
9\13    TOK     egy             egy\[Num][NOM]        egy\[Num][NOM]
9\17    TOK     vaskapu         vaskapu\[N][NOM]      vaskapu\[N][NOM]
9\24    PUNCT   ,               ,\WPUNCT  ,\WPUNCT
9\26    TOK     elzárva         elzár\[Pre][V][HIN] elzár\[Pre][V][HIN]
9\34    TOK     a               a\[Det]   a\[Det]
9\36    TOK     terem
        terem\[N][NOM]|terem\[V][e3]|tér\[N][PSe1][ACC]|tér\[N][PSe1][NOM]
        terem\[N][NOM]
9\42    TOK     bejáratát               bejárat\[N][PSe3][ACC]
        bejárat\[N][PSe3][ACC]
9\51    PTERM_P .       EOS     .\SPUNCT  .\SPUNCT
#               )SENT   </S>
#               (SENT   <S>
9\53    TOK     A       BOS     a\[Det]   a\[Det]
9\55    TOK     parkettás       parkettás\[A][NOM]  parkettás\[A][NOM]
9\65    TOK     padló           padló\[N][NOM]        padló\[N][NOM]
10\1    TOK     megremegett
        megremegett\[MIB][NOM]|megremeg\[Pre][V][Me3]     megremeg\[Pre][V][Me3]
10\12   PTERM_P .       EOS     .\SPUNCT  .\SPUNCT
#               )SENT   </S>
#               (SENT   <S>
10\14   TOK     A       BOS     a\[Det]   a\[Det]
```

6.4.3. *Procedure to delete the non-token rows from the raw lemmatized Hungarian text*

```
Sub egrics()
'
'
   Dim elsobetu As String

'#, DIM, PUNC sorok törlése,
   Selection.HomeKey Unit:=wdStory
   Do
      Selection.Find.ClearFormatting
      With Selection.Find
         .Text = "DIG"
         .Replacement.Text = ""
         .Forward = True
         .Wrap = wdFindContinue
         .Format = False
         .MatchCase = False
         .MatchWholeWord = False
         .MatchWildcards = False
         .MatchSoundsLike = False
         .MatchAllWordForms = False
      End With
      Selection.Find.Execute
      Selection.HomeKey Unit:=wdLine
      Selection.EndKey Unit:=wdLine, Extend:=wdExtend
      Selection.Delete Unit:=wdCharacter, Count:=1
      Selection.HomeKey Unit:=wdLine
      Selection.MoveRight Unit:=wdCharacter, Count:=1, Extend:=wdExtend
      elsobetu = Selection.Text
      Selection.MoveLeft Unit:=wdCharacter, Count:=1
   Loop Until elsobetu = "@"


End Sub
```

6.4.4. *Lemmatized Hungarian text with the rows of non-tokens removed*

<table>
<tr><td>2\1</td><td>TOK</td><td>LOUVRE</td><td>BOS</td><td>LOUVRE\UNKNOWNTAG</td><td>LOUVRE\UNKNOWNTAG</td></tr>
<tr><td>2\9</td><td>TOK</td><td>PÁRIZS</td><td></td><td>Párizs\[N][NOM]</td><td>Párizs\[N][NOM]</td></tr>
<tr><td>3\1</td><td>TOK</td><td>Jacques</td><td></td><td>Jacques\UNKNOWNTAG</td><td>Jacques\UNKNOWNTAG</td></tr>
<tr><td>3\9</td><td>TOK</td><td>Sauniere</td><td></td><td>Sauniere\UNKNOWNTAG</td><td>Sauniere\UNKNOWNTAG</td></tr>
<tr><td>3\19</td><td>TOK</td><td>a</td><td></td><td>a\[Det]</td><td>a\[Det]</td></tr>
<tr><td>3\21</td><td>TOK</td><td>neves</td><td></td><td>neves\[A][NOM]</td><td>neves\[A][NOM]</td></tr>
<tr><td>3\27</td><td>TOK</td><td>kurátor</td><td></td><td>kurátor\[N][NOM]</td><td>kurátor\[N][NOM]</td></tr>
<tr><td>3\35</td><td>TOK</td><td>rogyadozó</td><td></td><td>rogyadozó\[MIF][NOM]</td><td>rogyadozó\[MIF][NOM]</td></tr>
<tr><td>3\45</td><td>TOK</td><td>lábbal</td><td></td><td>láb\[N][INS]</td><td>láb\[N][INS]</td></tr>
<tr><td>3\52</td><td>TOK</td><td>esett</td><td></td><td>esett\[A][NOM]|esett\[MIB][NOM]|esik\[V][Me3]</td><td>esik\[V][Me3]</td></tr>
<tr><td>3\58</td><td>TOK</td><td>be</td><td></td><td>be\[Pre]</td><td>be\[Pre]</td></tr>
<tr><td>3\61</td><td>TOK</td><td>a</td><td></td><td>a\[Det]</td><td>a\[Det]</td></tr>
<tr><td>3\63</td><td>TOK</td><td>múzeum</td><td></td><td>múzeum\[N][NOM]</td><td>múzeum\[N][NOM]</td></tr>
<tr><td>3\70</td><td>TOK</td><td>Nagy</td><td></td><td>nagy\[A][NOM]|Nagy\[N][NOM]</td><td>nagy\[A][NOM]</td></tr>
<tr><td>4\1</td><td>TOK</td><td>Galériába</td><td></td><td>galéria\[N][ILL]</td><td>galéria\[N][ILL]</td></tr>
<tr><td>4\11</td><td>TOK</td><td>a</td><td></td><td>a\[Det]</td><td>a\[Det]</td></tr>
<tr><td>4\13</td><td>TOK</td><td>boltíves</td><td></td><td>boltíves\[A][NOM]</td><td>boltíves\[A][NOM]</td></tr>
<tr><td>4\22</td><td>TOK</td><td>bejárón</td><td></td><td>bejáró\[A][SUP]|bejáró\[MIF][SUP]|bejárón\[Adv]|bejáró\[N][SUP]</td><td>bejáró\[N][SUP]</td></tr>
<tr><td>4\30</td><td>TOK</td><td>keresztül</td><td></td><td>keresztül\[NU]|kereszt\[N][ESS]|keresztül\[Adv]|keresztül\[Pre]</td><td>keresztül\[NU]</td></tr>
<tr><td>4\41</td><td>TOK</td><td>Rávetette</td><td>BOS</td><td>Rávetet\[Pre][V][TMe3]|Rávet\[Pre][V][TMe3]</td><td>Rávetet\[Pre][V][TMe3]</td></tr>
<tr><td>4\51</td><td>TOK</td><td>magát</td><td></td><td>maga\[Pro][ACC]</td><td>maga\[Pro][ACC]</td></tr>
<tr><td>4\57</td><td>TOK</td><td>a</td><td></td><td>a\[Det]</td><td>a\[Det]</td></tr>
<tr><td>4\59</td><td>TOK</td><td>legközelebb</td><td></td><td>közel\[FF][A][FOK][NOM]</td><td>közel\[FF][A][FOK][NOM]</td></tr>
<tr><td>4\71</td><td>TOK</td><td>eső</td><td></td><td>eső\[A][NOM]|eső\[MIF][NOM]|eső\[N][NOM]</td><td>eső\[MIF][NOM]</td></tr>
<tr><td>5\1</td><td>TOK</td><td>festményre</td><td></td><td>festmény\[N][SUB]</td><td>festmény\[N][SUB]</td></tr>
<tr><td>5\13</td><td>TOK</td><td>egy</td><td></td><td>egy\[Num][NOM]</td><td>egy\[Num][NOM]</td></tr>
<tr><td>5\17</td><td>TOK</td><td>Caravaggióra</td><td></td><td>Caravaggióra\UNKNOWNTAG</td><td>Caravaggióra\UNKNOWNTAG</td></tr>
<tr><td>5\31</td><td>TOK</td><td>A</td><td>BOS</td><td>a\[Det]</td><td>a\[Det]</td></tr>
<tr><td>5\33</td><td>TOK</td><td>hetvenhat</td><td></td><td>hetvenhat\[Num][NOM]</td><td>hetvenhat\[Num][NOM]</td></tr>
<tr><td>5\43</td><td>TOK</td><td>éves</td><td></td><td>éves\[A][NOM]</td><td>éves\[A][NOM]</td></tr>
<tr><td>5\48</td><td>TOK</td><td>férfi</td><td></td><td>férfi\[N][NOM]</td><td>férfi\[N][NOM]</td></tr>
<tr><td>5\54</td><td>TOK</td><td>az</td><td></td><td>az\[Det]|az\[Pro][NOM]</td><td>az\[Det]</td></tr>
<tr><td>5\57</td><td>TOK</td><td>aranyozott</td><td></td><td>aranyozott\[MIB][NOM]|aranyoz\[V][Me3]</td><td>aranyozott\[MIB][NOM]</td></tr>
<tr><td>5\68</td><td>TOK</td><td>keretnél</td><td></td><td>keret\[N][ADE]</td><td>keret\[N][ADE]</td></tr>
<tr><td>6\1</td><td>TOK</td><td>fogva</td><td></td><td>fogva\[NU]|fog\[V][HIN]</td><td>fogva\[NU]</td></tr>
<tr><td>6\7</td><td>TOK</td><td>maga</td><td></td><td>maga\[Pro][NOM]</td><td>maga\[Pro][NOM]</td></tr>
<tr><td>6\12</td><td>TOK</td><td>felé</td><td></td><td>felé\[Adv]|felé\[NU]|fel\[N][POS][NOM]|ő_felé\[NU]</td><td>felé\[Adv]</td></tr>
<tr><td>6\17</td><td>TOK</td><td>rántotta</td><td></td><td>rántotta\[N][NOM]|ránt\[V][TMe3]</td><td>ránt\[V][TMe3]</td></tr>
<tr><td>6\26</td><td>TOK</td><td>a</td><td></td><td>a\[Det]</td><td>a\[Det]</td></tr>
<tr><td>6\28</td><td>TOK</td><td>műremeket</td><td></td><td>műremek\[N][ACC]</td><td>műremek\[N][ACC]</td></tr>
<tr><td>6\39</td><td>TOK</td><td>letépte</td><td></td><td>letép\[Pre][V][TMe3]</td><td>letép\[Pre][V][TMe3]</td></tr>
<tr><td>6\47</td><td>TOK</td><td>a</td><td></td><td>a\[Det]</td><td>a\[Det]</td></tr>
<tr><td>6\49</td><td>TOK</td><td>falról</td><td></td><td>fal\[N][DEL]</td><td>fal\[N][DEL]</td></tr>
<tr><td>6\57</td><td>TOK</td><td>és</td><td></td><td>és\[Con]</td><td>és\[Con]</td></tr>
<tr><td>6\60</td><td>TOK</td><td>hátrazuhanva</td><td></td><td>hátrazuhan\[Pre][V][HIN]</td><td>hátrazuhan\[Pre][V][HIN]</td></tr>
<tr><td>7\1</td><td>TOK</td><td>elterült</td><td></td><td>elterül\[Pre][V][Me3]|elterült\[MIB][NOM]</td><td>elterül\[Pre][V][Me3]</td></tr>
<tr><td>7\10</td><td>TOK</td><td>a</td><td></td><td>a\[Det]</td><td>a\[Det]</td></tr>
<tr><td>7\12</td><td>TOK</td><td>földön</td><td></td><td>föld\[N][SUP]</td><td>föld\[N][SUP]</td></tr>
<tr><td>7\19</td><td>TOK</td><td>a</td><td></td><td>a\[Det]</td><td>a\[Det]</td></tr>
<tr><td>7\21</td><td>TOK</td><td>vászon</td><td></td><td>vászon\[N][NOM]</td><td>vászon\[N][NOM]</td></tr>
<tr><td>7\28</td><td>TOK</td><td>alatt</td><td></td><td>alatt\[Adv]|alatt\[NU]</td><td>alatt\[NU]</td></tr>
<tr><td>8\1</td><td>TOK</td><td>Pontosan</td><td>BOS</td><td>Pontosan\[Adv]</td><td>Pontosan\[Adv]</td></tr>
<tr><td>8\10</td><td>TOK</td><td>az</td><td></td><td>az\[Det]|az\[Pro][NOM]</td><td>az\[Pro][NOM]</td></tr>
<tr><td>8\13</td><td>TOK</td><td>történt</td><td></td><td>történik\[V][Me3]|történt\[MIB][NOM]</td><td>történik\[V][Me3]</td></tr>
<tr><td>8\22</td><td>TOK</td><td>amire</td><td></td><td>ami\[Pro][SUB]|amire\[Con]</td><td>amire\[Con]</td></tr>
<tr><td>8\28</td><td>TOK</td><td>Sauniere</td><td></td><td>Sauniere\UNKNOWNTAG</td><td>Sauniere\UNKNOWNTAG</td></tr>
<tr><td>8\37</td><td>TOK</td><td>számított</td><td></td><td>számított\[MIB][NOM]|számít\[V][Me3]</td><td>számít\[V][Me3]</td></tr>
<tr><td>8\48</td><td>TOK</td><td>a</td><td></td><td>a\[Det]</td><td>a\[Det]</td></tr>
<tr><td>8\50</td><td>TOK</td><td>közelben</td><td></td><td>közelben\[Adv]</td><td>közelben\[Adv]</td></tr>
</table>

6.4.5. *Lemmas with the tags of the word types*

LOUVRE\UNKNOWNTAG
Párizs\[N][NOM]
Jacques\UNKNOWNTAG
Sauniere\UNKNOWNTAG
a\[Det]
neves\[A][NOM]
kurátor\[N][NOM]
rogyadozó\[MIF][NOM]
láb\[N][INS]
esik\[V][Me3]
be\[Pre]
a\[Det]
múzeum\[N][NOM]
nagy\[A][NOM]
galéria\[N][ILL]
a\[Det]
boltíves\[A][NOM]
bejáró\[N][SUP]
keresztül\[NU]
Rávetet\[Pre][V][TMe3]
maga\[Pro][ACC]
a\[Det]
közel\[FF][A][FOK][NOM]
eső\[MIF][NOM]
festmény\[N][SUB]
egy\[Num][NOM]
Caravaggió\UNKNOWNTAG
a\[Det]
hetvenhat\[Num][NOM]
éves\[A][NOM]
férfi\[N][NOM]
az\[Det]
aranyozott\[MIB][NOM]
keret\[N][ADE]
fogva\[NU]
maga\[Pro][NOM]
felé\[Adv]
ránt\[V][TMe3]
a\[Det]
műremek\[N][ACC]
letép\[Pre][V][TMe3]
a\[Det]
fal\[N][DEL]
és\[Con]
hátrazuhan\[Pre][V][HIN]
elterül\[Pre][V][Me3]
a\[Det]
föld\[N][SUP]
a\[Det]
vászon\[N][NOM]
alatt\[NU]
Pontosan\[Adv]
az\[Pro][NOM]
történik\[V][Me3]
amire\[Con]
Sauniere\UNKNOWNTAG
számít\[V][Me3]
a\[Det]
közelben\[Adv]
mennydörög\[V][HIN]
lecsapódik\[Pre][V][Me3]
egy\[Num][NOM]
vaskapu\[N][NOM]
elzár\[Pre][V][HIN]
a\[Det]
terem\[N][NOM]
bejárat\[N][PSe3][ACC]
a\[Det]
parkettás\[A][NOM]
padló\[N][NOM]
megremeg\[Pre][V][Me3]
a\[Det]
távol\[A][INE]
megszólal\[Pre][V][Me3]
a\[Det]
riasztócsengő\[N][NOM]
a\[Det]
kurátor\[N][NOM]
egy\[Num][NOM]
másodperc\[N][TER]
levegő\[N][NOM]
után\[NU]
kapkod\[V][HIN]
fekszik\[V][Me3]
a\[Det]
föld\[N][SUP]
és\[Con]
felmér\[Pre][V][TMe3]
a\[Det]
helyzet\[N][PSe3][ACC]
még\[Adv]
élet\[N][INE]
van\[V][e1]
Kimászik\[Pre][V][Me3]
a\[Det]
vászon\[N][NOM]
alól\[NU]
és\[Con]
végigpásztázik\[Pre][V][HIN]
a\[Det]
terep\[N][ACC]
rejtekhely\[N][NOM]
után\[NU]
néz\[V][Me3]
hátborzongató\[A][NOM]
közelség\[N][INE]
megszólalt\[MIB][NOM]
egy\[Num][NOM]
hang\[N][NOM]
ne\[Adv]
mozdul\[V][Pe3]
a\[Det]
négykézláb\[Adv]
álló\[MIF][NOM]
kurátor\[N][NOM]
megdermed\[Pre][V][Me3]
és\[Con]
lassan\[Adv]
elfordít\[Pre][V][TMe3]
a\[Det]
fej\[N][PSe3][ACC]
mindössze\[Adv]
tizenöt\[Num][NOM]
lépésnyi\[A][SUB]
a\[Det]
bezárult\[MIB][NOM]
kapu\[N][SUP]
kívül\[NU]
támadó\[MIF][PSe3][DAT]
sziluett\[N][PSe3][NOM]
tornyosul\[V][Me3]
ő_előtt\[NU]
és\[Con]

6.4.6. *Macro to remove the affixes from the words tagged with \unknown tag*

```
Sub langdon()
    Selection.Find.ClearFormatting
    With Selection.Find
        .Text = "Teabing"
        .Replacement.Text = ""
        .Forward = True
        .Wrap = wdFindContinue
        .Format = False
        .MatchCase = False
        .MatchWholeWord = False
        .MatchKashida = False
        .MatchDiacritics = False
        .MatchAlefHamza = False
        .MatchControl = False
        .MatchWildcards = False
        .MatchSoundsLike = False
        .MatchAllWordForms = False
    End With
    Selection.Find.Execute
    Selection.MoveRight Unit:=wdCharacter, Count:=1
    Selection.EndKey Unit:=wdLine, Extend:=wdExtend
    Selection.MoveLeft Unit:=wdCharacter, Count:=1, Extend:=wdExtend
    Selection.Delete Unit:=wdCharacter, Count:=1
End Sub
```

6.4.7. Hungarian lemmatized text with the \unknown tags removed

```
LOUVRE
Párizs\[N][NOM]
Jacques
Sauniere
a\[Det]
neves\[A][NOM]
kurátor\[N][NOM]
rogyadozó\[MIF][NOM]
láb\[N][INS]
esik\[V][Me3]
be\[Pre]
a\[Det]
múzeum\[N][NOM]
nagy\[A][NOM]
galéria\[N][ILL]
a\[Det]
boltíves\[A][NOM]
bejáró\[N][SUP]
keresztül\[NU]
Rávetet\[Pre][V][TMe3]
maga\[Pro][ACC]
a\[Det]
közel\[FF][A][FOK][NOM]
eső\[MIF][NOM]
festmény\[N][SUB]
egy\[Num][NOM]
Caravaggió
a\[Det]
hetvenhat\[Num][NOM]
éves\[A][NOM]
férfi\[N][NOM]
az\[Det]
aranyozott\[MIB][NOM]
keret\[N][ADE]
fogva\[NU]
maga\[Pro][NOM]
felé\[Adv]
ránt\[V][TMe3]
a\[Det]
műremek\[N][ACC]
letép\[Pre][V][TMe3]
a\[Det]
fal\[N][DEL]
és\[Con]
hátrazuhan\[Pre][V][HIN]
elterül\[Pre][V][Me3]
a\[Det]
föld\[N][SUP]
a\[Det]
vászon\[N][NOM]
alatt\[NU]
Pontosan\[Adv]
az\[Pro][NOM]
történik\[V][Me3]
amire\[Con]
Sauniere
számít\[V][Me3]
a\[Det]
közelben\[Adv]
mennydörög\[V][HIN]
lecsapódik\[Pre][V][Me3]
egy\[Num][NOM]
vaskapu\[N][NOM]
elzár\[Pre][V][HIN]
a\[Det]
terem\[N][NOM]
bejárat\[N][PSe3][ACC]
a\[Det]
parkettás\[A][NOM]
padló\[N][NOM]
megremeg\[Pre][V][Me3]
a\[Det]
távol\[A][INE]
megszólal\[Pre][V][Me3]
a\[Det]
riasztócsengő\[N][NOM]
a\[Det]
kurátor\[N][NOM]
egy\[Num][NOM]
másodperc\[N][TER]
levegő\[N][NOM]
után\[NU]
kapkod\[V][HIN]
fekszik\[V][Me3]
a\[Det]
föld\[N][SUP]
és\[Con]
felmér\[Pre][V][TMe3]
a\[Det]
helyzet\[N][PSe3][ACC]
még\[Adv]
élet\[N][INE]
van\[V][el]
Kimászik\[Pre][V][Me3]
a\[Det]
vászon\[N][NOM]
alól\[NU]
és\[Con]
végigpásztázik\[Pre][V][HIN]
a\[Det]
terep\[N][ACC]
rejtekhely\[N][NOM]
után\[NU]
néz\[V][Me3]
hátborzongató\[A][NOM]
közelség\[N][INE]
megszólalt\[MIB][NOM]
egy\[Num][NOM]
hang\[N][NOM]
ne\[Adv]
mozdul\[V][Pe3]
a\[Det]
négykézláb\[Adv]
álló\[MIF][NOM]
kurátor\[N][NOM]
megdermed\[Pre][V][Me3]
és\[Con]
lassan\[Adv]
elfordít\[Pre][V][TMe3]
a\[Det]
fej\[N][PSe3][ACC]
mindössze\[Adv]
tizenöt\[Num][NOM]
lépésnyi\[A][SUB]
a\[Det]
bezárult\[MIB][NOM]
kapu\[N][SUP]
kívül\[NU]
támadó\[MIF][PSe3][DAT]
sziluett\[N][PSe3][NOM]
```

6.4.8. *Lemmas and their tags in the lemmatized Hungarian texts with some superfluous characters*

```
LOUVRE
Párizs\[N
Jacques
Sauniere
a\[Det]
neves\[A
kurátor\[N
rogyadozó\[MIF
láb\[N
esik\[V
be\[Pre]
a\[Det]
múzeum\[N
nagy\[A
galéria\[N
a\[Det]
boltíves\[A
bejáró\[N
keresztül\[NU]
Rávetet\[Pre
maga\[Pro
a\[Det]
közel\[FF
eső\[MIF
festmény\[N
egy\[Num
Caravaggió
a\[Det]
hetvenhat\[Num
éves\[A
férfi\[N
az\[Det]
aranyozott\[MIB
keret\[N
fogva\[NU]
maga\[Pro
felé\[Adv]
ránt\[V
a\[Det]
műremek\[N
letép\[Pre
a\[Det]
fal\[N
és\[Con]
hátrazuhan\[Pre
elterül\[Pre
a\[Det]
föld\[N
a\[Det]
vászon\[N
alatt\[NU]
Pontosan\[Adv]
az\[Pro
történik\[V
amire\[Con]
Sauniere
számít\[V
a\[Det]
közelben\[Adv]
mennydörög\[V
lecsapódik\[Pre
egy\[Num
vaskapu\[N
elzár\[Pre
a\[Det]
terem\[N
bejárat\[N
a\[Det]
parkettás\[A
padló\[N
megremeg\[Pre
a\[Det]
távol\[A
megszólal\[Pre
a\[Det]
riasztócsengő\[N
a\[Det]
kurátor\[N
egy\[Num
másodperc\[N
levegő\[N
után\[NU]
kapkod\[V
fekszik\[V
a\[Det]
föld\[N
és\[Con]
felmér\[Pre
a\[Det]
helyzet\[N
még\[Adv]
élet\[N
```

6.4.9. *Procedure to remove unnecessary characters from the tags*

```
Sub amagyar()
'
'
Do
   Selection.Find.ClearFormatting
   With Selection.Find
      .Text = "]["
      .Replacement.Text = ""
      .Forward = True
      .Wrap = wdFindContinue
      .Format = False
      .MatchCase = False
      .MatchWholeWord = False
      .MatchKashida = False
      .MatchDiacritics = False
      .MatchAlefHamza = False
      .MatchControl = False
      .MatchWildcards = False
      .MatchSoundsLike = False
      .MatchAllWordForms = False
   End With
   Selection.Find.Execute
   Selection.EndKey Unit:=wdLine, Extend:=wdExtend
   Selection.MoveLeft Unit:=wdCharacter, Count:=1, Extend:=wdExtend
   Selection.Delete Unit:=wdCharacter, Count:=1
Loop Until Not Selection.Find.Found
End Sub
```

6.4.10. Lemmas with their tags in the Hungarian lemmatized texts

LOUVRE
PárizsN
Jacques
Sauniere
aDet
nevesA
kurátorN
rogyadozóMIF
lábN
esikV
bePre
aDet
múzeumN
nagyA
galériaN
aDet
boltívesA
bejáróN
keresztülNU
RávetetPre
magaPro
aDet
közelFF
esőMIF
festményN
egyNum
Caravaggió
aDet
hetvenhatNum
évesA
férfiN
azDet
aranyozottMIB
keretN
fogvaNU
magaPro
feléAdv
rántV
aDet
műremekN
letépPre
aDet
falN
ésCon
hátrazuhanPre
elterülPre
aDet
földN
aDet
vászonN
alattNU
PontosanAdv
azPro
történikV
amireCon
Sauniere
számítV
aDet
közelbenAdv
mennydörögV
lecsapódikPre
egyNum
vaskapuN
elzárPre
aDet
teremN
bejáratN
aDet
parkettásA
padlóN
megremegPre
aDet
távolA
megszólalPre
aDet
riasztócsengőN

6.5. Afterwords of Harranth, 1987

Nachwort

»Bruder dem Bruder –
doch weh dem, den wir hassen«

Die *Dschungelbücher* spielen nur zum Teil im Dschungel, sie wurden nicht für junge Leser geschrieben, und es stimmt nicht, was seine Kritiker Rudyard Kipling vorwarfen: Er hat weder Gewalt verherrlicht noch die »weiße Rasse« als überlegen dargestellt. Wie konnte es zu so vielen Missverständnissen und Vorurteilen kommen?

Es ist das Schicksal vieler Klassiker, verunstaltet, verstümmelt und bis zur Unkenntlichkeit bearbeitet zu werden. Kaum einem anderen Werk wurde aber so schwer zugesetzt wie den *Dschungelbüchern.* Die zuvor in verschiedenen Zeitungen veröffentlichten Erzählungen erschienen 1894 und 1895 in Buchform und machten ihren Autor mit einem Schlag berühmt. Die erste deutsche Übersetzung, 1898, entstand nach dem säbelrasselnden Zeitgeschmack des Kaiserreichs und verdrehte ungeniert viele Aussagen Kiplings ins Gegenteil. Auch in der Folge wurde das Original radikal gekürzt und mit Erfindungen der Nachdichter gespickt. Als 1933 die Nationalsozialisten an die Macht kamen, verschwanden die Namen der jüdischen Übersetzer, und ein bewährter Faschist »bearbeitete« den Text ganz nach den ideologischen Zielsetzungen des Dritten Reichs. Diese Fassung erschien dann auch nach 1945 und bis in die jüngste Vergangenheit unverändert sowohl in der Bundesrepublik als auch in der DDR. Und alle Kritiker verurteilten Kipling unter Berufung auf diese Ausgaben, die ebenso wenig den ursprünglichen *Dschungelbüchern* glichen wie die kitschigen Spielfilme über Mowgli und den Elefantenboy, die vielfältige Vermarktung durch Walt Disney und die Billig-Serien fürs Fernsehen. Kaum zu glauben: Die hier vorliegende Ausgabe war bei ihrem Erscheinen 1987 nach fast 95 Jahren die erste, die sich bei den Erzählungen und Gedichten streng ans Original hielt, Kiplings Forderung an sich selbst zu achten versuchte kein Wort zu viel und keines zu wenig – und die bemüht war, den unverwechselbaren rhythmischen Klang seiner Sprache nachzuempfinden.

Vor hundert Jahren umspannte das britische Empire die ganze Welt, war der indische Subkontinent eine riesige britische Kolonie – das muss man bedenken, wenn man Kiplings Weltsicht beurteilt. Aber unterscheidet sich die Realität von heute wirklich so sehr von dem, was in den *Dschungelbüchern* steht? Das Leben ist ein Kampf, sagt Kipling, in dem keinem der Sieg geschenkt wird. Der Stärkere besiegt den Schwachen, der Klügere den Dummen, der Flinkere den Langsamen. Stärke beweist sich aber nicht nur an Kraft, sondern auch an Mut und Geist; Klugheit nicht nur an Wissen, sondern auch an List und Schläue; Flinksein nicht nur an Tempo, sondern auch an Gewandtheit und Anpassungsfähigkeit. Wer wen besiegt, hat also nicht unbedingt allein mit Vernunft und Gerechtigkeit zu tun: Das ist das Gesetz des Dschungels, eines Dschungels, so groß wie die Welt. Wir sind »Bruder dem Bruder, doch weh dem, den wir hassen! «, heißt es im Jagdgesang des Wolfsrudels. Das Gesetz mag gnadenlos sein, aber der angeblich so unbelehrbare Imperialist Kipling lässt uns nicht im Zweifel, wem seine Sympathie gehört: Ob Baloo oder der Kleine Toomai, ja selbst Mowgli – ausgerechnet die liebenswertesten Helden der *Dschungelbücher* sind keineswegs perfekt. Sie achten das Gesetz, das schon, aber sie nehmen es hin und wieder nicht so schrecklich genau.

Wolf Harranth

6.6. The process of digitization

6.6.1. Scanning

To carry out text recognition, RECOGNITA PLUS 5.0 [9] was used. The choice fell on this software because through its settings we had access to several languages, and were able to use the same software for texts in different languages.

Details of the process of scanning is beyond the scope of this work, however one particular detail should be mentioned. Along the analysis the apostrophe was considered as a valid character (Chapter 2.1.1) because this character is used to indicate abbreviation in all the languages encountered in this project. Since the apostrophe was added to the set of the valid characters it had to be handled very carefully, because in several cases it was used for typographic purposes (Table 24a and b), substituted quotation marks (Table 24d), while in other cases it was misspelled (Table 24c), and in several cases the apostrophe itself was substituted with a similar but unknown character. All the incorrect usages had to be distinguished from the correct spelling (Table 24f).

Table 24. Examples of correct and incorrect appearances of the apostrophe in digitized text.

Misplaced apostrophe
(a) The remarkable poem of 'The Raven' was
(b) 'secret' drawer
(c) "How? – in what way?'*
(d) " 'We will suppose,' said the miser, 'that his symptoms are such and such; now, doctor, what would you have directed him to take?'
Correct apostrophe at the beginning and end of the words
(e) 'cause, 'ting, thinkin', likin' flyin', an' didn', 'bout
Correct apostrophe in the middle of the words
(f) G'night, sumf'n, more'n a minute longer, per'aps, don't

The scanning was always followed by a number of proofreading and correcting stages. If only a poor quality character recognition was carried out then the proofreading and the correction took an extremely long time, which in some cases was not worth its while. In these cases the worst option – typing the text – was unavoidable.

6.6.2. *Typing*

When the printed form of the text was in such a bad condition that the scanning, the text recognition, the proofreading, and the correction of the text would have taken too much time scanning was decided against and the text was finally typed.

'Text unscannable' was mainly encountered in heavily used books. In addition, some of the e-texts were not convertible either to .doc or .txt format, so they had to be printed and scanned. Text recognition did not work either if the quality of the original e-document and/or the printout was not good enough.

6.6.3. *Texts and tools*

Taken together, texts to be analyzed are highly dependent on their availability. In many cases the analysis was not carried out according to the original plan, simply because we had no access to the text.

For example, THE DA VINCI CODE project seems unfinished for at least two reasons. The condensed German and French texts were not available either in printed or digitized form and we still do not have access to German and French lemmatizer programs. For similar reasons, as was mentioned in Chapter 4.1.6 the German translation of TOM SAWYER was not available in digitized form at the time of the analysis. As detailed in THE JUNGLE BOOKS project the different adaptations of the text required several normalizations to reach comparable texts.

As the above mentioned examples show the comparison of the different adaptations of novels, consequently the conclusions drawn are highly dependent on the texts and tools available.

7. Sources – novels, short stories

BROWN, D. (2003) The Da Vinci Code. New York: Doubleday.

BROWN, D. and BORI, E. (2004) The Da Vinci Code. Translated by Bori, E. (2004) A Da Vinci-kód. Budapest: Gabo.

BROWN, D. and ROCHE, D. (2004) The Da Vinci Code. Translated by Roche, D. Da Vinci Code. (2004). Paris: JC Lattes.

BROWN, D. and POLL, P. (2004) The Da Vinci Code. Translated by van Poll, P. (2004) Sakrileg. Germany: Gustav Lübbe Verlag.

BROWN, D. (2004) The Da Vinci Code. (2004) Reader's Digest Association Inc.

BROWN, D. (2005) The Da Vinci Code. A Da Vinci-kód. 2005 Budapest: Reader's Digest Kiadó Kft.

CARROLL, L. (1866) Alice's Adventures in Wonderland. http://www.gutenberg.org/dirs/etext91/alice30.txt

CARROLL, L., KOSZTOLÁNYI, D. and SZOBOTKA, T. (1974) Alice Csodaországban. Fordította Kosztolányi Dezső. A fordítást az eredetivel egybevetve átdolgozta Szobotka Tibor (1974) Móra Ferenc Könyvkiadó, Budapest.
http://www.mek.oszk.hu/00300/00348/html/

CARROLL, L. (1871) Through the Looking-Glass and What Alice Found There.
http://etext.lib.virginia.edu/etcbin/ot2www-ebooks?specfile=/texts/english/ebooks/ebooks.o2w&act=text&offset=43068673&textreg=2&query=through+the+looking+glass&id=CarGlas
http://www.gutenberg.org/dirs/etext91/lglass19.txt

CARROLL, L., RÉVBÍRÓ, T. and TÓTFALUSI, I. (1980) Alice Tükörországban. Fordította Révbíró Tamás. A versbetéteket Tótfalusi István fordította (1980) Móra Ferenc Könyvkiadó, Budapest.
http://www.mek.oszk.hu/02900/02914/

CARROLL, L. (2004a) Alice au Pays des Merveilles. e-version created: 2004. Ebooks libres et gratuits http://www.ebooksgratuits.com/ebooks.php

CARROLL, L. (2004b) De l'Autre côté du miroir. Traduction de Jacques Papy. e-version created: 2004. http://www.ebooksgratuits.com/ebooks.php

DEFOE, D. (1719) THE ADVENTURES OF ROBINSON CRUSOE. e-version created: 2004. http://www.gutenberg.org/cache/epub/12623/pg12623.txt

GÁRDONYI, G. (1899) Egri csillagok. e-version created: 1997. http://mek.oszk.hu/00600/00656/index.phtml

KERTÉSZ, I. (1975) Sorstalanság. Magvető, Budapest.

KERTÉSZ, I. and VIRAGH, C. (1996) Roman eines Schicksallosen. Aus dem Ungarischen von Christina Viragh. (1996) Rowohlt Taschenbuch Verlag, Hamburg.

KERTÉSZ, I., WILSON, C. C. AND WILSON, K. M. (1992) Fateless. Translated by Christopher C. Wilson and Katharina M. Wilson (1992) Hydra Books, Northwestern University Press, Evanston, Illinois.

KIPLING, R. (1961) *The Jungle Books.* New American Library. A division of Penguin Books USA Inc. New York, USA. http://www.gutenberg.org/files/236/236.txt

KIPLING, R., BENEDEK, M. and WEÖRES, S. (1976) A dzsungel könyve. A fordítás a MACMILLAN, LONDON KIADÓ 1930. évi kiadásából készült. Benedek Marcell fordítása, a verseket Weöres Sándor fordította. Tizedik kiadás. Móra Könyvkiadó, Budapest. http://www.mek.oszk.hu/00400/00424/00424.htm

KIPLING, R., BENEDEK, M. and WEÖRES, S. (2002) A dzsungel könyve. A fordítás a MacMillan, London kiadó 1930. évi kiadásából készült. Benedek Marcell fordítása, a verseket Weöres Sándor fordította. Ciceró Könyvstúdió, Budapest.

KIPLING, R., BENEDEK, M. and WEÖRES, S. (2007) Riki-Tiki-Tévi és más történetek. A dzsungel könyvének második része. A fordítás a MacMillan, London kiadó 1930. évi kiadásából készült. Benedek Marcell fordítása, a verseket Weöres Sándor fordította. Ciceró Könyvstúdió, Budapest.

KIPLING, R. and MIKUSCH, D. VON (1951) Die Dschungelbücher. Dieser Band enthält: „Das Dschungelbuch“ und „Das neue Dschungelbuch“ in der von Dagobert von Mikusch durchgesehenen Originalübersetzung. Mit Genehmigung des Paul List Verlages.

KIPLING, R. and HAEFS, G. (1987) Die Dschungelbücher. Neu übersetzt und herausgegeben von Gisbert Haefs. Haffmans Verlag AG Zürich.

KIPLING, R. and HARRANTH, W. (2004) Das Dschungelbuch. Aus dem Englischen von Wolf Harranth (1987). Cecilie Dressler Verlag GmbH & KG, Hamburg.

KIPLING, R. (1965a) Das Dschungelbuch. In Die Dschungelbücher. Deutsche Buchgemeinschaft. e-version created: 2006. Digitized from a printed edition in 1965 based on Kipling (1951).
http://gutenberg.spiegel.de/?id=5&xid=3275&kapitel=1#gb_found

KIPLING, R. (1965b) Das neue Dschungelbuch. In Die Dschungelbücher. Deutsche Buchgemeinschaft. e-version created: 2006.
http://gutenberg.spiegel.de/?id=5&xid=3276&kapitel=1#gb_found

KIPLING, R, FABULET, L. and D'HUMIERES, R. (1899a) Le Livre de la jungle. Traduit de l'anglais par Louis Fabulet et Robert d'Humières. Mercure de France.
http://www.ebooksgratuits.com/ebooks.php

KIPLING, R., FABULET, L. and D'HUMIERES, R. (1899b) Le Second Livre de la jungle. Traduit de l'anglais par Louis Fabulet et Robert d'Humières. Mercure de France.
http://www.ebooksgratuits.com/ebooks.php

ORCZY, B. (1903) The Scarlet Pimpernel. (2000) Signet Classic.

ORCZY, B. (1966) The Scarlet Pimpernel. Reader's Digest Best Loved Books for Young Readers. (1966) The Reader's Digest Association, Inc.

TWAIN, M. (1876) The Adventures of Tom Sawyer. e-version created: 2006. http://www.gutenberg.org/files/74/74.txt

TWAIN, M. and KOROKNAY, I. (1977) Tom Sawyer kalandjai. Fordította: Koroknay István. A fordítást átnézte: Karinthy Frigyes. e-version created: 2006.
http://mek.oszk.hu/04100/04170/index.phtml#

TWAIN, M. (2007) Les Aventures de Tom Sawyer. e-version created: 2007. http://www.ebooksgratuits.com/ebooks.php

TWAIN, M. (1966) The Adventures of Tom Sawyer. Reader's Digest Best Loved Books for Young Readers. (1966) The Reader's Digest Association, Inc.

8. References

ÁBRAHÁM, KNÉ and JILLY, V. (1999) The School-Leaving Examination in Hungary. Fekete, H. (ed.). In English Language Education in Hungary. A Baseline Study. Fekete, H., Major, É. & Nikolov, M. (eds.) The British Council Hungary, Budapest.

ASTON, G. and BURNARD, L. (1998) The BNC Handbook: Exploring the British National Corpus with SARA. Edinburgh, UK: Edinburgh University Press.

BAAYEN R. H. (1993) Statistical Models for Word Frequency Distributions: A Linguistic Evaluation. *Computers and the Humanities* 26. 347–363.

BAAYEN, R. H. (1996a) The Randomness Assumption in Word Frequency Statistics. In Perissinotto, G. (ed), Research in Humanities Computing 5. Oxford: Oxford University Press: 17–31.

BAAYEN R. H. (1996b) The Effect of Lexical Specialization on the Growth Curve of the Vocabulary. *Computational Linguistics* 22: 455–480.

BAAYEN, R. H. (2001) Word Frequency Distributions. Kluwer Academic Publishers, Dordrecht, Netherlands.

BAAYEN, R. H., HALTEREN, H. and TWEEDIE F. (1996) Outside the Cave of Shadows: Using Syntactic Annotation to Enhance Authorship Attribution, *Literary and Linguistic Computing* 11: 121–131.

BALÁZS, J. (1985) A szöveg. Gondolat, Budapest

BART, I. and KLAUDY, K. (ed.) (1985) A fordítás tudománya. Tankönyvkiadó, Budapest.

BEAUGRANDE, R. and DRESSLER, W. (1981) Bevezetés a szövegnyelvészetbe. Siptár, P. (ford.) (2000) Corvina, Budapest.

BERTSEKAS, D. P. and TSITSIKLIS, J. N. (2008) Introduction to Probability, 2nd Edition. Athena Scientific, USA.

CARTER, R. and MCCARTHY, M. (1991) Vocabulary and Language Teaching. London: Longman Group UK.

CARRINGTON, C. (1955) Rudyard Kipling: His Life and Work. Macmillan & Co., London.

COOK, G. (1994) Discourse and Literature: The Interplay of Form and Mind. Oxford University Press, Oxford.

CSERNOCH, M. (2004) Another Method to Analyze the Introduction of Word-Types in Literary Works and Textbooks, The 16th Joint International Conference of the Association for Literary and Linguistic Computing and the Association for Computers and the Humanities Göteborg University, Göteborg 44-45. http://www.hum.gu.se/allcach2004/AP/html/prop83.html

CSERNOCH, M. (2005) Természetes nyelvi szövegek összehasonlítása első-rendű statisztikai modellekkel. Publicationes Universitatis Miskolcinensis, Sectio Philosophica, Tomus X. – Fasciculus 3. Miskolc 2005.

CSERNOCH, M. (2006a) The introduction of word types and lemmas in novels, short stories and their translations.
http://www.allc-ach2006.colloques.paris-sorbone.fr/DHs.pdf
Digital Humanities 2006. The First International Conference of the Alliance of Digital Humanities Organisations. (5–9 July 2006, Paris).

CSERNOCH, M. (2006b) Frequency-based Dynamic Models for the Analysis of English and Hungarian Literary Works and Coursebooks for English as a Second Language. Teaching Mathematics and Computer Science. Debrecen, Hungary, 53–70.

CSERNOCH, M. (2007a) Seasonalities in the Introduction of Word-types in Literary Works. Publicationes Universitatis Miskolcinensis, Sectio Philosophica, Tomus XI. – Fasciculus 3. Miskolc 2006–2007, 11–34.

CSERNOCH, M. (2007b) Dinamikusan kezelhető statisztikai modellek irodalmi művek szóalakjainak vizsgálatára. Alkalmazott Matematikai Lapok 24 (2007), 57–77.

CSERNOCH, M. (2007c). Newly introduced word-types and lemmas in Dan Brown's The Da Vinci code and its translations. Across Languages and Cultures 8 (2), 195–220.

CSERNOCH, M. (2007d) Condensed versions of literary works. In When grammar minds language and literature. University of Debrecen. 107–118.

CSERNOCH, M. (2008a) Újonnan bevezetett szóalakok és lemmák Dan Brown The Da Vinci Code című művében és fordításaiban. Fordítástudomány. 10: 18–41.

CSERNOCH, M. (2008b) A novel way for the comparative analysis of adaptations based on vocabulary rich text segments: the assessment of Dan Brown's The Da Vinci Code and its translations. Digital Humanities 2008. 95–96. http://www.ekl.oulu.fi/dh2008/Digital%20Humanities%202008%20Book%20of%20Abstracts.pdf

CSERNOCH, M. (2010) The Role of the Newly Introduced Word Types int the Translations of Novels. Proceedings of the International Multiconference on Computer Science and Information Technology. ISBN 978-83-60810-27-9. ISSN 1896-7094. pp. 389–396

CSERNOCH, M. and KORPONAYNÉ, N. I. (2005) A Comparative Analysis of the Word Types of the New Headway Coursebooks. Publicationes Universitatis Miskolciensis. Sectio Philosophica. Tomus X. – Fasciculus 2. E Typographeo Universitatis Miskolc, 3–10.

CUNNINGSWORTH, A. (1995) Choosing your Coursebook. Oxford, UK Heinemann Publishers.

É. KISS, K. (2002) The Syntax of Hungarian, Cambridge Syntax Guides, Cambridge University Press, Cambridge.

GENETTE, G. (1995) Narrative Discourse. Cornell University Press, Ithaca, New York.

GUEST, P. G. (1961) Numerical Methods of Curve Fitting. Cambridge University Press, Cambridge, UK.

HAJTMAN, B. (1971) Bevezetés a matematikai statisztikába. Akadémiai Kiadó Budapest.

HATIM, B. and MASON, I. (1993) Discourse and the Translator. Longman Inc., New York.

HERDAN, G. (1964) Type-token Mathematics. Mouton, The Hague.

HORNBY, A. S., COWIE, A. P. and GIMSON, A. C. (1987) Oxford Advanced Learner's Dictionary of Current English. Oxford University Press, Oxford, Great Britain.

HOPPENSTAND, G. (2000) The Scarlet Pimpernel. Introduction. Signet Classic.

JAMES, W. (1975) Webster's New World Dictionary of the American Language. Plume, New York.

JOHNSON, N.L. KOTZ, S. and KEMP, A.W. (1992) Univariate Discrete Distributions, 2nd Edition. New York: John Wiley.

KENNEDY, G. (1998) An Introduction to Corpus Linguistics. Longman, London and New York.

KIEFER, F. AND É. KISS, K. (1994) (ed.) The Syntactic Structure of Hungarian, Syntax and Semantics vol. 27, Academic Press, San Diego-New York.

LEECH, G. (1991) The States of Art in Corpus Linguistics. In Aijmer and Altenberg (1991): 8–29.

LORGE, I. (1949). Semantic count of the 570 commonest English words. Columbia University Press, New York.

MACMILLAN (2002) Macmillan English Dictionary for Advanced Learners. International Student Edition. Macmillan Publishers Limited, Oxford.

MCENERY, T., XIAO, R. and TONO, Y. (2006) Corpus-Based Language Studies. An advanced resource book. Routledge.

MESZÉNA, GY. and ZIERMANN, M. (1981) Valószínűség elmélet és matematikai statisztika. Közgazdasági és Jogi Könyvkiadó, Budapest.

NEUFELDT, V. (editor in chief); Guralnik, D. B. (editor in chief emeritus) (1991) Webster's New World Dictionary of American English. Third College Edition. Prentice Hall, New York.

OAKES, M. P. (1998) Statistics or Corpus Linguistics. Edinburgh University Press.

ORAVECZ, CS. and DIENES, P. (2002a) Large scale morphosyntactic annotation of the Hungarian National Corpus. In Béla Hollósi and Judit Kiss-Gulyás (eds) Studies in Linguistics, Volume VI., pages 277–298, Debrecen, 2002.

ORAVECZ, CS. and DIENES, P. (2002b) Efficient Stochastic Part-of-Speech tagging for Hungarian. In Proceedings of the Third International Conference on Language Resources and Evaluation, pages 710–717, Las Palmas, 2002.

OXFORD, R. L. and SCARCELLA, R. C. (1994) Second Language Vocabulary Learning Among Adults: State of the Art in Vocabulary Instruction. System Vol. 22. No. 2.

PAPP, F. (1974) Szövegszó, szóalak, lexéma. Magyar Nyelvőr 98. kötet: 76–82.

PETŐFI, S. J. (1990) Szöveg, szövegtan, műelemzés. (Textológiai tanulmányok) Országos Pedagógiai Intézet, Budapest.

PRÓSZÉKY, G. (1989) Számítógépes nyelvészet. Számítástechnika-Alkalmazási Vállalat, Budapest.

PRÓSZÉKY, G. AND KIS, B. (1999) Számítógéppel – emberi nyelven. Intelligens szövegkezelés számítógéppel. SZAK Kiadó, Budapest.

RAYSON, P. (2003) Matrix: A statistical method and software tool for linguistic analysis through corpus comparison. PhD thesis, Lancaster University.

RAYSON, P. (2005) Wmatrix: a web-based corpus processing environment. Computing Department, Lancaster University. http://www.comp.lancs.ac.uk/ucrel/wmatrix/

RIBYCKI, J. (2003) Burrowing into Translation: Character Idiolects in Henryk Sienkiewicz's Trilogy and its Two English Translations. Conference Abstract, The 16th Joint International Conference of the Association for Literary and Linguistic Computing and the Association for Computers and the Humanities Göteborg University, Sweden.

RYBICKIE, J. (2006) Burrowing into Translation: Character Idiolects in Henryk Sienkiewicz's Trilogy and its Two English Translations. Journal of The Association for Literary and Linguistic Computing, Volume 21 Number 1 April 2006.

RUSSELL, S. J.; and NORVIG, P. (1995) Artificial Intelligence. A Modern Approach. Prentice Hall.

SIMIGNÉ, F. S. (2006) A fordítás mint közvetítés. STÚDIÓ Rendezvények és Nyelvtanfolyamok, Miskolc.

SINCLAIR, J. (1991). Corpus, concordance, collocation. Oxford University Press, Oxford, Great Britain.

SINCLAIR, J. (1995). Corpus typology – a framework for classification. In Melchers, G. and Warren, B. (eds.) Studies in Anglistics. Almqvist & Wiksell, Stockholm, pp. 17–33.
SINCLAIR, J. (1995). Corpus typology – a framework for classification. In Melchers, G. and Warren, B. (eds.) Studies in Anglistics. Almqvist & Wiksell, Stockholm, pp. 17–33.
SINGLETON, D. (1999) Exploring the Second Language Mental Lexicon. Cambridge: Cambridge University Press.

SMITH, N. (1997). Improving a Tagger, in Garside, R., Leech, G., and McEnery, A. (eds.) Corpus Annotation: Linguistic Information from Computer Text Corpora, Longman, London, pp. 137–150.

SCHMITT, N. (2000) Vocabulary in Language Teaching. Cambridge University Press, Cambridge, UK.

SCHMITT, N. and MCCARTHY, M. (eds.) (1997) Vocabulary: Description, acquisition, and pedagogy. Cambridge University Press, Cambridge.

SOLT, GY. (1971) Valószínűségszámítás. Műszaki Könyvkiadó, Budapest.

SNYDER, L. (2008) Fluency with information technology. Skills, Concepts, and Capabilities. Third Edition. Pearson.

UNDERWOOD, A. and RADCLIFFE, J. (august 2nd 2008) The new readers' guide to the works of Rudyard Kipling. Her majesty's servants. http://www.kipling.org.uk/rg_majservants1.htm

WORTHING, A. G. and GEFFNER, J. (1959) Treatment of Experimental Data. John Wiley and Sons, Inc., New York.

YONGQI, P. G. (2003) Vocabulary Learning in a Second Language: Person, Task, Context and Strategies. Teaching English as a Second or Foreign Language Vol. 7. No.2.

9. E-sources

[1] Merriam-Webster OnLine.
http://www.m-w.com/dictionary/corpus (1th August 2010)

[2] Project Gutenberg.
http://promo.net/pg/ (1th August 2010)

[3] University of Virginia Library, Electronic Text Center.
http://etext.lib.virginia.edu/ebooks/ebooklist.html (1th August 2010)

[4] Magyar Elektronikus Könyvtár.
http://www.mek.iif.hu
http://www.mek.oszk.hu (1th August 2010)

[5] Digitális Irodalmi Akadémia.
http://pim.hu/object.d8f182da-fdfa-45ba-914f-2688ce822346.ivy (1th August 2010)

[6] ebooks Libres & Gratuits.
http://www.ebooksgratuits.com/ (1th August 2010)

[7] Projekt Gutenberg-DE.
http://gutenberg.spiegel.de/index.php?id=6 (1th August 2010)

[8] Projekt Gutenberg-DE. Mark Twain: Tom Sawyers Abenteuer und Streiche
http://gutenberg.spiegel.de/?id=5&xid=5445&kapitel=1#gb_found (1th November 2010)

[9] Recognita.
http://www.recognita.hu (1th August 2010)

[10] Alice Tükörországban.
http://mek.oszk.hu/02900/02914/usmarc.html
http://mek.oszk.hu/02900/02914/02914.htm (1th August 2010)

[11] The 'Code' Breakers. Newsweek.
http://www.msnbc.msn.com/id/10509652/site/newsweek/ (1th August 2010)

[12] SNCF.
http://www.sncf.com (1th August 2010)

[13] Danken, B. (1987) Kiplings unsterblicher Klassiker. Zeit Online.
http://www.zeit.de/1987/46/Kiplings-unsterblicher-Klassiker (1th August 2010)

[14] Reader's Digest.
http://www.rd.com/ (1th August 2010)

Acknowledgement

This work was supported by the University Foundation established by the K&H Bank.

METALINGUISTICA

Editor/Herausgeber: András Kertész

Bd./Vol. 1 András Kertész (Hrsg.): Sprache als Kognition - Sprache als Interaktion. Studien zum Grammatik-Pragmatik-Verhältnis. 1995.

Bd./Vol. 2 Tibor Laczkó: The Syntax of Hungarian Noun Phrases. A Lexical-Functional Approach. 1995.

Bd./Vol. 3 Péter Pelyvás: Subjectivity in English. Generative Grammar Versus the Cognitive Theory of Epistemic Grounding. 1996.

Bd./Vol. 4 András Kertész (Hrsg.): Metalinguistik im Wandel. Die 'kognitive Wende' in Wissenschaftstheorie und Linguistik. 1997.

Bd./Vol. 5 Gábor Alberti: Argument Selection. 1997.

Bd./Vol. 6 Zsuzsanna Iványi: Wortsuchprozesse. Eine gesprächsanalytische Untersuchung und ihre wissenschaftsmethodologischen Konsequenzen. 1998.

Bd./Vol. 7 Piroska Kocsány / Anna Molnár (Hrsg.): Wort und (Kon)text. 2001.

Bd./Vol. 8 Éva Sáfár: Persuasive Texte. Eine vergleichende Untersuchung sprachlicher Argumentationsstrategien. 2001.

Bd./Vol. 9 András Kertész (ed.): Approaches to the Pragmatics of Scientific Discourse. 2001.

Bd./Vol. 10 Zsuzsanna Iványi / András Kertész (Hrsg.): Gesprächsforschung. Tendenzen und Perspektiven. 2001.

Bd./Vol. 11 Peter Plöger: Wissenschaft durch Wechselwirkung. Bausteine zu einem diskursiven Modell der Wissenschaften. 2002.

Bd./Vol. 12 Anna Molnár: Die Grammatikalisierung deutscher Modalpartikeln. Fallstudien. 2002.

Bd./Vol. 13 László Hunyadi. Hungarian Sentence Prosody and Universal Grammar. On the Phonology – Syntax Interface. 2002.

Bd./vol. 14 Marcello La Matina: Texts, Pictures and Scores. Some Aspects of a Philosophy of Languages. 2002.

Bd./Vol. 15 Krisztina Károly: Lexical Repetition in Text. A Study of the Text-Organizing Function of Lexical Repetition in Foreign Language Argumentative Discourse. 2002.

Bd./Vol. 16 László Tarnay / Tamás Pólya: Specificity Recognition and Social Cognition. 2004.

Bd./Vol. 17 Gábor Tolcsvai Nagy: A Cognitive Theory of Style. 2005.

Bd./Vol. 18 Lajos Marosán: The Meaning of Word Classes. 2006.

Bd./Vol. 19 Marina Rakova / Gergely Pethõ / Csilla Rákosi (eds.): The Cognitive Basis of Polysemy. New Sources of Evidence for Theories of Word Meaning. 2007.

Bd./Vol. 20 Gábor Tolcsvai Nagy (ed.): Function and Genres. Studies on the Linguistic Features of Discourse Types. 2008.

Bd./Vol. 21 Enikõ Tóth: Mood Choice in Complement Clauses. A Semantic Approach with Special Reference to Hungarian. 2008.

Bd./Vol. 22 András Kertész / Csilla Rákosi (eds.): New Approaches to Linguistic Evidence. Pilot Studies. Neue Ansätze zu linguistischer Evidenz. Pilotstudien. 2008.

Band 23 Gizella Boszák: Realisierung der valenzbestimmten Korrelate des Deutschen. 2009.

Band 24 Mária Csernoch: Vocabulary Richness of Novels and Their Adaptions. 2011.

www.peterlang.de

Peter Lang · Internationaler Verlag der Wissenschaften

Kerstin Anna Kunz

Variation in English and German Nominal Coreference

A Study of Political Essays

Frankfurt am Main, Berlin, Bern, Bruxelles, New York, Oxford, Wien, 2010.
XXI, 418 pp., num. tab. and graph.
Saarbrücker Beiträge zur Sprach- und Translationswissenschaft.
Edited by Alberto Gil, Johann Haller and Erich Steiner. Vol. 21
ISBN 978-3-631-61017-6 · hardback € 72,80*

The topic of this work is nominal coreference in English and German. Its focus is on coreference relations that establish textual coherence and continuity above the local level of the clause. The book shows how linguistic options for creating coreference in English and German can be interpreted against the background of their motivating factors. It discusses mental text processing, German-English systemic contrasts and register peculiarities as possible sources for variation on different linguistic levels. Hermeneutic and example-based observations are complemented by a corpus-linguistic analysis of English and German political essays and German translations from the English originals. The study finally highlights linguistic and functional correlations of coreference instantiations in English and German texts, additionally shedding light on coreference strategies employed in translations. It thus yields an incentive for future research as well as providing a wealth of insights for language and translation teaching.

Content: Variation in nominal coreference in English and German · Influencing Factors: Mental text processing, Systemic contrasts English-German, Register, Process of translation · Corpus-linguistic study of political essays · English and German originals, German translations from the English originals

Frankfurt am Main · Berlin · Bern · Bruxelles · New York · Oxford · Wien
Distribution: Verlag Peter Lang AG
Moosstr. 1, CH-2542 Pieterlen
Telefax 00 41 (0) 32 / 376 17 27

*The €-price includes German tax rate
Prices are subject to change without notice

Homepage http://www.peterlang.de